Tois Pasin ho Kairos

Tois Pasin ho Kairos

Judaism and Orthodox Christianity Facing the Future

Edited by

Nicholas de Lange
Elena Narinskaya
Sybil Sheridan

LEXINGTON BOOKS/FORTRESS ACADEMIC
Lanham • Boulder • New York • London

Published by Lexington Books/Fortress Academic
Lexington Books is an imprint of The Rowman & Littlefield Publishing Group, Inc.
4501 Forbes Boulevard, Suite 200, Lanham, Maryland 20706
www.rowman.com

86-90 Paul Street, London EC2A 4NE, United Kingdom

Copyright © 2023 by The Rowman & Littlefield Publishing Group, Inc.

All rights reserved. No part of this book may be reproduced in any form or by any electronic or mechanical means, including information storage and retrieval systems, without written permission from the publisher, except by a reviewer who may quote passages in a review.

British Library Cataloguing in Publication Information Available

Library of Congress Cataloging-in-Publication Data

Names: De Lange, N. R. M. (Nicholas Robert Michael), 1944– editor. | Narinskaya, Elena, editor. | Sheridan, Sybil, editor.
Title: Tois Pasin ho Kairos : Judaism and Orthodox Christianity facing the future / edited by Nicholas de Lange, Elena Narinskaya, and Sybil Sheridan.
Description: Lanham : Lexington Books/Fortress Academic, [2023] | Includes bibliographical references and index. | Summary: "This book presents a comprehensive, comparative view of the contemporary challenges facing Judaism and Orthodox Christianity. Bringing together contributions by many experts, writing within their own tradition, essays are arranged in pairs to bring out the living dialogue between these ancient faiths"— Provided by publisher.
Identifiers: LCCN 2023002598 (print) | LCCN 2023002599 (ebook) | ISBN 9781978714014 (cloth) | ISBN 9781978714021 (epub)
Subjects: LCSH: Orthodox Eastern Church—Relations—Judaism. | Judaism—Relations—Orthodox Eastern Church. | Religion and sociology.
Classification: LCC BM535 .T554 2023 (print) | LCC BM535 (ebook) | DDC 296.3/96—dc23/eng/20230213
LC record available at https://lccn.loc.gov/2023002598
LC ebook record available at https://lccn.loc.gov/2023002599

To the memory of

Father Ephrem Lash

Rabbi John Rayner

*who were deeply influential in the dialogue
between Jews and Orthodox Christians*

Contents

Introduction *Elena Narinskaya and Sybil Sheridan*	ix
Chapter 1: A 'City Whose Gates Are Always Open'?: Visions for Jerusalem in Orthodox Christianity *Nikita Banev*	1
Chapter 2: Jerusalem: A Jewish Perspective *Marc Saperstein*	13
Chapter 3: Jewish and Eastern-Rite Christian Relations in Israel: A Sketch of Contexts and Interests *Petra Heldt*	23
Chapter 4: The Encounter between the Greek Orthodox Church and the Jews in Israel *David Rosen*	35
Chapter 5: The Greek Orthodox Church under Israeli Sovereignty *Michael G. Azar*	41
Chapter 6: Women in the Synagogue *Miri Freud-Kandel*	53
Chapter 7: Women in the Orthodox Churches: Modernity and Change *Mary B. Cunningham*	65
Chapter 8: Orthodoxia and Orthopraxia: On the Issue of Blood *Elena Narinskaya*	77
Chapter 9: *Kashrut—Niddah—Milah*: On the Issue of Blood *Sybil Sheridan*	89

viii   *Contents*

Chapter 10: Judaism and Homosexuality   99
    René Pfertzel

Chapter 11: Orthodoxy and Homosexuality: Mapping the Vectors   109
    Misza Czerniak

Chapter 12: Confronting Environmental Crisis: What Do Jewish
    Traditions Teach about Using the World?   121
    Tanhum Yoreh

Chapter 13: Confronting Environmental Crisis: What Do Orthodox
    Christian Traditions Teach about Using the World?   133
    Elizabeth Theokritoff

Chapter 14: The Challenge of COVID-19: Reflections of an
    Orthodox Congregational Rabbi   145
    Michael J. Harris

Chapter 15: The Challenge of COVID-19 to Rituals around Death
    in Orthodoxy   155
    Ian Graham

Chapter 16: Euthanasia and Assisted Dying: What Jewish Texts
    Can Teach Us   163
    Sylvia Rothschild

Chapter 17: Do We Have the Right to End Our Own Life?:
    Orthodox Christian Responses to the Debate on Euthanasia and
    Assisted Dying   173
    Joanna Burton

Index   185

About the Editors and Contributors   187

Introduction

Elena Narinskaya and Sybil Sheridan

Tois Pasin o Kairos – to everything, a season. This reference to the famous passage in Ecclesiastes (3:1–11) seemed appropriate for this, the second volume on Jewish–Christian Orthodox dialogue developed from the seminars held in the Faculty of Divinity in Cambridge. Like the title of the first volume, *Elonei Mamre,* it derives from a shared scriptural heritage, though here we have chosen to use the Greek formulation of the phrase as a balance to the Hebrew title of Elonei Mamre.

The Ecclesiastes passage holds a dichotomy within its verses. A set time for every activity – a repeated and regulated 'time' to birth and to die, to plant and pull up – the regularity of human activity and the predictability of human emotions. 'There is nothing new under the sun' (Eccl 1:9). This sentiment is set well within our organised religious traditions with its focus on the ritual year, the consistency of worship and the attention to a fixed liturgy which is intrinsic in both faiths. Yet at the same time, by pairing each action with its opposite, the passage remains open to the irregular and unpredictable. There is a time to tear down and a time to build up, a time to keep and a time to discard. Both faiths have a vulnerable history, have encountered and overcome deep traumas. Such traumas do not pass without imprinting themselves in some manner upon the faith, and religious survival depends on adaptability to external circumstances. There is a time for practised custom and a time for innovation; a time for tradition, yes, but there is also a time for change.

The foundation for this book is at least two decades of experience in dialogue and academic exchanges between Jewish and Orthodox Christian scholars and practitioners. Why such a marginal and exclusive selection for the dialogue? It is for two reasons. We believe that we found a niche for dialogue that is less explored. We often hear about Jewish–Catholic dialogue, or a Jewish–Protestant dialogue, but we rarely hear about Jewish–Orthodox

Christian dialogue. Is it because Orthodox Christianity is seen to be the closest to Judaism, and therefore it is more difficult to find the space for the dialogue? Or is it because Orthodox Christianity is projecting itself as being closed to any kind of dialogue, be it within its own boundaries, or outside of them? We, as a group, find it valuable and important to ask ourselves and others these questions, and to constantly find new answers to them.

We meet twice a year, usually in November and May, staying together the whole day, sharing our views and responding to the views of others. We also share a meal and informal communications, gelling as a group, developing personal relationships, and learning about the others as well as about our own religious tradition.

The members of the group are invited personally. The main criterion of becoming a member is being a religious practitioner, a believer if you wish, and the ability to present the foundations of one's belief in a manner that is substantiated with theological, scriptural, historical, philosophical, or linguistic background. In lay terms, the core foundation of the group is religious curiosity, continuous discovery of one's own religious tradition, and marvelling at the beauty and splendour of the beliefs and traditions of the other. Stable membership over continued meetings has contributed to the building up of mutual trust – a vital ingredient for dialogue.

As members of this group, and as practising Jews or Orthodox Christians, we understand that we share an enormous religious legacy of a difficult past and a complex present. This understanding allows us to help each other in furthering our knowledge about this world, the experience of the divine in it, and most importantly, to follow on our religious journey accompanied by likeminded people who are as curious about themselves as they are about the others around them. We do realise that we share a lot of common knowledge about God, whether it is found in our scriptures, or conveyed to us through the teachings of the fathers of the church or rabbinical discourses.

Why do we meet again and again? The answer to this can be as simple or as complex as you like. First, we meet because we are invited by our welcoming facilitator, Professor Nicholas de Lange, with whom some of us have developed, firstly, perhaps, academic admiration, but later personal friendships. Secondly, we meet to discuss the topics of interest to us, again not just intellectually and academically, but also personally and experientially. We want to learn about our God, we want to learn about how the others see the divine, and how they express their relationship with our God. We learn to recognise our God in the writings of our fathers, be they Christian saints, ascetics, or rabbinical sages. We learn from our scriptures, and we share the common experience of journeying together through our religious traditions, our experiences of it. But most importantly we witness to and partake of the reality of Judaism and Christianity as a living tradition of continuous

Introduction xi

renewal, freshness and endless discovery of new horizons and depth of its understanding.

The twenty-first century is one that confronts us with many challenges, of which we have chosen four to present in this volume. They are modern Israel, gender and sexuality, climate change and issues around death: euthanasia/ assisted dying and the challenge of the Covid 19 pandemic. Unlike the first volume, these are areas of innovation. While both faiths will look back to their classical texts, to precedent, the issues throw up demands that require a response beyond that of tradition. Perhaps more than in the first volume, where the focus on God and worship were areas held as of equal significance by Jews and Orthodox Christians alike, these areas demonstrate an imbalance in the experience and impact of the two faiths. The experience of Jews in Israel is inevitably very different to that of Christians, but what is troubling is the apparent lack of dialogue between Jews and Orthodox Christians in that country. While encounters between Jews and Catholics or Jews and Protestants are well established, those between Jews and the Orthodox (both Greek and Russian) go little beyond ceremonial appearances together. Why that should be is beyond the scope of this book, but it is an area that deserves close scrutiny. We did not manage to find any Orthodox Christian in Israel who was willing or able to write about their experience of dialogue and that is why we invited Petra Heldt, one of the few non-Orthodox, to contribute her chapter.

We had difficulty also on the subject of homosexuality. To find a Jewish writer was easier, as the progressive wings of the faith, Liberal, Masorti and Reform, have come to accept lesbian and gay individuals within the religious fold. However, it remains a difficult subject in a traditional faith context, and in Orthodoxy – both Jewish and Christian – homosexuality remains taboo and writing about it only marginally less so. With climate change, the Orthodox Church appears well in advance of Judaism, incorporating a special day for the protection of the environment with attendant prayers and ritual. Both faiths, however, share similar experiences when it comes to death. COVID has affected us all, and our responses to it have been remarkably similar. So too, the challenge faced in faith communities by the possibilities of euthanasia and assisted dying.

In coming to grips with these challenges, it is to be noted how close is the methodology of both the Jewish and the Orthodox Christian contributors. Their use of classical texts and their method of interpretation follow very similar lines. The conclusions may be different, but each can recognise the pathway of the other. It is hoped that through this book the reader will also come to recognise this and understand that, despite our often tormented history, we share and have always shared so much.

We begin our book with two chapters on Jerusalem. Marc Saperstein gives a historical and very personal account of the significance of the Holy City to Jews. The history in Nikita Banev's article is of a very different experience, but both understand the challenge between the idealised Jerusalem of our faith and the reality of today's divided city. These chapters create the context for the modern encounter between Judaism and Christianity reflected in the chapters by Petra Heldt and David Rosen that follow, and Michael Azar's article on the experience of the Orthodox Church under the control of the State of Israel demonstrates that all is not holy in the Holy Land.

In talking about God and the experience of the divine in our respective religious traditions one cannot possibly neglect the topic of our humanity. We took our time in identifying this topic as important enough to be selected for a book on challenges of modernity.

We also narrowed the topic to three areas: the position of women in religious institutions, impurity laws and the issue of homosexuality. We present these painful and often scandalous topics in religious circles, not to add fuel to the debates, but to open the door for serious discussion on the matter.

We asked Miri Freud-Kandel to write on women in Judaism, and Mary Cunningham on women in Orthodox Christianity. They both write on contemporary challenges of being a woman in traditional religious communities, and look for a balance between challenges of the contemporary world and religious vocation.

Sybil Sheridan and Elena Narinskaya write on the issue of blood, a tricky subject indicating that in the most traditional religious environments change and modernity do not always happen in time. The issue of blood is the unfortunate legacy of the ritual impurity laws of Leviticus, which penetrated the rituals and practices in Jewish and Christian settings, and which are continued today.

Our contributors pose the question whether sacred traditions always have to be, by their nature, unchangeable. Another important subject that is discussed in these essays is the necessity of the ongoing discovery of the scriptural legacy of Judaism and Christianity, as well as an ongoing process of renewal and rediscovery of one's own religious tradition, at every moment of one's life. This is essential in the attempt to keep our religious legacy alive, current and flourishing.

If we are to appreciate the multiple gifts of God, we need to open a serious discussion about our experiences as sexual beings. We do not presume to exhaust the discussion of the topic in the two essays about homosexuality, one written by a Jewish Rabbi, René Pfertzel and the other by Misza Cherniak, an Orthodox Christian humanist activist. We give them a voice in this book, we admire their courage in putting their names and their reputations on the

Introduction xiii

record, and we also hope that the conversations that we emphasise as important for contemporary times can be continued further.

Two chapters on the environment follow, examining the traditional beliefs and practices in Judaism and Orthodox Christianity. Tanhum Yoreh and Elizabeth Theokritoff clearly agree on the need to reform the way humanity relates to the world around us, and both of them search their religious tradition for an answer, yet their conclusions are very different. Yoreh focuses on the Jewish ideal of Shabbat, while Theokritoff sees the solution in a renewed asceticism. But when it comes down to the practical application of each approach the resultant practice is very much the same.

Contemplating death is perhaps the only exercise that is encouraged in certain religious circles, while shied away from in the world. There are several reasons for it. First, death seems to be one of these huge elephants in the room that everyone is aware of, but the issue is too big, too heavy, too scary or simply too much to bring into conversation. And since our conversations are mostly relegated to small talk, we prefer not to mention death unless we are confronted by it. And guess what? Along came the COVID pandemic, and we were all confronted with it. We invited Father Ian Graham and Mother Joanna Burton, two Orthodox Christians, and two Jews, Rabbis Michael Harris and Sylvia Rothschild, to address the challenges of COVID, and to introduce the very serious and controversial topic of euthanasia to our readers.

What has become obvious throughout the centuries of religious discourse about death is that it enhances the experience of life, prioritises the valuable aspects of it, and refines the overall experience. 'Death, where is your sting?' – we sing in the Orthodox Paschal Hymn. Sheol, what is your purpose? – we find out in the rabbinical discourse.

Of course, the discussions introduced in these chapters are not exhaustive. The situation in Israel is a difficult one, but it is one that could change in future years. Our hope is that this book can in some small way be a catalyst for a Jewish–Orthodox Christian encounter that enhances and deepens the knowledge of each faith and that may in some small way change the narrative for the benefit of all. In the area of gender and sexuality, we have in this book only the very start of an exploration that will, in time, have to take on board the question of nonbinary and transgender individuals and their place in religious communities. When it comes to environmental issues, unless the world begins to take notice, our actions will be overtaken by events in the natural world itself. The COVID pandemic has brought with it the experience of many returning to faith, a focus on the essentials of life and a greater appreciation of spiritual matters. We do not know what the future holds, only that we have an opportunity to make of life something better and as believers we feel faith is the key.

We offer this collection of essays, a joint effort of Jewish and Orthodox Christian scholars and practitioners, as the fruit of a labour of promoting and testifying to the availability of religious dialogue. This book is a testament to dialogue in action, so to speak, in which religious practitioners and scholars of two Abrahamic faiths offer their insights into their respective traditions, and give feedback to each with respect and appreciation, and with a loving but critical view. It is valuable in the contemporary world to have experience of dialogue, especially dialogue of a religious nature. Jews and Orthodox Christians in this book address current issues that extend beyond the boundaries of religion, but that are common to all humanity. Hence, this book could be seen as a helping hand to the world that we live in, where religion for a change is not the cause of the problems, but the source of finding meaningful and insightful solutions to them.

This book is a first in addressing some of these areas of Jewish–Orthodox relations. It is a first, but it will not be the last book on the subject. Our dialogue group will continue, and as society changes in response to the very real challenges of our world, we and other groups will look further into our traditions to meet those challenges, and move further along the path together in recognition and mutual understanding.

To everything a season . . . a time for silence and a time to speak. . . .

Postscript: *Tois Pasin ho Kairos*, to everything a season. This book was written when the COVID-19 pandemic was at its height, and before the fighting in Ukraine had exploded into full-blown war. Many passages in the book would have been written differently in the present (June 2022) circumstances.

Chapter 1

A 'City Whose Gates Are Always Open'?

Visions for Jerusalem in Orthodox Christianity

Nikita Banev

On 22 January 1988, one month after the eruption of violence in Gaza and the West Bank, Jerusalem witnessed an unprecedented act of Christian solidarity: the heads of local churches issued what was to become the first of many joint statements calling on all leaders and people in authority to end hostilities and facilitate the cause of peace. The first signatory to this document, as well as to all subsequent joint statements, was the Greek Orthodox patriarch (May 2010: 13, 20–22). The Holy Places and the Holy City became the focus of the *1994 Memorandum of Their Beatitudes the Patriarchs and the Heads of Christian Communities in Jerusalem on the Significance of Jerusalem for Christians* – a key document in which the bishops articulated their vision for Jerusalem as a city, in the words of the Prophet Isaiah, 'whose gates are always open' (§6, May 2010: 50; see Isa. 60:11). In this, the heads of churches went beyond the obvious call to speak for the rights of their own Christian flock. More recently, in a statement of 14 May 2021, the Greek Orthodox Patriarch Theophilos III condemned the violence at the Al-Aqsa Mosque and the Sheikh Jarrah neighbourhood affirming the rights of the adherents of all three Abrahamic faiths to their Holy Places (WCC 2021). The resilience with which this new vision for Jerusalem is preached is remarkable, especially given the context in which Christians in the Holy Land, as a minority within the Palestinian minority, have to operate. In a brief summary for 2020, the *Report of the Committee on the Exercise of the Inalienable Rights of the*

Palestinian People to the UN speaks of ongoing 'arbitrary arrests, discrimination, administrative detention, including of children, restrictions on freedom of movement, violations of the right to worship, restrictions on access to education and health care and killings by Israeli security forces in the West Bank, including in East Jerusalem' (§9, at www.un.org).

There is here an obvious tension between the historical 'is' and the prophetic 'ought to be', between the Jerusalem-divided-by-a-wall and the Holy City 'whose gates are always open'. Taking a stance against the injustices of the first, it is to the potential in the second that the present text will be dedicated. It will provide a platform enabling the voices of local Christians to be heard (see May 2010 for the period 1988–2008). In order to show both what is traditional and what is new in their vision for a Jerusalem-after-the-end-of-Israeli-Palestinian-hostilities we will then turn to the phenomenon known as *hierotopy* – a special case of which is the setting up of 'new Jerusalem' sites across the Christian world (Lidov 2009). Here we will examine the efforts on the part of three centres in the Orthodox world – in Byzantium, Georgia and Russia – to re-create the Holy Places and to appropriate some of Jerusalem's sacred attributes for their own historical contexts.

Jerusalem as both a troubled earthly city and an enduring icon of messianic peace, a place which does not exclude, but gathers – despite all divisions, a powerful symbol of divine hospitality – this vision is one which Christians in the Holy Land evidently share, deferring, as they have been in promoting it over the course of the past 35 years, to the leadership of the Greek Orthodox Patriarchate. If in earlier centuries they had seen themselves in a more Christian-focused sense as the 'Guardians of the Tomb of Christ', now – without rejecting the earlier identification – they speak as defenders also of the 'unique pluralistic character' of Jerusalem itself (Easter Message, 23 March 1991; May 2010: 35). According to the *1994 Memorandum*, the city's vocation is to promote 'reconciliation and harmony among people, whether citizens, pilgrims or visitors' (§2, May 2010: 48). For Christians specifically, Jerusalem holds a twofold significance. As the 'Holy City with Holy Places', it provides them with a 'link with the history of salvation fulfilled in and through Christ'. Furthermore, it has 'a community of Christians that have been living there continually' since apostolic times (§10, May 2010: 51). These statements emphasise the local nature of the communities. It is their voices that we hear lamenting that the issue of who is in control of the city has 'become a source of conflict and disharmony'. Being at 'the heart of the Israeli-Palestinian and Israeli-Arab disputes', the situation of Jerusalem has become 'unenviable' and 'scandalizes many' (§2, May 2010: 48). Thus, the *1994 Memorandum* speaks of Jesus weeping over the earthly Jerusalem (Luke 19:41), because its people have 'completely lost sight of the path to peace'. The heavenly Jerusalem, in contrast, is a 'new' city (Rev 3:12, 21:2), which is 'from above' and is 'free' (Gal 4:26, cf. Heb 12:22). When it is revealed, 'God will wipe away all tears' (Rev 21:4) (§6, May 2010: 50). The *1994 Memorandum* explains the relationship between the two cities as follows: 'The earthly Jerusalem, in the Christian tradition, prefigures the heavenly Jerusalem as "the vision of peace"' (§7, May 2010: 51).

One is struck by the fact that Christian communities which remain divided for theological and historical reasons here speak with one voice. Furthermore, there is the emphasis on peace and reconciliation also with Jews and Muslims, for whom the Christian bishops are eager to secure the rights of human dignity and religious freedoms as for their own communities: 'Christians declare themselves disposed to search with Jews and Muslims for a mutually respectful application of these rights and for a harmonious coexistence, in the perspective of the universal spiritual vocation of Jerusalem.' (§13, May 2010: 53)

The *1994 Memorandum* is remarkable with its call for preserving the religious diversity in the earthly city – Old Jerusalem – as an abiding symbol of peace and justice, which are attributes of the Jerusalem-to-come, the New Jerusalem. This is because

> every exclusivity is against the prophetic character of Jerusalem. . . . The experience of history teaches us that in order for Jerusalem to be a city of peace, it cannot belong exclusively to one people or to only one religion. Jerusalem should be open to all, shared by all. Those who govern the city should make it 'the capital of humankind'. This universal vision of Jerusalem would help those who exercise power there to open it to others who also are fondly attached to it and to accept sharing it with them. (§5, May 2010: 49–50)

Jerusalem – here designated as 'capital of humankind' – thus embodies a political project of local independence. The protected – because endangered – status of the city is presented as divinely sanctioned. Jerusalem, concludes the document, is a 'symbol and a promise of the presence of God'. With the express aim of securing for Jews, Christians and Muslims the right to be 'at home' and 'at peace with one another', the bishops appeal to the international community to safeguard Jerusalem's character as 'an open city that transcends local, regional or world political troubles' (§14, May 2010: 53).

Placed in the context of the history of the Greek Orthodox Patriarchate, which claims unbroken continuity with the apostolic church, this vision for Jerusalem as an 'open city' must be seen as inaugurating an important change. As is well known, in the centuries that followed the destruction of the Temple by the Romans until the Muslim conquest of the city – that is, while the city was in Roman and Byzantine control – Jews were, in the best of cases, only allowed to visit but never again to settle. Their return, and the possibility to rebuild the Temple, entered the Roman agenda only once, during the brief reign of the emperor Julian (361–63 CE). In all other cases, from Constantine onwards, the building of the church of the *Anastasis* opposite the ruins of the Temple was meant to symbolize the demise of Judaism – and thus of king David's (old) Jerusalem. As the historian Eusebius put it, with the coming of the new David, that is, Constantine, Christians obtained what the prophets had longed for – a 'fresh new – *kainēn kai nean* – Jerusalem' (*Life of Constantine* III, 33. tr. Cameron & Hall, 135), which Jews could no longer call their home. Eusebius was following the line established by earlier apologists such as Melito in the second century who claimed that 'the Jerusalem below was precious, but it is worthless now because of the Jerusalem above' (*On Pascha* 45, tr. Hall. Oxford 1979, cited in Pahlitzsch 2011: 240). The issue is left out of the *1994 Memorandum*. One Greek scholar has spoken, with relief, that 'today the attitude of Orthodox thought toward Jerusalem and the Jews has completely changed' (Karavidopoulos 1988: 192). In the *1994 Memorandum,* this is taken for granted and the appeal is made directly to the period after the Muslim conquest. The reference is to the 'historical *firmans* of the Ottoman emperors' and the 'rights of property ownership, custody and worship' defined in them (§11, May 2010: 52). This is the Status Quo agreement between the faith communities with regard to sharing the Holy Places for which the bishops seek recognition and respect from the Israeli state and the international community (Roussos 1995).

In contrast to the exclusion of Jews, one could speak here of continuity in terms of sharing with Islam. From the period before the crusades, archaeologists have established shared use of church buildings in Jerusalem and Bethlehem (Verstegen 2019). The mosque built over the sixth-century refectory in St Catherine's monastery on Mt Sinai, where the minaret was placed opposite the bell tower, also testifies to this practice. This phenomenon shocked many travellers who came from Western lands, where such a practice was unknown. The significance of such arrangements has been highlighted recently with reference to the Saidnaiya Greek Orthodox convent near Damascus:

> The thaumaturgic icon of Our Lady of Saidnaiya has for more than eight hundred years met with a response which cuts across the confessional divisions within Christianity, and even across the deeper divisions between Christianity and Islam. It has brought together in a common religious activity groups of people normally antagonistic to each other: the Muslim subjects of Saladin and the crusaders against whom they fought . . . ; Latin Catholic clergy and the Orthodox clergy whom they considered schismatic; and the many varieties of

oriental Christians whose relations with each other and with the Orthodox were often stormy. Moreover, control of the shrine has never been a contentious issue. It is a not inconsiderable achievement. (Hamilton 2000: 215)

The vision for a new Jerusalem 'shared by all' can thus be linked in part to lived experience – past and present – in the Holy Land. At the same time, however, it must be seen as something radically new. Positive assessments of religious coexistence, such as the one quoted above, lend credibility to the voices we hear in the *1994 Memorandum* and other joint statements. Their historical accuracy, however, can be fully accepted in only one sense: they record how Christians in the Holy Land today imagine their future while at the same time looking back – selectively, as we have seen – for historical precedent. Thus, there can be no question of reviving the myth of interfaith utopia (in agreement with Cohen 2008). No local Christian community can afford to do so. The appeal to the Status Quo and the historical *firmans* of Ottoman emperors acknowledges the lower level of interfaith conflict when the city was in Muslim control. This, however, does not invalidate the fact that the calendars of each church commemorate martyrs from this period as well; Greek Orthodox, Copts or Armenians will not forget their names. The phenomenon of sharing individual sites, for what must have been and remains a segregated form of religious worship, is also quite different from the currently espoused vision of sharing – together – the Holy City. The factors which have brought about the sense of solidarity to which the joint statements bear testimony are also unprecedented in their political and sociological complexity. Palestinians, Muslim and Christian, as the oppressed minority, feel strongly that they share a common identity as they struggle to survive in the face of an aggressive Jewish Israeli majority. Such an identity fits well with the popular narrative defining Palestinians as the people of the land who, regardless of religious affiliation, throughout history have had to resist foreign oppression (Mana 2012: 179). Monitoring closely, from distant headquarters, is the international community. All this has created the urgency for local Christians to act – together – to do what they can to secure a vision for their own future. The language used by the Christian leaders – and its ineffectiveness in terms of *Realpolitik* – mirrors that of the UN, whose resolutions to promote a two state solution remain largely ineffective on the ground.

The articulation of a new vision, however, does not mean a complete break with tradition – something impossible in Jerusalem. Rather, we can say that the new is also traditional to the extent to which it includes elements of the past (the experience, for example, of shared religious sites). What is novel is the total rejection of exclusive political or religious claims over the Holy City. In a much more fundamental sense, this change, too, must be seen as part of an ongoing process of reconceptualizing Jerusalem, which has been taking place throughout Christian history.

One key aspect of the sanctity of Jerusalem, which the joint statements of the heads of churches seek to protect, is access to the Holy Places. Hence the commitment in the *1994 Memorandum* to safeguarding the local communities' rights of 'ownership and custody'. Thus, the text continues, Christians of the 'entire world, Western or Eastern, should have the right to come on pilgrimage to Jerusalem' (§11, May 2010: 52). Here there is historical continuity, but there is also an issue which has been left out of focus: the exporting of relics which accompanied the growth of pilgrimage to the Holy Land from the fourth century CE onwards.

Very soon, Constantinople would boast more relics than any other place in the Christian world, acquiring the reputation of being not just the New Rome, or the city of the Mother of God, but also a New Jerusalem (Klein 2006). The first title it owed to its political prominence, the second and the third to the extraordinarily rich collection of relics, eventually amounting to more than 3,600 items from at least 476 different saints (Ousterhout 2004: 4). Chief among these were the relics associated with Christ's life and death – the crown of thorns, large pieces of the cross, two nails from the crucifixion, the lance that pierced his side, an ampulla with Christ's blood, the purple robe of derision, the reed with which a sponge with vinegar was offered, his sandals, and the *mandylion* imprint of his face – the majority of which were kept in the church of the Virgin of the Pharos located inside the imperial palace (Pahlitzsch 2011: 246). Further relics of Christ's closest associates were also gathered in the city: St John the Baptist, St Lazarus the Friend of Christ, and above all the Virgin Mary, the Mother of God. Thus, on the eve of the sack of Constantinople by the Fourth Crusade (1204 CE), the city was hailed as 'Jerusalem, Tiberias, Nazareth, Mount Tabor, Bethany and Bethlehem' (Nikolaos Mesarites, *Epitaphios* §13, tr. Angold 2017: 152). It was as if, with their relics, the Virgin Mary 'Theotokos', Christ and the saints had all arrived to confirm the people of Byzantium as the New Israel, and Constantinople as Jerusalem – the main stage of divine action in the world. Housed in the palace, the main dominical relics were beyond the reach of the population except on special feast days when they were exhibited for public veneration. This arrangement further contributed to the sacralisation of the rule of the emperor, providing what has been interpreted as 'symbolic identification' of the imperial palace as heavenly Jerusalem itself (Carlie 2006).

The connection with Jerusalem looks very different if we examine it not from the centre but from the periphery of the Christian *oikoumene*. At Mtskheta, the capital of medieval Georgia, it was the mantle of Christ which was believed to be the country's most sacred relic. Because of it, the city became known as Georgia's Jerusalem. This was understood both as signifying the presence of the Heavenly Jerusalem and as a copy of the earthly one, with its Golgotha at the Mtskheta Holy Cross Monastery, the Jordan at the Mtkvari River as well as Gethsemane, Bethlehem, Bethany, Tabor, the Church of St Stephen the Protomartyr and even a small chapel called 'Antioch' (Chkhartishvili 2009). Historical scrutiny cannot confirm the tradition of the arrival at Mtskheta of the mantle of Christ with a Georgian Jew who had been in Jerusalem at the time of the crucifixion. Only subsequent accounts of miracles testify to the relic's presence under the so-called 'Living' or 'Life-giving' pillar from which the imposing eleventh-century Sveti-Tskhoveli cathedral at Mtskheta takes its name. What is certain is that soon after the conversion of the country, Georgian monks became a constant presence in the Holy Land. Witness to this are some of the earliest known Georgian inscriptions discovered in Palestine (dating from the mid-sixth century, Braund 1994: 285). Such Jerusalem connections – real as well as legendary – played a major role in the formation of Georgian identity, of which the complex at Mtskheta was to become a key element – emancipating Georgia from the jurisdiction of Antioch and circumventing the influence of its neighbour Armenia.

By contrast, the gathering of relics in Constantinople did not result in duplicating the Jerusalem Holy Places on the Bosphorus. The emperor Justinian may well have thought to have surpassed Solomon with building the magnificent Hagia Sophia but, nevertheless, no attempt was ever made to re-create in Constantinople the Tomb of Christ or other of the major Jerusalem sites. The capital of the empire was politically and religiously secure in its identity as New Rome. The importing of relics cannot be viewed as somehow putting it in a position of needing legitimation from distant Jerusalem, as appears to have been more the case with Georgia (Pahlitzsch 2011: 253–54).

The subject of Christian–Jewish relations provides further basis for comparison between the new Jerusalems on the Bosphorus and at Mtskheta. While in Roman and Byzantine law Jews were accorded legal protection, they were denied settlement in Jerusalem, and there were also attempts at forced mass conversions (De Lange 2018). The Georgians, in contrast – with their cherished account of a Jew bringing the mantle of Christ – have retained a uniquely positive image of key members of their ancient Jewish community being among the first to convert to Christianity, well before the fourth century. Tombstones with Hebrew inscriptions at Mtskheta confirm a Jewish presence in the city from the third until the fifth century (Mgaloblishvili & Gagoshidze 1998). These Jews had evidently kept their religion and identity. Thus, as opposed to the case at Jerusalem in Palestine, Jews were present and remained welcome in Mtskheta well after the Christianisation of the country. Researchers today accept the view that hatred of Jews was not a feature of medieval Georgian society. Concurring with previous assessments of the situation prior to Georgia's becoming part of the Russian empire and church in 1801 CE, one of the few Jewish scholars who has researched the topic confirms that 'the absence of evidence regarding church incitement against the Jews, or religious persecutions, expulsions or riots, is proof of the tolerant attitude of the Georgian people toward the Jews' (Aaron Krikheli, cited in Ben-Oren 1992).

When a new Jerusalem finally came to be designed on Russian soil, it had to outshine all previous attempts in the Christian Orthodox world. In 1658, the Moscow patriarch Nikon (1652–66) started building a full-scale copy of the Jerusalem *Anastasis* (Price 2000; Kain 2017). He placed his 'New Resurrection' monastery near the river Istra, renamed 'Jordan'. The places around also acquired Biblical names: Tabor, Hermon, Sinai, Mount of Olives, Garden of Gethsemane, etc. The complex was created with almost scientific accuracy following the plans of Jerusalem buildings, which became available in Moscow thanks to detailed descriptions, three-dimensional models and printed architectural drawings.

The fascination with the Holy Land was not a new phenomenon in Russia. The first account of a Russian pilgrim to (Old) Jerusalem is that of the abbot Daniel, who travelled between 1104 and 1107 in the aftermath of the capture of Jerusalem by the First Crusade (Price 2000: 251–52). His descriptions are valuable both for the information they give of the places he visits but also because of the religious and cultural sensitivities associated with what he sees or, indeed, does not see. Thus, the Holy Places are in the care of Christians. Greek monks reside in the major monasteries but some of the sites are in the hands of Latin clergy. The crusader massacres have ensured that the Holy Land is free from Jews and Muslims, which do not appear in his account; the only 'Saracens' he mentions are robbers who threaten pilgrims on their way. Most revealing is his account of the Holy Saturday celebration at the *Anastasis* with the coming of the 'Easter fire'. A great multitude of people from all tongues and nations fills the church. The service is conducted by the Greek monks but Latin clergy sing on the side in their own tongue. Daniel did not know Greek or Latin, but he was clearly able to recognize the members of the different churches. He then describes how the miraculous fire was distributed to the faithful, including, firstly, Baldwin I, the Crusader King of Jerusalem. Daniel had asked for permission to place – on behalf of all Russian people – his own candle inside the Tomb of Christ. His request was granted: the candle had to be on the floor and he was only allowed to enter the sacred space barefoot. At the end of the service, he was ecstatic to see his candle ablaze with the miraculous fire.

The popularity of Daniel's descriptions in Russia reveals a perception of Jerusalem in which the unique sanctity of the place is clearly acknowledged, signalled by the ritual removing of shoes at the Tomb of Christ. The religious demarcation of the sacred was also made clear: the Holy Places belong to Christians, and among them the Orthodox are the ones favoured by divine grace. The Latin clergy were singled out not just because of their language but also because they had placed their lamps high up but still failed to obtain grace – the miraculous fire had passed them by. The sacred city is in this instance shared only by Christians and clear lines are set which define the degrees of access to it.

At the end of the seventeenth century, these features reappear in patriarch Nikon's new Jerusalem at Moscow with its full-size copy of the *Anastasis* church and the surroundings of his *Voskresensky* monastery landscaped as a new Palestine. The project was a success, but Nikon ended up condemned and deposed at the Moscow council of 1666, at which the patriarchs of Jerusalem and Antioch were also present. Nikon's work had been so meticulous that he was charged with arrogance for pretending to have set up not just a 'model' (*obrazetz*) of Jerusalem but for seeking to supplant the original Jerusalem (Price 2000: 260–61). His chief transgression, however, was that in doing so he had also claimed for himself the title 'Patriarch of New Jerusalem', thus appearing to challenge the seniority of the Eastern patriarchs (Kain 2017: 392). Simple believers were said to have been 'scandalized' by the degree of presumed similarity between the 'new' holy places at Moscow and those in Palestine. Many were even prepared to believe that the Romanov Tsar and Tsarina were now their new Constantine and Helena (Kain 2017: 393). As for outsiders who were denied access, the council of 1666 condemned the group which had resisted Nikon's liturgical reforms. Excluded from the new-Moscow-Jerusalem, they became known as 'Old Believers'.

In the fourth century, not all Christians agreed that pilgrimage to Jerusalem was essential to their faith. Christ, as Gregory of Nyssa famously wrote, had not required it of those whom he called 'blessed' in his Sermon on the Mount (*Letter* 2, 2–3, Matt. 5; Bitton-Ashkelony 2005: 53). What mattered for being a good disciple of Christ was not the place (*topos*) but the way (*tropos*). Cappadocia, or indeed Constantinople, could offer examples of equal or even greater sanctity. The basic soundness of this theology did not, however, prevent the spectacular growth of pilgrimage in Late Antiquity. This was followed by the emergence of new Jerusalem sites across the Christian world. Concluding our brief review, we note that something always appears to have been lost in the *translations* of Jerusalem which fill the pages of history. Constantinople acquired relics but did not seek to replicate Holy Places; Georgia – one main relic with a major cathedral and a rudimentary complex of sites; and Moscow – no major relic but the most spectacular re-creation of the Holy Places in the Orthodox world. In all cases, the translation of the sacred posed a problem of exclusivity. In the fourth century, the building of the Constantinian church of the *Anastasis* right opposite the ruined Temple was seen as a 'fresh new' Jerusalem – marking also the line separating Jews as 'outsiders' from the initiated Christians. In Constantinople, the keeping of major relics inside the imperial palace had a similar effect, supported by the legislation excluding Jews from settling in Jerusalem and, later, non-Nicene Christians from worshipping inside the walls of Constantinople. In Georgia, uniquely, a more inclusive climate seems to have developed around the Holy Places at Mtskheta, especially with regard to Jews, whose ancestors were credited with contributing to the Christianisation of the country. In Russia, striving to consolidate its reputation as 'Third Rome', the creation of the most ambitious replica of the Jerusalem Holy Places coincided with one of the most violent episodes in Orthodox Christian history. In the long history of realizing new Jerusalem(s), the Jews and Muslims missing from abbot Daniel's account of his twelfth-century pilgrimage to the Holy Land effectively correspond to the Old Believers excluded from the new Moscow-Jerusalem at the end of the seventeenth century. The horrors accompanying the arrival of the crusaders in the Holy Land presage the apocalyptic persecution unleashed against the Old Believers. As background to both, we find the exclusive sacredness of Jerusalem's Holy Places, old and new. Can there be a different *tropos*? As at the dawn of Christian history, the Jerusalem church is offering a new vision: "We invite each party to . . . consider the religious and national aspirations of others in order to give back to Jerusalem its true universal character and to make of the city a holy place of reconciliation for humankind." (*1994 Memorandum*, May 2010: 53)

BIBLIOGRAPHY

Angold M. 2017. *Nicholas Mesarites: His Life and Works (in Translation)*. Liverpool: Liverpool University Press.

Ben-Oren G. 1992. 'The History of the Jews of Georgia until the Communist Regime', in *In the Land of the Golden Fleece. The Jews of Georgia – History and Culture*. Tel Aviv. Online at: https://dbs.anumuseum.org.il/skn/en/c6/e162313/Place/Georgia (accessed 5 August 2021).

Bitton-Ashkelony B. 2005. *Encountering the Sacred: The Debate on Christian Pilgrimage in Late Antiquity*. Berkeley: University of California Press.

Braund D. 1994. *Georgia in Antiquity. A History of Colchis and Transcaucasian Iberia 550 BC–AD 562*. Oxford: Clarendon Press.

Carlie M. C. 2006. 'Constantinople and the Heavenly Jerusalem?: Through the Imperial Palace', *Byzantinistica* 2/8, 85–104.

Chkhartishvili M. 2009. 'Mtskheta as New Jerusalem: Hierotopy in the Life of St Nino', in *New Jerusalems*, ed. A. Lidov, 131–50. Moscow: Indrik.

Cohen M. R. 2008. *Under Crescent and Cross: The Jews in the Middle Ages*. Princeton: Princeton University Press.

De Lange N. 2018. 'Byzantium', in *The Cambridge History of Judaism, vol. 6*, ed. R. Chazan, 76–97. Cambridge: Cambridge University Press.

Hamilton B. 2000. 'Our Lady of Saidnaiya: An Orthodox Shrine Revered by Muslims and Knights Templar at the Time of the Crusades', in *Studies of Church History 36*, ed. R. N. Swanson, 207–15. Woodbridge: Boydell Press.

Kain K. 2017. 'New Jerusalem in Seventeenth-century Russia: The Image of a New Orthodox Holy Land', *Cahiers du Monde russe* 58/3, 371–94.

Karavidopoulos J. 1988. 'Jerusalem in the Orthodox Theological Tradition', *Greek Orthodox Theological Review* 33/2, 189–200.

Klein H. A. 2006. 'Sacred Relics and Imperial Ceremonies at the Great Palace of Constantinople', in *Visualisierungen von Herrschaft. Fruhmittelalterliche Residenzen – Gestalt und Zeremoniell*, ed. F. A. Bauer, 79–99. Istanbul.

Lidov A. 2009. *New Jerusalems: Hierotopy and Iconography of Sacred Spaces*, ed. A. Lidov. Moscow: Indrik.

Mana A. et al. 2012. 'Perceptions of Collective Narratives and Identity Strategies: The Case of Palestinian Muslims and Christians in Israel', *Mind & Society* 11, 165–82.

May M. 2010. *Jerusalem Testament: Palestinian Christians Speak, 1988–2008*. Grand Rapids, Michigan: Eerdmans.

Mgaloblishvili T. & I. Gagoshidze. 1998. 'The Jewish Diaspora and Early Christianity in Georgia', in *Ancient Christianity in the Caucasus*, vol. 1, 39–58. Richmond: Curzon Press.

Ousterhout R. 2004. 'Sacred Geographies and Holy Cities: Constantinople as Jerusalem', in *Herotopy: Studies in the Making of Sacred Spaces*, ed. A. Lidov, 1–12. Moscow: Indrik.

Pahlitzsch J. 2011. 'Zur ideologischen Bedeutung Jerusalems für das orthodoxe Christentum', in *Konflikt und Bewältigung: Die Zerstörung der Grabeskirche zu Jerusalem im Jahre 1009*, ed. Th. Pratsch, 239–55. Berlin: De Gruyter.

Price R. 2000. 'The Holy Land in Old Russian Culture', in *Studies of Church History 36*, ed. R. N. Swanson, 250–62. Woodbridge: Boydell Press.

Roussos S. 1995. 'The Greek Orthodox Patriarchate and Community of Jerusalem', in *The Christian Heritage in the Holy Land*, ed. A. O'Mahony et al., 211–24. London: Scorpion Cavendish.

Verstegen U. 2019. 'How to Share a Sacred Place – The Parallel Christian and Muslim Usage of the Major Christian Holy Sites at Jerusalem and Bethlehem', in *Ambassadors, Artists, Theologians: Byzantine Relations with the Near East from Ninth to the Thirteenth Centuries*, ed. Z. Chitwood & J. Pahlitzsch, 29–44. Mainz: Schnell & Steiner.

WCC 2021. World Council of Churches, News and Resources, at: www.oikoumene .org (accessed 5 August 2021).

Chapter 2

Jerusalem

A Jewish Perspective

Marc Saperstein

It would be an interesting exercise to ask a group of Jews and of Christians how important Jerusalem is in the Bible. My guess is that the response of both would be that it is extremely important. Although a word-count is not overly sophisticated as a test, it can sometimes be revealing. 'Jerusalem' appears 750 times in the Hebrew Bible, 'Zion' 150 times; including 'city of David', 'Holy City', 'Shalem' there are altogether more than 1,000 biblical mentions. Yet the biblical reality is more complicated. 'Jerusalem' hardly appears in the Torah, or in the books of Joshua, Judges, Esther, or the Wisdom Literature. Virtually all the references are in Samuel, Kings, Ezra–Nehemiah, the Prophets and Psalms. The absence of a specific reference in the Torah is especially striking (Kalimi & Richardson 2014).

King David was the key to this transformation, through his decision to establish a new political base in territory independent of all the existing tribes. It was a decision often emulated in subsequent history, as can be seen in the cities of Baghdad, Cairo, and Washington, DC – in each case a decision to establish a new center of political control independent of existing locations. The idea that Jerusalem would become not only the center of kingship but also the core of a religious cult – and eventually the only place for proper worship – was indeed dramatic, its influence obvious in the Prophets and Psalms.

Of course, this role of Jerusalem as the unique center for all Jewish political and religious life lasted only through the reign of Solomon; after his death, with the division of the kingdom, the ten tribes of the Northern Kingdom had little connection with Jerusalem. After the devastating conquest of the Northern Kingdom by the Assyrian army led by Sennacherib in 721 BCE and the expulsion of the ten tribes from their homeland, Jerusalem was

14 *Marc Saperstein*

also besieged by the Assyrians. According to the biblical account, 185,000 Assyrian forces were struck to their death overnight by an angel, and once again Jerusalem became the unique center of Jewish political and religious life (2 Kings 18:13–19:36).

The unique role of Jerusalem was dramatically ended with the conquest of Judea by Babylonian forces and the destruction of the Temple in the early sixth century BCE. Little is known of Jewish religious life in the land of Israel following these devastating events; Jews remained in Palestine during the Babylonian exile, but no known texts were produced there for two generations. Although Jewish leadership was shifted to Babylon, memories of Jerusalem remained strong, as can be seen in Psalm 137:

> By the rivers of Babylon, there we sat and wept, as we remembered Zion. . . . If I forget you, O Jerusalem, let my right hand wither; let my tongue stick to my palate if I cease to think of you, if I do not keep Jerusalem in memory even at my happiest hour. Remember, O Lord, against the Edomites the day of Jerusalem's fall; how they cried, 'Strip her [Jerusalem], strip her to her very foundations!'

Yet simply refusing to forget Jerusalem during this period in exile is not such a great commitment. More important was the realization that Jewish religious and political life could actually continue in a totally different environment, without Jerusalem and its Temple.

A major transformation occurred when the Babylonians were defeated by Cyrus the Great of Persia, king of the Achaemenid Empire, who permitted Jews to return to their homeland (Ezra 1:30). The prophet Zechariah powerfully articulated from Babylonia a divine command for a return to Jerusalem under the reign of the subsequent Persian king, Darius: 'Proclaim! Thus said the Lord of Hosts: I am very zealous for Jerusalem – for Zion. . . . I have returned to Zion, and I will dwell in Jerusalem. Jerusalem will be called the City of Faithfulness, and the mount of the Lord of Hosts the Holy Mount' (Zech 8:3).

The books of Ezra and Nehemiah present the restoration of Jerusalem as an actual process:

> I arrived in Jerusalem. . . . I surveyed the walls of Jerusalem that were breached, and its gates, consumed by fire. . . . Then I said . . . 'You see the bad state that we are in – Jerusalem lying in ruins, and its gates destroyed by fire. Come, let us rebuild the wall of Jerusalem and suffer no more disgrace. I told them of my God's benevolent care for me . . . and they said, 'Let us start building'. (Neh 2:11, 13, 17–18)

With the Temple rebuilt in Jerusalem, there were two centers of Jewish life, Jerusalem and Babylonia, along with Jewish communities in the northern part of Israel. Despite some serious temporary problems recorded in the books of the Maccabees, Jerusalem could be said to be thriving once again for more than five hundred years.

This period came to an end with the Roman conquest of the Holy Land, and specifically of Jerusalem. A dramatic rabbinic response is focused on the figure of Johanan ben Zakkai. Originally from the Galilee, he settled in Jerusalem at the time when the Roman forces were in control of the Holy Land. A revolt by Jews starting in 66 CE led Roman forces to confront the rebels. With Jerusalem surrounded by a powerful army, Ben Zakkai argued that Jews should not resist the Romans, but allow them to take control over Jerusalem, while Jewish practices would continue elsewhere. Sneaking outside the city, he was brought to Vespasian and asked for permission to live with his disciples in the town of Yavneh; the Roman general granted his request. Soon afterward, the Romans breached the walls of the city, and Jerusalem came under Roman control. Here is a story indicating that there are more important Jewish values than even the city of Jerusalem and that Jerusalem is not essential for continued Jewish life (Babylonian Talmud, *Gittin* 56a–b).

The Roman conquest of Jerusalem was described in detail by Josephus, who presents the Roman destruction, including of the Temple, in shattering detail. In the wake of this disaster, important questions emerged. Does God's presence remain at the site of the Temple in ruins? Or is it withdrawn? Does the divine presence, the *Shekhinah*, remain with the Jews in their exile, perhaps even in hated Rome? Or has the holiness of the sacred city been temporarily removed from the earth, residing now only in the heavenly Jerusalem?

Around the year 129 CE, the Roman emperor Hadrian visited the Middle East and ordered that a new Roman city bearing his name, Aelia Capitolina, be built on the ruins of Jerusalem, with a Greek temple on what had been the Temple Mount. This inspired a revolt in 132 led by Shim'on Bar Kokhba, which took the Romans three years to suppress but had devastating consequences. The Romans prohibited the Jews from returning to Jerusalem except on the holy day of *Tisha b'Av*, the archetype of Jewish mourning. This policy regarding Jerusalem was maintained after Rome became Christian: Jews were allowed to visit Jerusalem, but not to live there.

A Rabbinic source of late antiquity states:

These are the ones who rend their garments and may not repair them. . . . Those who rend at the [sight of the ruined] cities of Judea, the Holy Temple, or Jerusalem. . . . On seeing Jerusalem in its ruin, one recites, 'Zion is become a wilderness, Jerusalem a desolation' (Isa. 64:9). On seeing the Holy Temple in its ruin. one recites, 'Our holy and beautiful house where our fathers praised Thee,

16 *Marc Saperstein*

is burned with fire and all our pleasant things are laid waste' (Isa. 64:10), and then rends his garment. (Babylonian Talmud, *Mo'ed Katan* 26a)

A brief interruption in this pattern was the intrusion into the Christian-held Holy Land by the Persians in the early seventh century. Not surprisingly, the Jews were extremely supportive of Persian control, and the Persians considered the Jews to be partners against the Byzantine Christians. It did not take much time for the Byzantine armies to regain control, and with the Persians leaving the Holy Land, the Jews were once again in the hands of their adversaries.

With the Muslim conquest of Jerusalem and the Holy Land, the Jews were compelled to make another important decision about support. Umar ibn al-Kattab, the second caliph after the death of Mohammed, expanded Islam from a principality in Arabia into a world power. He led his armies to extraordinary military victories, conquering significant components of the Byzantine and Persian empires. His army entered Jerusalem with little resistance in 638. At that time the Temple Mount had no practical religious significance, as the Christian holy places in Jerusalem were elsewhere, but, based on the tradition that Muhammad had visited Jerusalem on his 'Night Journey' (Qur'an 17:1), Umar recognized the Temple Mount as a holy site.

Under Muslim control, the 'Pact of Umar' permitted Jews to live in Jerusalem along with Muslims and Christians, which was certainly an improvement over Christian policy. But there was a consensus that Jewish life was not to be centered in Jerusalem until the Messianic Age; the Jewish population was still primarily in northern Palestine and Babylonia. For most Jews, the idea of rebuilding the Temple remained as part of the future messianic age.

Yet there were exceptions. A powerful expression of a belief in Jerusalem's unique importance for Jewish life was expressed by the Karaite Daniel al-Kumisi, at the end of ninth century:

> Know, then, that the scoundrels who are among Israel say one to another, 'It is not our duty to go to Jerusalem until He shall gather us together, just as it was He who had cast us abroad'. These are the words of those who would draw the wrath of the Lord and who are bereft of sense. . . . The Lord Himself has commanded the men of the Exile to come to Jerusalem and to stand within it at all times before Him, mourning, fasting weeping, and wailing wearing sackcloth and bitterness, all day and all night, as it is written, *Upon your walls, O Jerusalem, I have appointed watchmen, who shall never be silent by day or by night* (Isa. 62:6). (Nemoy 1952: 35–36)

This was certainly a minority view.

Jerusalem 17

The First Crusade had a major negative impact on Jews in Jerusalem. Jews fought alongside the Muslims to protect the sacred city, but the Crusaders conquered their opponents, with some 10,000 Muslims and many Jews killed (Prawer 1988: 23–24). Some surviving Jews fled to Ashkelon and to Fustat in Egypt.

Under Christian control, only a small number of Jews were permitted to live in Jerusalem, although they were allowed to visit the holy city, usually without problems. Following are examples of three well-known twelfth-century Jews.

In his masterpiece the *Kuzari*, Judah Halevi wrote that 'Jerusalem can be rebuilt only when Israel yearns for it to such an extent that they embrace her stones and dust' (5:27). One of his best-known poems, entitled 'Jerusalem', begins:

> Beautiful heights, joy of the world, city of a great king,
> For you my soul yearns from the lands of the West,
> My pity collects and is roused when I remember the past,
> Your glory in exile, and your temple destroyed. . . .
> How shall I kiss and cherish your stones?
> Your earth will be sweeter than honey to my taste. (Goldstein
> 1971: 129)

Undoubtedly with this in mind, he decided to leave Spain for the Holy Land in the middle of the century. He spent some time in Egypt, then continued travelling eastward, apparently landing in Christian-controlled Palestine in 1141. It is unclear whether he reached Jerusalem; the legend is that he was struck down by a horseman, probably a Crusader, as he walked through the gates of the city. There is no contemporary documentary evidence that confirms this (Halkin 2010: 237).

A generation later, Moses Maimonides, who also grew up in Muslim Spain, then lived in Morocco, decided in 1165 to embark with other family members on a pilgrimage to Jerusalem. There was apparently no problem in visiting the city and viewing the Temple Mount from the Mount of Olives, but it was clear that remaining there would not be permitted, and so – despite a strong commitment to the sanctity of the Land of Israel and Jerusalem – Maimonides decided to settle in Egypt, where he spent the rest of his life. In his *Mishneh Torah*, a codification of the entirety of Jewish law, he wrote that 'the sanctity of the Sanctuary and of Jerusalem derives from the Divine Presence, which could not be banished. . . . Even though the Sanctuary is today in ruins because of our iniquities, we are obligated to reverence it in the same manner as if it was standing' (Book 8, *The Book of Temple Service*, 6:16, 7:7, cited in Peters 1985: 279).

18   *Marc Saperstein*

A few years later, in 1170, the celebrated traveler Benjamin of Tudela described Jerusalem in rather mundane terms:

> Jerusalem is a small city fortified by three walls. It is full of people whom the Mohammedans call Jacobites, Syrians, Greeks, Georgians, and Franks, and people of all tongues. . . . There are about 200 hundred Jews who dwell under the Tower of David in one corner of the city. . . . The city contains two buildings, from one of which – the hospital – there issue forth four hundred knights [Crusaders]; all the sick who come there are lodged and cared for in life and in death. The other building is called the Temple of Solomon. . . . Three hundred knights are quartered there. . . . In Jerusalem is the great church called the Sepulcher, and here is the burial place of Jesus, unto which the Christians make pilgrimages. (Adler, ed. 1907: 82–83)

In all three cases, despite powerful feelings for Jerusalem, the possibility of a Jewish return to the Holy City had to be pushed into the future.

With the return of Muslim control of Jerusalem in 1187, the Jewish community remained and continued to grow. Moses Nahmanides had to flee from Spain following his powerful defence of Jewish thought in the 'Disputation of Barcelona' of 1263, held at the royal court of King James I of Aragon. He decided to settle in Palestine. Shortly after his arrival in Jerusalem he addressed a rather bleak letter to his son, in which he described the desolation of the Holy City, where there was no synagogue, but there were 'ten men who meet and on the Sabbaths they hold the services at their home.' Jerusalem, he wrote, 'is more desolate than the rest of the country. . . . But even in this destruction, it is a blessed land' (Kobler 1953: 1.226). Reports of Nahmanides's presence brought more residents to Jerusalem. Before long, a synagogue was ready for use in time for the High Holy Days.

Following the expulsion of Jews from Spain in 1492, a significant number who left Spain, and – five years later – Jews who left Portugal following the mass forced conversion in 1497, expressed their revulsion toward Christianity by settling in the Ottoman Empire, creating important new communities in Salonika and Istanbul. A generation later, when the Ottomans took control of the Holy Land, many Jews moved there to live, creating a major community in Safed, which clearly outshone the smaller yet important community in Jerusalem.

The most dynamic movement of seventeenth-century Judaism was associated with the messianic claims of Sabbatai Zevi. Born and educated in Smyrna, he moved on to Salonika, and then to Constantinople, Egypt, and Jerusalem, which at that time had about two or three hundred Jewish families. He remained in Jerusalem for most of 1663; he did not yet formally claim to be the Messiah, but more than a few of the Jews, strongly impressed by him, became active members of a developing movement. Sabbatai was placed under a ban by the majority of the Jerusalem rabbis and formally expelled from Jerusalem, but the rabbis could not stop the growth of the Sabbatean movement, which developed in its center in Turkey (Scholem 1973: 180–86, 248, 251).

The eighteenth century brought two extremely important and influential religious leaders: Israel ben Eliezer 'Ba'al Shem Tov', the founder of Hasidism, and Elijah ben Solomon, 'the Vilna Gaon'. Jerusalem apparently had very little significance for these giants, although some of their followers relocated to the Promised Land. Moses Mendelssohn's important book *Jerusalem* contains virtually nothing about the distant city and its meaning; his major theme is an attempt to reconcile traditional Jewish loyalty to God with philosophical rationalism. In a recent academic book of more than 1,100 pages on the early modern period, the only references to 'Jerusalem' pertain to the book by Moses Mendelssohn (Karp & Sutcliffe 2018: 666–69, 1077). It seems as if in the early modern era of Europe the ancient Jerusalem had all but disappeared.

This changed dramatically in 1840 (5600 in the Jewish era, supposedly counting from the creation of the world), which had a traditional significance as a date on which the Messiah was expected in Jerusalem (Zohar, *VaYera* 1:117). As 5600 grew near, messianic expectations became more fervent. Under the rule of Mohammed Ali, Jews had been given permission to worship in public at the graves of holy rabbis and to rebuild Sephardic synagogues in Jerusalem. A letter sent from Jerusalem to Jews in the Diaspora reported that people in Jerusalem were asserting that the redemption had already begun (Morgenstern 1992: 442–43).

But the year 5600, so fervently awaited in Jerusalem, turned out to be a time of crisis, with epidemics and famine in Jerusalem. Needless to say, the Messiah did not come to Jerusalem in 5600.

The reality for Jews in Jerusalem changed dramatically during World War I when, in December 1917, the British Army took control of what had been for many centuries a Muslim entity. For the first time, Jews were permitted full religious expression in Palestine under Christian control. The emergence of a powerful Zionist movement raised significant questions about authentic policy, especially when in 1948 the British Mandate ended and leaders of the new Jewish State, under Zionist control, had to make some important decisions. Many of these decisions pertained to Jerusalem.

As the British prepared to leave, the United Nations made it clear that a new Jewish state would not include the Temple Mount and the old city of Jerusalem, as these were inhabited mainly by Muslims, with a significant Christian population. Most of the holy sites were located in the Arab section of divided Jerusalem. Was a new Jewish state more important than the Temple

20   *Marc Saperstein*

Mount? Should Jewish Jerusalem be limited to new territory that had little historical significance? Should Jews accept the United Nations proposal of internationalization for Jerusalem?

Some of the Jewish militants were opposed to any partition, insisting that all of biblical Israel, including even territory east of the Jordan River, belonged to the Jewish people. At the other extreme, Jewish leaders such as Martin Buber and Rabbi Judah Magnes, the first Chancellor of Jerusalem's Hebrew University, supported a bi-national state, shared by Jews and Arabs. The largest consensus was for partition, a division into Jewish Jerusalem and Arab Jerusalem. Most of the holy sites were in the Arab section, and some of the ultra-Orthodox Jews, who were opposed in principle to a Jewish State in premessianic times, preferred to live in the Old City, under Arab sovereignty.

With the 'establishment of an independent Jewish State in Palestine' – a phrase used by the United Nations on November 29, 1947, and by the Declaration of Independence on May 14, 1948, adding 'to be called Israel' – various problems arose, especially for the Orthodox Jews. Should the new government permit Jewish buses, or private automobiles, to travel in Jerusalem during the Sabbath? Should restaurants in Jewish Jerusalem be permitted to serve nonkosher food? Should there be a universal educational system, based on traditional Jewish literature? These were not problems in Tel Aviv, or in many of the new *Kibbutzim*, which were secular institutions, but they were indeed problems in Jewish Jerusalem. How complicated Jerusalem had become!

At this point, I shift to vivid personal memories, beginning with my visit to Jerusalem in 1967. After my undergraduate degree, I received a scholarship for a year of graduate study in Cambridge, UK, before beginning my five-year program leading to rabbinical ordination. In the spring of 1967, my father had his first sabbatical – after serving as congregational rabbi in the same Lynbrook, Long Island congregation since 1933 – and my parents invited me to visit them during the spring break. They were staying at the Hebrew Union College building on 13 King David Street, where I joined them. There was nothing between their temporary home and the walls of the Old City except for a no-man's land. The walls of the Old City were clear, but Jews simply could not go there to visit the site of ancient Jerusalem.

In May 1967, soon after my visit, Naomi Shemer introduced a powerful new song: *Yerushalayim shel Zahav*, 'Jerusalem of Gold'. It was a song of yearning: 'Captured in her dream, the city sits in solitude, and in its midst: a Wall, . . . How the cisterns have dried, the markets are empty, and no one remembers the Temple Mount in the Old City'. Then, in early June, when I was back in Cambridge, the 'Six-Day War' was fought; Israel took control of the Old City, and before the end of the month, Jews were permitted to enter the Old City and visit the Temple Mount. Naomi Shemer's song seemed no

Jerusalem 21

longer consistent with the new reality, and she added a final verse: 'We have returned to the cisterns, to the market, to the square; a ram's horn [*shofar*] calls out on the Temple Mount in the Old City. . . .' Clearly, many complex problems needed to be solved, but this was a time when the power of Jerusalem seemed to be transcendent.

The almost messianic dimensions of June 1967 became more ambiguous and disturbing when decisions had to be made about Israel's governance of the Old City. Many Jews wanted to live in the 'Old City', or more broadly in East Jerusalem, and its environment. The Hebrew University restored its original site on *Har haTsofim*, Mount Scopus, overlooking the Old City from the East; the original Hadassah Hospital on the mountain was restored. But other matters, especially within the Old City, became more complicated.

There was no question that the existing Muslim religious sites, especially the Dome of the Rock, built in the late seventh century on the site of the ancient Temple, would remain intact, and that there would be no Jewish interference with Muslim worship there. The consensus was that Jews (and Christians) would remain outside the Muslim shrine and that the Jewish connection with the site would be expressed through prayer standing at the 'Western Wall'. There were internal issues: Jewish women were required to pray in a different area from men; men – including Christians – had to have their heads appropriately covered.

There were Jews who believed that the Israeli military victory and its impact on the Old City represented the first stages of messianic recovery of the Holy Mount and rebuilding of The Temple. One group, called *Ne'emanei Har Ha-Bayit* (The Faithful of the Temple Mount), insisted on their right to pray within the actual confines of the ancient Temple. In 1984 there was a failed attempt by the *Lifta* Gang, led by Shlomo Barda and Yehuda Etzion, to blow up the Muslim Dome of the Rock in order to catalyse the construction of the third Temple in its place. The Shin Bet security agency thwarted the plot (Gorenberg 2000: 131–37).

There were various unsuccessful plans to begin the building of the Third Temple, including by Christian groups. None of these have made any significant impact on Jews either in Israel or in the Diaspora.

Fortunately, the Holy One has not forced or permitted us to make this decision. I am rather certain that most contemporary Jews would not support a rebuilding of the biblical Temple and restoration of the sacrificial cult in Jerusalem, even if Muslims decided to move the Dome of the Rock to different premises.

BIBLIOGRAPHY

Adler N. M. ed. 1907. *The Itinerary of Benjamin of Tudela: Travels in the Middle Ages.* London.

Goldstein D. 1971. *The Jewish Poets of Spain 900–1250.* Harmondsworth: Penguin Books.

Gorenberg G. 2000. *The End of Days: Fundamentalism and the Struggle for the Temple Mount.* New York: The Free Press.

Halkin H. 2010. *Yehuda Halevi.* New York: Nextbook/Schocken.

Kalimi I. & Richardson S. eds. 2014. *Sennacherib at the Gates of Jerusalem: Story, History and Historiography.* Boston: Brill.

Karp J. & Sutcliffe A. eds. 2018. *The Cambridge History of Judaism, Volume Seven: The Early Modern World, 1500–1815.* Cambridge: Cambridge University Press.

Kobler F. 1953. *Letters of Jews through the ages.* London: East and West Library.

Morgenstern A. 1992. 'Messianic Concepts and Settlement of Israel', in *Essential Papers on Messianic Movements and Personalities in Jewish History*, ed. M. Saperstein, 444–51. New York & London: New York University Press.

Nemoy L. 1952. *Karaite Anthology.* New Haven & London: Yale University Press.

Peters F. E. 1985. *Jerusalem.* Princeton: Princeton University Press.

Prawer J. 1988. *The History of the Jews in the Latin Kingdom of Jerusalem.* Oxford: Oxford University Press.

Scholem G. 1973. *Sabbatai Sevi: The Mystical Messiah: 1627–1676.* Princeton: Princeton University Press.

Chapter 3

Jewish and Eastern-Rite Christian Relations in Israel

A Sketch of Contexts and Interests

Petra Heldt

Recent scholarship often references Jews and eastern-rite Christians in Israel under three subject headings: religious relations between Jews and Byzantine Orthodox Christians, religious freedom, and Christians in the state of Israel. A standard reference work for religious relations between Orthodox Christians and Jews is the volume *Orthodox Christians and Jews on Continuity and Renewal* (Lowe 1994). The study focuses on the intellectual relationship between Israel and Byzantine Christianity; Oriental Orthodox churches and Uniate Christians, not included specifically, represent a similar attitude. The matter of religious freedom for Christians in the Middle East is recorded for nearly all eastern-rite Christians in the Middle East and beyond; relations with Jews in Israel are not prominent. There are a number of learned studies on the topic of Christians in the state of Israel (e.g., Ramon 2012). These often focus on action and reaction between governmental and eastern-rite Christians' issues, less on their respective historic and religious aspects. Thus, there is almost no work that examines the contributions of both Jews and eastern-rite Christians in Israel. The present study cannot fill this gap, but will sketch the contexts and interests that appear to shape interactions between eastern-rite Christians and Israel today.

Throughout history, eastern-rite Christendom has been closely involved with Israel, people, land and religion, basing itself on a theological tradition that follows values given to the Jewish people (Heldt 1994a). The modern Jewish state's respect for the representatives of eastern-rite Christians is exemplified on the diplomatic level by following the historic order of the ecclesiastical hierarchy in Jerusalem and honouring the Greek Orthodox patriarch as the supreme head of Christians in Jerusalem. Tradition, history, and protocol are indispensable for examining the contexts and interests of the two faiths.

The various eastern-rite hierarchs in Israel represent three historic branches: the prelates of the four Oriental Orthodox churches embody the Armenians, Copts, Ethiopians, and Syrians; the Greek Orthodox Patriarch of Jerusalem heads the Byzantine Orthodox Church in the Holy Land with its missions from some of the thirteen autocephalous Patriarchates, including those of Georgia, Greece, Rumania, Russia, and Serbia; and the religious leaders of the ten Uniate churches stand for branches of the Orthodox churches in union with Rome. All eastern-rite Christians have roots in nondemocratic countries in the Middle East and eastern Europe.

Eastern- and western-rite Christians together form one Christian Church, yet for more than a millennium and a half they have resided in dissimilar political contexts. These circumstances made for divergent interests which, in regard to relations with Israel, manifest themselves in forms of different agendas. Whereas eastern-rite Christians in the Middle East survived in areas often hostile to their faith, including Judaism, western-rite churches flourished and frequently enjoyed state support. Active relations between eastern-rite churches and Israel developed only recently in moments of political opportunities, whereas western-rite Christians and Israel established relations at the inception of the State of Israel.

The agenda for the dialogue between western-rite churches and Israel was set by the terror of the Shoah. Israel wanted to see anti-Judaism abolished from the theological books of the Church and anti-Semitism from the attitude of society. Since the late 1940s, the research of the Jewish scholar Jules Isaac (1948) on anti-Judaism and anti-Semitism in western Christian theology provided numerous points for this agenda. Israel's efforts were spearheaded by Jewish Ashkenazi scholars turned diplomatic officers, trained by the same western academia as their Christian ecclesiastical counterparts. Western Christians and Jews were equally familiar with western Christian theological intricacies and bias, against Jews, Judaism and the State of Israel, as well as with certain anti-Semitic sociopolitical programs of society at large. The success in establishing structural means for the betterment of relations between the two faiths and in redirecting western Christian theological thought and practice towards Jews and Judaism is particularly obvious in the Catholic documents *Nostra Aetate* of the Second Vatican Council in 1965 and the *Fundamental Agreement* between the State of Israel and the Holy See in 1993. The agenda of the western-rite churches focused, necessarily, on a segment of Christian theology that had been compromised by anti-Semitism and anti-Judaism.

At times, that western model of relations between Jews and Christians has been erroneously understood as representing the whole of Christendom. In fact, the separation of the Middle East from Europe in the early medieval period made for different theological developments in each part of the Church. The eastern Church held fast to two areas, the Holy Land and the Christian apostolic tradition. As it turned out, these two assets were invaluable for continuing the Christian tradition of honouring the Jewish Bible and Israel. The relations to Jews were characterized by a neighbourly attitude, apart from rare and locally isolated exceptions of anti-Jewishness. As the Mediterranean Sea became an impenetrable border, some European Christians, in the wake of fierce Muslim invasions, developed hostile attitudes against Jews, while others followed the Christian tradition of valuing Jews.

The separation of the Middle East from Europe in the mid-seventh century was the result of a new world order. In the Roman empire the Mediterranean Sea was seen as the middle of the Empire; in the new Islamic empire the sea became the all but impenetrable border between the Middle East and Europe. Christian life continued on the eastern and western shores under different political, social and religious systems. In Europe, the western-rite ecclesiasts acted often in close cooperation with the political leaders. The Church flourished. In the Middle East, Christians lived under the religious-political system of Islam with the law of the *dhimma*, which entailed segregation and humiliation of the non-Muslim population (Ayoub 1983, Bat-Yeor 1985). That protocol caused severe poverty for Christians and Jews, and often obliterated their respective cultures, including the loss of histories, languages, and arts.

From the mid-seventh until the mid-twentieth century eastern Christians and Sephardic Jews shared the struggle for survival and the aspiration for freedom. They were confined between hope and reality. The hope was to gain independence from foreign rule over Christian and Jewish lands and cultures. The reality was to be mindful of the political power and to protect life. The search for the blend of hope and reality has become a lasting task. That background, still relevant today, sets the agenda for relations between Israel and eastern-rite Christians in the Middle East.

In present-day Jerusalem eastern-rite Christian hierarchs represent numerous adherents who reside in three areas: the Middle East (plus Ethiopia and Kerala), eastern Europe and Russia, and the western world.

Middle-Eastern Christians, especially their ecclesiastical leaders, tend to be discouraged from relating to Israel: if they interact with Israel, their lives may need to be protected; in addition, they risk experiencing reprisals from their few western friends who wish to protect their own political, economic and cultural relations in the region. For the same reason, Israel safeguards its own political and economic interests in Arab and western countries. Good relations between Israel and eastern Christians generate a diplomatic conundrum.

26 *Petra Heldt*

The Oriental Orthodox churches often experience this challenge. With some ten million adherents in Egypt and a proud memory of its own preconquest history, the Coptic Orthodox church is arguably the most numerous church left in the Middle East. Coptic and Jewish overtures are not uncommon. In 2015, for instance, the Coptic Orthodox Pope Tawadros II broke a decades-old Egyptian ban on pilgrimages to Israel to take part in the funeral of Archbishop Dr Anba Abraham in Jerusalem. The archbishop himself had maintained good relations with Jews in Israel, in spite of a *fatwa* issued against him.

As political relations between Israel and Egypt improved, Coptic and Israeli bonds also grew closer, even against strong sensitivities among some non-Christian groups in Egypt who acted violently against the Coptic Christians (U.S. Department of State 2020). In the meantime, the Coptic Orthodox Church in Jerusalem gratefully recognizes the increase of Coptic pilgrimages to Israel. Interactions between Israel and the Coptic Church are increasing.

Armenian Orthodox relations with Israel are no less complex. On the one hand, Israel's interests in Turkey restrain Armenians' aspirations for Israel's recognition of the Armenian genocide of 1915; on the other hand, Armenia's relations with Iran control current perspectives for close relations between Israel and the Armenian Orthodox Patriarchate in Jerusalem. The ongoing legal disputes over Armenian lands in Israel are real, but are sometimes regarded as a proxy battle over bigger issues. Some Orthodox Jews express their dislike of clergy attire by spitting at it. Although some legal and moral matters need to be solved, everyday relations between Jews and Armenian Christians remain friendly. Israeli academia organizes symposia in memory of the Armenian genocide, and the Patriarch encourages Armenian priests to study for higher academic degrees at Israeli universities.

Meanwhile, the Byzantine Orthodox Church faces a truly intricate situation. Its thirteen patriarchs are sovereign over thirteen ecclesiastical territories spread throughout the world. The Greek Orthodox patriarch of 'the Holy City of Jerusalem and all Palestine, Syria, Arabia, and beyond the Jordan River, Cana of Galilee, and Holy Zion' is responsible, as his full title shows, for his faithful in territories of Israel, the Palestinian Authority and Jordan. Each of these three governments gives its legal stamp to his right of office. Consequently, the patriarchal position requires navigating the Church through some delicate waters. Almost all challenging issues derive from the *dhimma* protocol, which defines normative structure and relations between Muslim and non-Muslim. It is based on the *dhimma* pact attributed to the period of Caliph Umar (Ayoub 1983, 172–82; Bat Ye'or 1985, 47–77). The *dhimma* regulates *dhimmi* taxes and *dhimmi* life and sets *dhimmi* inferiority against Muslim superiority; all conquered lands are *fay* land, which means property of the Muslim community, administered by the Waqf which can lease it for the *kharaj* (land) tax.

In particular, two issues of the *dhimma* protocol are of interest to Orthodox Christians in Israel – the land and the *status quo*. The land issue has been turned into a prime political topic. Israel regards Jerusalem as its capital, and Judea and Samaria as areas to be defined at a final peace agreement. The Palestinian Authority holds the Islamic position on all of Israel, including Jerusalem, Judea and Samaria, as Muslim land.

The *status quo* originated in *firmans* issued by the sultans for dealings with *dhimmis* and referred to land properties, holy sites and the social position of people. By its nature, the *status quo* freezes the life of *dhimmis* and curtails their progress. The *firman* for holy places gained international recognition in the Treaties of Paris (1856) and Berlin (1878) (Cust 1929). Israel honors the *status quo* protocol for Christians but rejects both the *fay* claim on its own land and the *dhimma* for its inhabitants. Orthodox Christians, positioned differently, must oblige. The Orthodox patriarch of Jerusalem maneuvers through this maze with experience and prayer, supported by many faithful.

While matters of land and the *status quo* are relevant for all three territorial parts of the Jerusalem Patriarchate, it is mainly issues concerning Israel that get international attention. The affair around the Church of the Nativity in Bethlehem in 2002 was no exception.

Since the Oslo I Accord of 1993 Bethlehem is under the Palestinian Authority. In 2002 suspected Palestinians militants held some two hundred monks hostage in the church, which was put under a thirty-nine-day siege by the Israel Defense Forces. Israel negotiated an agreement. The siege affected Oriental, Byzantine and Catholic Christians, with the latter denying any hostage-taking. The Greek Orthodox Church called for an international 'solidarity day' for the people in the church and for the church itself, and for immediate intervention to stop the 'inhuman measures against the people and the stone of the church' (Dymond 2002). True to its aspiration for freedom and protection of life, the patriarchal call defended the church without naming any offenders. The damage to the church was estimated at US$1.4 million. In the process, Israel supported the Church, Arab and western countries remained largely silent or blamed Israel, local Christians kept quiet, and a number of their hierarchs relayed the Palestinian narrative. This pattern recurred in 2012, when the Church of the Nativity was put on the UNESCO World Heritage List. The management of the *status quo* of the Church was supplemented by an advisory committee formed by the Palestinian president. The governmental interference went without a word.

It is not because Israel operates by way of negotiations and equal treatment of the other that international fury greets it when it comes to issues of land and *status quo*. A point in case is the closure of the Holy Sepulchre by the Jerusalem patriarchs in February 2018. Amnon Ramon has analyzed the convoluted history behind this controversy (Ramon 2018). In the midst of heated business debates between Israel and the Orthodox patriarchate on land sales the mayor came with his own agenda and froze bank access for churches with outstanding payments of the municipality tax. The affair became an international issue and the two matters were conflated. In regard to the sales, oversimplified media reports put the two business partners into the dock. Arab and western voices argued, *inter alia*, that the church is not permitted to sell land to Israel (in reference to the disputed status of Jerusalem and Israel's perceived occupation of Arab land). There was no word about Ottoman land sales to churches, or *dhimma* stipulations, but elaborations on international law and human rights. The church came out of the international dock when the matter turned against Israel, that demanded the municipality tax from the church. Israel argued that tax law is equal for all inhabitants. The church referred to the *status quo*, which frees it from paying the municipality tax. In the end, the two parties negotiated the complex issue and partly solved the matter for the time being.

In addition, a Member of Knesset proposed a law suggesting transferring to the state land sold since 2010 by the church in return for compensation to the companies and promoters that had bought the land. Trying to comply with the electorate, the lawmaker failed to consider the position of the church and international complexity. The Church argued successfully, for the time being, against the proposal on grounds of discrimination (Greek Orthodox Synod; Surkes & Pileggi 2018).

This event, as convoluted as it is, shows Israel's commitment to interest-based negotiation for the mutual benefit of both parties; a stark contrast to the *status quo* protocol. The Orthodox hierarchy cannot but present itself as being *sui generis*. It takes the middle way between preserving relations with Israel and protecting the life of its adherents in non-Israeli lands.

Most of the ten Uniate churches derive from *fay*-claimed lands. Rome became an external support for advancing freedom on their native soil. An example is the Maronite Church of Lebanon, with more than a million adherents inside the homeland, some eleven thousand in Israel today and more elsewhere. In the midst of the Arab conquest, the Maronites three times established an independent state of Lebanon (between 676 and 1303).

In the 1940s the Maronite Archbishop of Beirut, Ignace Mubarak, openly supported Israel's struggle for independence (Phares 1995, 95–97). His booklet of 1945, *S.O.S. Lebanon. A Homeland for the Christians in the Near East*, caused huge interest (Phares 1995, 96). In 1946 a treaty was signed by the Christian presidents of Lebanon, Emile Edde and Alfred Naccache, the Maronite Patriarch Arida, and envoys of the Jewish Agency. 'The aim of the agreement was to establish an alliance between the Jewish people of the Yishuv and the Christian people of Lebanon' (Phares 1995, 97). In 1947, a document called for a Christian homeland in Lebanon and a Jewish homeland in Palestine. Pro-Arab pressure inside Lebanon and opposition from Arab and Middle East-oriented western Christians muzzled the initiative, and Archbishop Mubarak remained a lonely public voice calling for a Jewish–Lebanese alliance.

A similar scenario occurred in 1981, when Israel and the Phalange of the Lebanese Gemayal Maronite faction established relations. John Yemma of the *Christian Science Monitor* commented that 'Israel and its new Lebanese ally, the Falange, are trying hard to establish that the complex Lebanese crisis is simply a matter of Muslim vs. Christian, with Jew on the side of Christian. And again in 1989, when the Saudi-led Taif Agreement reoriented Lebanon towards the Arab world, defined it as a country with an Arab identity, and demanded the renunciation of relations with the West, including Israel, many Lebanese Christians, including Michel Aoun, the president of Lebanon since 2016, objected severely, other Maronite leaders acquiesced, together with western countries.

2014 was a turning point. In the wake of Archbishop Mubarak's history, some Maronite Christians in Israel wanted a change to the *status quo* in Israel. The Maronites argued that they were an Aramean ethnic group, not an Arab one, and opposed the Ottoman enforced registration as Arab Christians, at that time still upheld by Israel. The Aramean origin can be ascribed to churches in Aramean-speaking territories in the Middle East, namely to members of five Syrian churches (Maronite, East Syrian Orthodox, West Syrian Orthodox, East Syrian Uniate, West Syrian Uniate) and of two Greek churches (Greek Orthodox, Greek Uniate). In 2015 these seven churches numbered 5.4–8.9 million Christians worldwide (Weissblei 2017, 3).

After years-long negotiations the Jewish state allowed Israeli Christians to have their Population Registry entry changed from Arab to Aramean nationality. The Ministry of Interior ruled that 'the fact that the Aramean nation exists is evident' and that 'the conditions necessary to prove the existence of a nationality exist, including historical heritage, religion, culture, origin and shared language'. In fact, '[S]ome *80–90% of the Christian Arab population in Israel – i.e., an estimated 110,000–120,000 people*' (Weissblei 2017, 6 [emphasis added]) meet the criteria for changing their registered nationality to Aramean. In 2017 the bill passed the first reading in the Knesset Plenum. This time attempts were made to frustrate the Maronite initiative. The 2021 study of Rima Farah of Brandeis University debunks 'the traditional claims that this phenomenon is mainly a present-day attempt by Israel to separate Christians from Arab society' (Farah 2021, 1).

With political changes in the Middle East, relations between Israel and eastern-rite Christians also change. Developments in the Coptic, Byzantine and Maronite Church are a small manifestation of a larger process.

With the fall of the Soviet Union, eastern-rite Orthodox churches in Russia and eastern Europe began to relate officially to Israel. Studies on anti-Jewish sentiments and pogroms in Russia and eastern Europe during the nineteenth and twentieth centuries, shelved since 1917, have been-renewed by some ecclesiastical and secular scholars. Among these is the Romanian researcher Ioan Moga (2019) who reflects the church attitude that anti-Semitism was rooted in secular policies which sometimes penetrated the church and that ecclesiasts participated in anti-Semitic actions against the spirit of the Orthodox Christian tradition. The Russian scholar Dominic Rubin (Rubin 2010) documents important developments in the academic debate about Christian relations to Jews and Judaism among Orthodox Christians in Russia and eastern Europe in the twentieth century since the time when Vladimir Solovyov (Solovyov 2016) famously defended the Jews. In Romania, young researchers investigate aspects of that relation in liturgy (Moga 2019), or in the Church itself (Patru Forthcoming). Patru's work presents painstaking research on the attitude of the Romanian Orthodox Church towards Jews during the first half of the twentieth century. Frequently, Orthodox prelates from Russia, eastern Europe and western countries, together with Jewish academics and representatives of the World Jewish Congress, deliberate research on multiple aspects of Orthodox theology and Judaism. That dialogue enables the development of knowledge about the other and permits modern tendencies in anti-Semitism to be addressed.

The Yad Vashem Institute in Jerusalem sometimes gives directions to eastern Orthodox churches which relate intimately to the Shoah of the Jewish people through their own genocidal sufferings during WWII. In Yad Vashem they find guidance for commemorating those horrors. The Serbian Orthodox bishop of Pakrac and Slavonia, Jovan Ćulibrk, has been a pioneer in this research. The bishop studied at Yad Vashem and published his master's thesis on *Historiography of the Holocaust in Yugoslavia* (2014). As the Director of the Jasenovac Committee, which oversees the site of the Jasenovac extermination camp in Slavonia, Bishop Jovan initiates multiple educational activities between Serbia and Yad Vashem.

Orthodox churches from Russia and eastern Europe have sizeable properties in Israel since the time of the Ottomans. The subject of land, so convoluted for the eastern-rite church in the Middle East, appears to be a manageable business matter between Israel and the churches. The negotiations about renovations, sales, and rentals might be drawn out or demanding at times, but do show results.

Orthodox Christians in the United States of America, the British Commonwealth and western Europe have established flourishing academic activities, often in cooperation with Jewish scholars. The archbishop of Dallas, the South and the Bulgarian Diocese, Alexander Golitzin, is 'a scholar known for his original vision of Jewish and Christian mystical texts and traditions. . . . He formed . . . the "Theophaneia School", a theological forum on the Jewish roots of eastern Christian mysticism' (Orlov 2020, 1–2). Among the growing number of Orthodox scholars in western countries who contribute to understanding between the eastern-rite churches and Israel are Andrei Orlov at Marquette University, originally from Russia, and John A. McGauckin at Oxford University, archpriest of the Romanian Orthodox Patriarchate.

Academic contributions derive predominantly from scholars attached to the Byzantine Orthodox churches in Russia, eastern Europe and western countries. They are connected to autocephalous churches with little or no attachment to the Middle East. Their relation with Israel is unimpeded. Also the Oriental Orthodox churches maintain communities in western countries but stay under the authority of the respective patriarch located in the country of origin in the Middle East. Relations with Israel are under the control of the relevant oriental patriarchates.

The research reported in this study has explored the contexts and interests in the relations between Jews and eastern-rite Christians in Israel today. A critical assessment used throughout this research to evaluate those relations has been the recognition of tradition, history, and protocol. In the introductory part of this chapter two arguments were reviewed: that Christian tradition follows an affirmative outlook on Israel and acknowledges its own derivation from Israel; second, that historical development in the early medieval period divided Christendom into eastern- and western-rite halves, each half moving in slightly different directions, pushed by different engines. Eastern-rite Christians experienced the enforcement of the *dhimma* protocol in the Middle East; a free-moving and industrial society shaped western-rite Christians, falling to anti-Jewishness in the wake of the medieval Middle-Eastern conquest of southern Europe. The main body of the chapter assessed some current influence of historic protocol conditions on eastern-rite Christians for relations with the modern state of Israel. It was found that the State of Israel offers eastern-rite Christians a fair place in society, appreciated by, but sometimes falling short of, full response from eastern Christians who face the protocol from Middle-Eastern countries. The approach taken in this chapter has interesting implications for comprehending and acquiring further eastern-rite Christian and Jewish relations in Israel. Three suggestions are in place.

One proposition looks at a process of recognizing Orthodox Christians and Sephardic Jews as being on the trajectory of a shared Middle Eastern history. This process might explore features of common ground between the

32   *Petra Heldt*

two faiths, hitherto modestly investigated. Another implication derives from the analysis of Arab protocol that affects higher-ranking ecclesiasts more than laity. As this research has suggested, the freedom of Orthodox Christian laity advances the quality of life for both eastern Christians and Jews in Israel and should be further explored. At the same time, Arab protocol, attached severely to high-ranking eastern ecclesiasts, may be seriously considered in the course of action between Jews and eastern-rite Christians in Israel. A third implication originates in the observation of intransigent attitudes from many western-rite Christians and groups to relations between eastern-rite Christians and Jews in Israel. The account proposed here suggests that the structure of western representation in and of the Middle East is primarily determined by economic, political and cultural interests in the Middle East. Israel and the eastern churches may explore their own vibrant cultural processes for attracting western interests. Historically, interactions between Europe and the Middle East without Israel have often seen anti-Semitism resurfacing. Today is no exception. Eastern-rite Christians outside the Middle East often show strong academic traits which, together with their Middle-Eastern experience, should be explored for their potential to counter contemporary anti-Semitism.

BIBLIOGRAPHY

Ayoub M. 1983. 'Dhimma in Qur'an and Hadith', *Arab Studies Quarterly* 5:2, 172–82.
Bat Ye'or. 1985. *The Dhimmi. Jews and Christians under Islam.* London & Toronto: Associated University Presses.
Ćulibrk J. 2014. *Historiography of the Holocaust in Yugoslavia.* Belgrade.
Cust L. G. A. 1929. *The Status Quo in the Holy Places.* London.
Dymond J. April 20, 2002. 'Church seeks action on Bethlehem siege', BBC News. http://news.bbc.co.uk/2/hi/middle_east/1940575.stm/, accessed July 30, 2021.
Farah R. 2021. 'The Rise of a Christian Aramaic Nationality in Modern Israel', *Israel Studies* 26:2, 1–28.
Greek Orthodox Synod 2018, Paragraph 1 of the *Decisions of the Holy and Sacred Synod of the Jerusalem Patriarchate on Thursday February 9/22 2018.* https://en.jerusalem-patriarchate.info/blog/2018/02/22/decisions-of-the-holy-and-sacred-synod-of-the-jerusalem-patriarchate-on-thursday-february-9-22-2018/, accessed September 10, 2021.
Heldt P. 1994a. 'A Brief History of Dialogue between Orthodox Christians and Jews', in M. Lowe (ed.), *Orthodox Christians and Jews on Continuity and Renewal,* 211–24. Jerusalem: Ecumenical Theological Research Fraternity in Israel.
Heldt P. 1994b. 'Bibliography of Dialogue between Orthodox Christians and Jews', in M. Lowe (ed.), *Orthodox Christians and Jews on Continuity and Renewal,* 240–49. Jerusalem: Ecumenical Theological Research Fraternity in Israel.

Isaac J. 1948. *Jésus et Israël*. Paris.

Lowe M. (ed.) 1994. *Orthodox Christians and Jews on Continuity and Renewal. The Third Academic Meeting between Orthodoxy and Judaism. Including a History and Bibliography of Dialogue between Orthodox Christians and Jews*. Jerusalem: Ecumenical Theological Research Fraternity in Israel.

Moga I. 2019. 'Jüdische Elemente in der Tradition der Orthodoxen Kirche. Ein Beitrag im Zeichen des Dialogs', *Review of Ecumenical Studies* 11, 167–79.

Orlov A. A. (ed.) 2020. *Jewish Roots of Eastern Christian Mysticism. Studies in Honor of Alexander Golitzin*. Leiden & Boston: Brill.

Patru M. Forthcoming. *Das Ordnungsdenken im christlich-orthodoxen Raum. Nation, Religion und Politik im öffentlichen Diskurs der Rumänisch-Orthodoxen Kirche Siebenbürgens in der Zwischenkriegszeit* (1918–1940). Frankfurt am Main.

Phares W. 1995. *Lebanese Christian Nationalism*. Boulder, CO: Lynne Rienner Publishers.

Ramon A. 2012. *Christians and Christianity in the Jewish State. Israeli Policy towards the Churches and the Christian Communities (1948–2010)*. Jerusalem Institute for Policy Research, Pub no. 420. The Jerusalem Institute for Israel Studies and Jerusalem Center for Jewish-Christian Relations, Israel.

Ramon A. 2018. 'Why was the Church of the Holy Sepulcher closed?', tr. S. Vardi, https://rossingcenter.org/en/church-holy-sepulcher-closed/#_ftn1, accessed July 30, 2021.

Rubin D. 2010. *Holy Russia, Sacred Israel*. Brighton, MA: Academic Studies Press.

Solovyov V. S. 2016. *The Burning Bush: Writings on Jews and Judaism*, ed. and tr. G. Y. Glazov. Notre Dame, IN: University of Notre Dame Press.

Surkes S. & T. Pileggi. February 25, 2018. 'After Holy Sepulchre locked, bill allowing seizure of former Church land shelved', *The Times of Israel*, accessed September 10, 2021.

U.S. Department of State. May 2021. *2020 Report on International Religious Freedom: Egypt*. https://www.state.gov/reports/2020-report-on-international -religious-freedom/egypt/, accessed July 29, 2021.

Weissblei E. 2017. *Arameans in the Middle East and Israel: A Historical Background, Modern National Identity, and Government Policy*. Jerusalem.

Yemma J. April 30, 1981. 'Israel Pushes Informal Alliance with Falange in Lebanon', *Christian Science Monitor*. https://www.csmonitor.com/1981/0430 /043044.html, accessed July 20, 2021.

Chapter 4

The Encounter between the Greek Orthodox Church and the Jews in Israel

David Rosen

Historical and sociological factors (and sometimes also political ones) have led traditional religious communities in the Middle East as a whole to live in voluntary segregation from one other. The context of the Israeli–Arab conflict and the fact that the overwhelming majority of non-Jews in Israel are Arabs compounds this situation and means that very few of any religion engage in interreligious relations of any kind; and there are even fewer who have the educational competency to do so in any substantial manner. In addition, the fact that Christians in Israel are a minority within a minority presents various challenges and adds to this insularity. Nevertheless, one must mention in parenthesis the paradox that, despite these facts, there is a significant amount of interreligious collaboration and dialogue in Israel. However, it is the province of a tiny proportion of the population, and it is mostly unknown by the vast majority of Israelis, Jews as well as Arabs.

The case of the Greek Orthodox Church is additionally unique inasmuch as, while the rank and file are overwhelmingly Arab, the leadership is almost entirely Greek. In addition to the internal challenges that it poses, this situation means that, even when clergy are involved in any kind of interreligious dialogue with Jews, this does not normally involve or extend to the rank and file.

A new demographic component of the Church comes from the more recent immigration from the former Soviet Union of those who entered Israel under Israel's Law of Return who are practising Christians and for whom the Greek Orthodox Churches provide the religious context and services closest to those they knew in the lands of their birth. Estimates of their number vary from some sixty thousand (according to the Israel Bureau of Statistics) to four times that number according to some church estimates. However, this community has its own insecurities, often confronting suspicion or worse within the Jewish communities of which they are a part, and they do not serve as any kind of bridge between the church and the Jewish community – on the contrary.

History and politics have placed additional and unique demands upon the Greek Orthodox Church in Israel. Not least of these is the fact that formal procedures, established under Ottoman rule in the Holy Land, required the church to receive authorization for the position of patriarch by the temporal powers. The fact that the mandate of the Jerusalem Patriarchate covers three political entities – Jordan, the Palestinian Authority, and Israel – means that not only are their communities of disparate character and political orientation, but that the patriarchate itself is beholden to these three often conflicted political bodies. However, there is also a salutary side to this, as close interaction with civic and especially security authorities – while not without its difficulties – also provides opportunity for the development of good relations between church officials and their civic and security counterparts.

The majority of interactions between the Jewish community and the Greek Orthodox Church in the Holy Land (Israel and the West bank) take place in the context of tourism. Israeli tour guides study the history and teaching of the church and impart this knowledge to the myriads that they bring to visit churches and other holy sites, often developing close friendships with the clergy responsible for these places. Notwithstanding this, very few of the leadership, let alone of the Arabic-speaking rank and file, are involved in interreligious activity.

In addition to the above-mentioned sociological and historical factors, as well as the matters of language, self-confidence, and competency, there has also been theological resistance. Even intra-Christian dialogue has often been perceived as a threat to absolute theological affirmations and even as a slippery slope to syncretism.

The fact that the Ecumenical Patriarchate based in Istanbul has spearheaded a more open and dialogic approach both to intra-Christian and interreligious relations in the last half century has surely encouraged those in the Church in the Holy Land who are inclined to such. However, it has also played into a sense of rivalry, providing a pretext for more conservative clergy to distance themselves from Constantinople. Nevertheless, a number of the academic consultations of the Ecumenical Patriarchate (involving representatives of the Jerusalem Patriarchate, as well as most of the other national Orthodox churches) and IJCIC (the International Jewish Committee for Interreligious Consultations established in 1970 to represent world Jewry to the Holy See, to the WCC, and subsequently to the Orthodox Church) have taken place in Israel. The last of these was held in December 2017 on the subject of the significance of Jerusalem in the respective traditions. During this meeting, an honorary doctorate was conferred on His All-Holiness Patriarch Bartholomew by the Hebrew University.

A few individual members of the Jerusalem Patriarchate, such as its current secretary, Archbishop Aristarchos of Constantina, have been prominent in interfaith organizations such as the Jerusalem Rainbow Group, and the Patriarchate has collaborated with a number of practical interfaith activities, such as the 'Window to Mount Zion' of the Jerusalem Inter-Cultural Centre. Particularly notable regarding interfaith cooperation have been the sporadic fruits of the Alexandria summit in 2002. Facilitated by the archbishop of Canterbury at the time, Dr George Carey, and hosted by the then grand Imam of Al-Azhar Sayed Mohamed Tantawi, the summit was a joint Israeli–Palestinian initiative at the highest political level and with the blessing of Egyptian President Hosni Mubarak. Led by Israeli Deputy Minister Rabbi Michael Melchior and PA minister Sheikh Talal Sidr, the summit was an attempt to use religious leadership to end the violence during the second intifada and restart the stalled peace process. While it failed to do so, it was the first time that official religious leaders from the three Abrahamic faiths from the Holy Land had ever come together and provided for the subsequent establishment of the Council of the Religious Institutions of the Holy Land. The latter was established with three express goals: Firstly, to keep open avenues of communication between the official religious leadership; secondly, to work together to combat incitement and defamation against any and all of the religions; finally, to provide religious support for any diplomatic initiatives to bring about an end to the Israeli–Palestinian conflict, so that two nations and three religions may live in peace and flourish in the land. While there were notable successes regarding the first two goals, there was little or no interest on the part of the political authorities in any kind of practical engagement of the Council for any diplomatic purpose. Nevertheless, the role and prominence of the Jerusalem Patriarch was significant in this council. In addition, another council of the official heads of religions in Israel was also subsequently founded, which continues to bring officials from the different religions in Israel together annually around common concerns and nurtures personal contacts between the leadership. Here too, the Greek Orthodox Patriarchate has been prominent.

Arguably the most complex and vexing issue for the Church in Jerusalem concerns land sales. The Patriarchate has responsibility for about a hundred churches, monasteries, and other holy sites, visited by millions each year. The cost of this mission is significant and depends almost entirely on real estate revenues which are also essential to enable the church to maintain its extensive educational system, health facilities, charities, and youth centres. It sponsors and supports more than twenty schools west of the Jordan River attended by approximately fifteen thousand students, Muslims and Christians, as well as many schools in the Kingdom of Jordan.

The church operates the Patriarch Benedict Health Clinic in the Old City of Jerusalem that provides full health services, including an in-house pharmacy, either free of charge or at a highly discounted rate to anyone in need. It cares for Jerusalem residents, regardless of religious affiliation, who lack health insurance, as well as the elderly and visiting pilgrims. The patriarchate also supports the Four Homes of Mercy, which provide permanent housing and care to the disabled and chronically ill, currently ranging from ages four to ninety-four. When civil war broke out in Syria, the Patriarchate established the 'Orthodox Initiative' in Jordan to aid tens of thousands of refugees. The Jordanian government does not oversee these camps, and NGOs often have difficulty reaching them. The church distributes food and health parcels and maintains an unofficial school system, teaching men and women crafts and trades for future employment.

All of this the church would not be able to do without the sale of some of its extensive real estate holdings in the Holy Land from time to time. Indeed, the Patriarchate is often described as the second largest landowner in the State of Israel after the government. With the establishment of the state, and especially after the Six-Day War in 1967, the Church leased much property both to Israeli national bodies and to private entrepreneurs, mostly under agreements for a limited duration. This has led to challenges for the Patriarchate, first and foremost from Palestinian nationalist quarters, especially within the local church itself, who accuse it of selling off and selling out Palestinian national assets. However, it has also led recently to tensions with the State of Israel and Jewish homeowners living in apartments on these lands. As many of these leases come to an end, there has been concern not only regarding the church's overall intentions regarding these properties, but also due to the willingness of the church to enter into financial arrangements with independent real estate agents with no guarantees for homeowners living in buildings on these properties. This has led to proposals in the Knesset which are seen by the Patriarchate as limiting its freedom and undermining its financial security and future. As a result, the protests have been strong and have often exploited political tensions as well.

Nevertheless, generally speaking these issues do not significantly affect the personal relationships that exist between members of the Greek Orthodox Church and the Jewish population in Israel. Like all citizenry in the State of Israel, the local Christian communities are beneficiaries of the state's democratic institutions and modus operandi which are widely appreciated. While there is little theological and academic dialogue between the communities, a 'dialogue of life' is sustained of a positive nature that has never existed before in the Holy Land.

FURTHER READING

Estrin D. 2017. 'Greek Orthodox Church Sells Land in Israel, Worrying Both Israelis and Palestinians'. *NPR*, December 12, 2017. https://www.npr.org/sections/parallels/2017/12/02/565464499/greek-orthodox-church-sells-land-in-israel-worrying -both-israelis-and-palestinia//. Accessed November 21, 2022.

Katz I. & R. Kark 2007. 'The Church and Landed Property: The Greek Orthodox Patriarchate of Jerusalem'. *Middle Eastern Studies* 43: 383–408.

Lowe M. (ed.) 1994. *Orthodox Christians and Jews on Continuity and Renewal. The Third Academic Meeting between Orthodoxy and Judaism. Including a History and Bibliography of Dialogue between Orthodox Christians and Jews.* Jerusalem.

Mack M. 2012. 'Christian Palestinian Communities in Israel: Tensions between Laity, Clergy, and State', in *Sacred Space in Israel and Palestine: Religion and Politics*, ed. M. J. Breger, Y. Reiter and L. Hammer. London and New York, 284–309.

Mack M. 2020. 'United by Faith, Divided by Language: The Orthodox in Jerusalem', in *Arabic and Its Alternatives: Religious Minorities and Their Languages in the Emerging Nation States of the Middle East (1920–1950)*, ed. H. Murre-van den Berg, K. Sánchez Summerer and T. C. Baarda. Leiden, 247–60.

Roussos S. 2008. 'The Greek Orthodox Patriarchate of Jerusalem: Church-State Relations in the Holy Land between the Palestinian-Israeli Conflict', in *Christianity in the Middle East: Studies in Modern History, Theology, and Politics*, ed. A. O'Mahony. London, 219–31.

Theros P. N. 2019. 'Don't Blame the Orthodox Patriarchate for Nasty Political Games in the Holy Land'. *Foreign Policy*, February 8, 2019. https://foreignpolicy .com/2019/02/08/dont-blame-the-orthodox-patriarchate-for-nasty-political-games -in-the-holy-land-israel-ateret-cohanim-settlers-azaria-knesset-rehavia/. Accessed November 21, 2022.

Chapter 5

The Greek Orthodox Church under Israeli Sovereignty

Michael G. Azar

The Greek Orthodox Patriarchate of Jerusalem comprises what is widely regarded as the most ancient, historically most populous, and geographically most significant Christian community in the Holy Land. Yet, the current state of the Patriarchate is marked by centuries of subjugation and marginalization. Since the end of Roman rule in Palestine in the seventh century, the Patriarchate has been subjected to a series of Muslim, Catholic, Protestant and Jewish rulers. Most of these governments, officially secular or otherwise, have tolerated the Patriarchate, in their own ways and to varying degrees, but few have equitably cared for its well-being and continued growth. If the local Orthodox Church has survived, it has more often done so despite government policies, not because of them. This is as true of the current government as it was under many preceding.

The near-millennium after Roman rule witnessed a Christianity that held tenaciously to its Greco-Roman roots and character while becoming thoroughly Arabized in culture and language (Panchenko 2021). However, with the advent of the Ottoman *millet*, the Patriarchate's leadership (including the monastic Brotherhood of the Holy Sepulcher, which oversees the holy places and from which the patriarch is drawn, the synod of bishops, which oversees the affairs of the Patriarchate, and the patriarch himself) became increasingly and exclusively Greek, 'not only in its traditions and atmosphere, but also in its membership' (Bertram & Young 1926: 74). The people remained primarily Arab in their identity, and, by the twentieth century, this Greek-Arab divide grew into competing nationalisms and differing approaches to church governance, with the Ottoman-supported leadership entrenched in a Greek national identity, and the Arab people, with Russian encouragement, demanding a greater say in the Patriarchate's leadership and affairs (Kildani 2010). Nonetheless, despite their disagreements with each other, both the Greek leadership and Arab people had in their common and explicit interest the stymieing of European-supported Protestant and Catholic missionary activities, which had grown in number and successes over the preceding century, drawing the vast majority of converts not from Jews or Muslims, but Orthodox.

After World War I, everything changed. The Ottoman Empire gave way to European governments, which, it did not go unnoticed by the Patriarchate, had favored the previous century's missionaries. The Bolsheviks ensured a jarring and sudden end to what had been an ample flow of both Russian finances (for schools and other projects) and Russian pilgrims (a tremendous source of income to the Jerusalem Patriarchate). Greece, though by no means a major power, began to see itself as the successor of Russia in its role as protector of the Patriarchate's leadership (but not people, as with the Russians) and solidified further the notion that Greeks were divinely 'chosen' to oversee and protect the holy sites. Together, the Patriarchate's leadership and Greece both saw in the new British government of Palestine the best hope of preserving Orthodox care for the holy sites as dictated by the Ottoman-era 'Status Quo' (Papastathis 2013). The Arab faithful, meanwhile, hoped also to see in the new government sympathies for their grievances against Greek hegemony – but, despite a few affable ears and optimistic concessions, such hopes would, ultimately, go unrealized. It was more conducive to British interests, as it had been for the Ottomans and would be for the Israelis, to retain a Greek-Arab divide within the Patriarchate.

The Patriarchate that the British now encountered was one that owned unparalleled swaths of land in Palestine but financially was in disarray (Katz & Kark 2007). The new government saw here an opportunity both to stabilize the Patriarchate's finances and fulfill its own desire for the 'establishment of a national home for the Jewish people' (Balfour Declaration) – an objective that the Greek Secretary of State had publicly affirmed five months before Balfour (Papastathis 2013: 76). Thus, with Greek support and British oversight (and outright pressure), the Patriarchate's leadership sold large swaths of practically and ideologically important land to Zionist organizations. The Arab Orthodox, who disproportionately by this time made up much of Palestine's urban, educated classes, reacted strongly against what they understood as two sides of the same foreign problem: Greek hegemony of church and Jewish hegemony of land (Robson 2011). As the 1920s unfolded into 1930s and 1940s, Orthodox Arabs solidified a notably disproportionate place at the forefront of Palestinian nationalism (and Arab nationalism elsewhere), showing little distinction in their contentions with the British, Zionists, and Greeks. Each, they felt, were depriving Palestine's less able communities of their political, national, and ecclesial rights (Tamari 2014).

Nonetheless, by the end of British rule, Palestinian Orthodox struggles 'ended in defeat, with Palestine lost and Greek control of the church undiminished' (Robson 2011: 6). Almost as a result of being in the 'wrong place at the wrong time', the Orthodox were disproportionately affected by the violence that ensued (1947–1949). Many of the Palestinian refugees who fled, either by financial means as war loomed or by Jewish and Israeli force, were the educated, urban, and upper classes, of whom the Orthodox were a major part. Galilee fell under Israeli control and is now where the majority of Israel's Christians live, but by 1948, it was marked more by its Catholic, rather than Orthodox, presence (Betts 2009). Jaffa, on the other hand, which had previously served as a major Orthodox intellectual center and meeting point, ceased to be so after it was violently taken by Jewish/Israeli forces explicitly in favor of re-creating it as a Jewish city. Other major Orthodox centers around Jerusalem and Bethlehem were close to (or on) the Green Line and dwindled accordingly. As a result of these catastrophes, the Orthodox community leaders who had previously resisted British-supported Greeks and Zionists diminished both in number and influence. It is notable that in recent years, contrary to earlier periods, the most prominent Palestinian Christian religious leaders have typically been Protestant or Catholic, but no longer Orthodox.

Some 90% of the Patriarchate's vast territory after 1948 was now in Israel, but its leadership (based in Old City Jerusalem), the vast majority of expenditures, and its people (some 60,000 vs. 6,000) were now in Jordan (Bialer 2005). With the financially strapped leadership therefore in 'enemy territory' with no significant support internationally (paling in comparison to local Protestants and Catholics), Israel had a prime chance to gain large swaths of practically, politically, and ideologically valuable land, and so Israeli authorities moved quickly, explicitly aware of the Patriarchate's weaknesses. They openly contemplated establishing a separate ecclesial authority for the Orthodox communities in Israel; they initially classified much of the Patriarchate's land as 'absentee land' (which under the 1950 Absentee Property Law they would be able to expropriate for state use); they withheld most of the Patriarchate's income from its land (even while requiring taxes); and they exploited the now centuries-old fears of the Patriarchate that the far more financially and politically able Catholic Church would gain more control of the holy sites. Each of these moves served as bargaining chips in negotiations for the Patriarchate's land and open support abroad. And with each of these chips, Israel was tremendously successful, especially in obtaining valuable land necessary to build its new capital in Jerusalem (Bialer 2005).

Meanwhile, with the Patriarchate leadership now under a national Arab government in Jordan, the Arab Orthodox were able to get a few concessions from the Greek synod and the Brotherhood, but not nearly as many as they had hoped (Tsimhoni 1993). And any further hopes came to a jarring halt in 1967: the Israelis (like the British and Ottomans before them) could profit far more from preserving the Orthodox Greek–Arab divide rather than alleviating it. And for the more nationalistically minded Greeks who had resented earlier concessions to Arabs, Israel was welcomed and even praised alongside Greece as a sibling nation (Isodoros of Nazareth 1971). The close connection between the hierarchy and the Israeli authorities that thereafter periodically developed was not simply a religious cooperation between Christians and Jews (despite attempts to characterize it as such, especially among Israel's Christian supporters), but an ethnic cooperation between Greeks and Jews that grew into a national cooperation between Greece and Israel. Still, this relationship would later come under considerable strain, especially over issues of land.

While there have been many cordial moments of cooperation between the Israeli government and the churches, the driving motive behind its overall approach since its 1948 and 1967 victories has not been the well-being of the churches themselves, but a concern for the country's standing abroad and relations between Jews and Christians elsewhere (Ramon 2021). As such, Israel has made little progress in developing a clear and consistent official policy toward the churches under its sovereignty. While this lack of policy has often been misleadingly characterized by the government, and praised by its supporters (especially among Christian Zionists), as a sort of 'live and let live' aspect of Israel's commitment to the freedom of worship, the government has in fact used the lack of policy time and again as a bargaining chip. This approach allows the government to exert pressure when suitable, while technically maintaining the 'freedom of worship' practice on which its perception around the world depends so heavily. To state it simply, Israel's *lack of* policy has, in many ways, *been* its policy. This, together with the government's 'divide and rule' approach to non-Jewish communities under its purview in general (Ramon 2021), has caused numerous problems for both the leadership and people of the Orthodox Patriarchate, as it has for other non-Jewish communities.

The government has the ability to tax and/or appropriate valuable and strategic church land and buildings; it has the ability to withhold finances; it has the exclusive right to grant clergy visas. On each of these the churches' ability to function depends entirely; yet, it is precisely these powers that the government has previously employed to influence church cooperation, particularly regarding land sales and leases below market price (Ramon 2021). Despite the generally cordial relationship between them (which should be neither denied nor unduly stressed), the current Orthodox patriarch, Theophilos III, has more than once accused the Israeli government of employing pressure, unprecedented legal action, or explicit support of settler enterprises in ways

The Greek Orthodox Church under Israeli Sovereignty 45

that ensure both Israel's ability to obtain Patriarchate land and Jerusalem's path toward becoming an exclusively Jewish city (e.g., Patriarch Theophilos III 2018).

Even beyond such external pressures, Israel has in the past demonstrated its willingness to interfere in the internal affairs of the Patriarchate in ways that serve its own interests – particularly, again, when it comes to the sensitive matter of the Patriarchate's unrivaled land holdings. This was exemplified by the government's refusal to recognize Patriarch Theophilos's election for over two years (November 2005–December 2007), after Patriarch Eirenaios, the immediate predecessor, had been deposed as part of the fallout over church land that had been transferred to Israeli developers. As a Member of Knesset admitted openly at the time, 'The State of Israel . . . is interfering in an improper manner, impairing freedom of worship and the principles of its own Declaration of Independence. . . . The excessive involvement of the government in the affairs of the Patriarchate are [*sic*] due to the fact that this Patriarchate owns property and extensive land in the State of Israel' (Quoted in Ramon 2021: 195).

Even in the lead-up to Patriarch Eirenaios's own election in 2001, Israel attempted to remove from the candidate list those thought not to favor the state's objectives, constituting 'the first time since the nineteenth century that the sovereign or occupying power had intervened directly in the Patriarchal election' (Roussos 2005: 115). Though hardly a major threat, a clear and driving concern of Ariel Sharon's government at the time, as it has undoubtedly been for each Israeli government, was the potential for further Arabization of the Patriarchate and therefore 'Palestinian control over the Patriarchate's property' (Roussos 2005: 114). There are many reasons why the Patriarchate has yet to see major changes in the ethnic makeup of its leadership, some more practical than ideological, but Israel has repeatedly made clear that the Greek–Arab divide better serves its interests than any alternatives.

While Israel does not severely restrict freedom of religion – and often falsely claims to be the only such government in the region – its discriminatory policies nonetheless clearly and consistently promote the flourishing of Jewish communities and identity over and above all others. It does not in any way devote equal time, energy, and resources to other communities under its sovereignty, of which the Orthodox are already a fading minority. While the history of Israeli policies has been to inspire Jews to immigrate, it has served equally well either to encourage or to force others to emigrate.

Despite the rhetoric of a 'united' Jerusalem, in the aftermath of the June 1967 War, Israel did not merely 'unite' the municipalities of Jordanian Jerusalem and Israeli Jerusalem; rather, it added just under 28 square miles from at least 27 surrounding Palestinian villages to its new, unilaterally-defined city (Seidemann 2017). Overall, the government's driving motive was to acquire land with as few Palestinians as possible. In fact, soon after the June 1967 War, when Israel was drawing the boundaries of a new Jerusalem, a large group of mostly Christian dignitaries (at least half likely Orthodox) in Bethlehem petitioned the Israeli government also to annex Bethlehem, which, they noted, had always been united with Jerusalem in Christian thought. The request was received favorably by some within the government (as it would benefit the Israeli–Christian relationship *abroad*), but it was ultimately rejected 'on demographic grounds', in order to avoid the 'addition of a large Arab population' (Ramon 2021, 95; see *Davar*, October 2, 1967). Christian or not, they were still Arab: that remains a determining factor in Israeli policy.

This policy of land-but-not-people had a devastating effect on the Orthodox Christian strongholds surrounding Jerusalem (namely, the Ramallah and Bethlehem areas). The route along which Israel chose to draw Jerusalem's new boundary in the 1960s and 1970s ensured that much of the land fell within Israel while many of its owners did not. This phenomenon allowed the state to wield its 1950 Absentee Property Law in order to build a ring of Jewish neighborhoods around the city. When Israel announced these building plans, Metropolitan Diodoros (later, Patriarch Diodoros [1981–2000]) joined two Catholic bishops in protest. They feared that the plans would both exclude many Christians from the Holy City and surround Christian neighborhoods elsewhere (*The Catholic Review*, April 16, 1971). A major proponent of Catholic–Jewish relations in the U.S. denounced the bishops as 'alarmists', but noted sarcastically that their concerns would have 'some semblance of rationality', if the planned construction were to be 'a series of military fortifications or a row of police stations, and not a scattering of apartment houses' (*NC News Service*, April 22, 1971).

Subsequent history has shown that Metropolitan Diodoros's concerns were justified and his opponent's prescient. The Wall that Israel has been building since the Second Intifada demonstrates that the government continues to hold strongly to a land-but-not-people policy, and the communities closest to it continue to be devastated. The current settlements, or 'neighborhoods', of Gilo and Har Homa, for example, are built in part on land once part of the predominantly Orthodox villages of Beit Jala and Beit Sahour respectively, but the people themselves remain divided from this land and Jerusalem's holy sites by the nearly-thirty-foot Wall (only able to enter the other side with special permits). The Wall itself, in order to preserve as much land as possible on the Israeli-controlled side, unnaturally penetrates into urban areas, as most clearly seen, perhaps, around Rachel's Tomb: though this pilgrimage site was once within the Bethlehem area, the Wall has snaked through streets to ensure that it now remains accessible only from the Israeli side. What is now left for the Palestinian side is a neighborhood surrounded on three sides by the Wall. For centuries preceding, this neighborhood was the main thoroughfare for

The Greek Orthodox Church under Israeli Sovereignty 47

pilgrimage traffic entering the Bethlehem area on the way from Jerusalem to Hebron, but it is so no longer.

Israel's prejudicial control of water throughout the West Bank ensures that Jewish settlements receive disproportionately far more water than Arab communities. Throughout the West Bank, one can stand within sight of, on one side, reservoir tanks on top of flat Palestinian buildings (which conserve water for use during the frequent shut-off periods) and, on the other side, Israeli settlements with typically far greener vegetation and sloped, Spanish tile roofs without tanks. One such point is near Aboud, a Ramallah-area village home to an Orthodox church originally built in the fourth century. From a hilltop outside of the village, where there is a holy site dedicated to St Barbara (one of the most celebrated saints in the Arab Orthodox world), one can see, while overlooking both Aboud and the nearby Beit Aryeh-Ofarim settlement, that it is frequently ethnicity, not need, that determines water distribution.

Suffice it to say that the local economy can hardly flourish under these Israeli restrictions and disparities, and it is that economy that has been cited regularly (along with numerous other effects of Israeli military occupation) as a key reason why so many Christians emigrate from the West Bank (PSR 2020). Since, as noted earlier, those most prone to emigration have been the educated and upper classes, of which the Orthodox have been a disproportionate part, the Orthodox population (nearly 50% of the West Bank's Christians) has been particularly affected. The situation is exacerbated even further in Gaza, where Orthodox Christians (who gather freely at the ancient church of St Porphyrios, a fifth-century bishop of Gaza) make up the vast majority of the Christian population. There, the Israeli blockade (in cooperation with Egypt on the southern border) makes life hardly manageable, whatever the problems with the Hamas government. The effects of COVID-19 closures remain to be seen fully, but the outlook is pessimistic. Christians of the West Bank are disproportionately involved in the hard-hit tourism industry: most hotels are Christian-owned and two-thirds of the tour guides are Christians (though Christians are no more than 3% of the population). Though tourism was at a standstill during the pandemic, these guides did not receive unemployment pay (despite paying most taxes to the same Israeli government that offered unemployment pay to citizens on the other side of the Wall).

Though it would significantly help the dwindling Christian communities, Israel does not currently give permanent visas to foreign spouses who wish to reside in the West Bank or Gaza. Rather, spouses must apply for permission to stay at least twice a year, and at other times they have to leave the country and return (usually an unpleasant and costly back-and-forth bus trip to Jordan) in order to re-enter under a tourist visa. During the COVID-19 pandemic many of these people were unable to return to their homes with their families because Israel, like many other countries, for much of the pandemic

48   *Michael G. Azar*

was, in theory, only allowing citizens and permanent residents to enter the country. To the government, these foreign-born spouses are neither, despite many attempts to become so and despite having lived in their Palestinian homes for years. There is currently no clear system in place for these spouses to normalize their visas and reside securely in their homes, and those few who are able to achieve something akin to a more permanent residency often do so amid a myriad of legal fees. Furthermore, even more severe regulations were published in February 2022 (but are awaiting implementation at the time of writing) that will make the difficult process even more impossible to navigate. The new regulations will not, however, affect the ability of foreign Jews to continue to move into nearby settlements, with functional government mechanisms (under the 1950 Law of Return), no fees, and even financial incentives.

For those Palestinians within Jerusalem's boundaries – again, traditionally an Orthodox epicenter – matters have been considerably better. They have access to Israeli health insurance and other governmental benefits; they can freely travel within and outside of Jerusalem and can use, with an Israeli-issued laissez-passer, Ben Gurion Airport (unlike most Palestinians elsewhere). But even here Israeli policies still encourage emigration, as they reveal a 'concerted effort to accelerate the growth and the development of the Israeli sector, while adopting policies designed to artificially cap the development of Palestinian East Jerusalem' (Seidemann 2017: 188). Palestinians are nearly 40% of the city's population, but warrant only around 10–12% of the municipal budget, which leaves a significant gap in infrastructure and basic city services. As of 2017, only about half the Palestinian residents were connected to the city's water grid, and thus the telltale mark of rooftop water tanks is still easily visible in Arab neighborhoods (Seidemann 2017).

While East Jerusalem residents were able, generally speaking, to keep their property once Jerusalem's new border was drawn after the June 1967 war, their ability to do so, as well as their status as residents, has been under continual strain since. Though not immigrants, they are designated as permanent residents, the status obtained by foreign nationals living within Israel. They are allowed to apply for citizenship, but few do, and the majority of applications have been denied until recently. In recent years, undoubtedly as part of a 'divide and rule' policy, Israel has been pushing Christians specifically to take the citizenship, but should these Arab residents of Jerusalem (Christian or otherwise) apply for Israeli citizenship, they are required to give up citizenship elsewhere. By contrast, Israel continues to accept dual citizenship for Jews. What serves to encourage one to immigrate serves to encourage the other to emigrate.

The reasons for which an East Jerusalemite can lose a residency permit are numerous, particularly for those who reside in the ever-valuable property of

The Greek Orthodox Church under Israeli Sovereignty 49

the Old City, where building permits are notoriously far harder for non-Jews to obtain. Should Palestinians of East Jerusalem wish to move elsewhere while maintaining their property in Jerusalem, they encounter numerous difficulties, as Israeli authorities are able to summon the Absentee Law to confiscate property. East Jerusalemites who own property in the West Bank cannot spend the majority of their time in those properties but must reside in their Jerusalem home or risk losing it along with their Jerusalem IDs (without which they cannot enter Jerusalem freely), health insurance, and other government benefits. To ensure compliance, suspected Jerusalemites regularly endure unexpected police visits (often in the middle of the night) to confirm their primary residence. By contrast, Jewish Jerusalemites are under no such watch, and the Absentee Law is not a constant, looming threat, even if they wish to reside outside of their Jerusalem properties.

Arab Orthodox Christians who are citizens of the State of Israel (primarily in the north) have a far better relationship with the government (despite spending the first two decades after 1948 under strict military control), and it is to these residents that Israeli officials often, and misleadingly, point as evidence of flourishing Christian communities and equal treatment for all, Jew and non-Jew alike, under Israeli democracy. Yet, as minority societies everywhere can attest, lack of *official* discrimination does not necessarily entail a lack of *real* discrimination. Arab citizens of Israel encounter a variety of issues that serve as regular reminders that they live in a *Jewish* state, a point which the 2018 Nation State Law made ever clearer, and a point about which the Arab-Jewish riots in May 2021 recently reminded Israeli society.

One of the most pressing forms of discrimination has been Israel's 'Family Reunification Law', which Israel first passed in 2003. In practice, this law prohibits residents from Gaza, the West Bank, or Jordan from moving to Israel (including East Jerusalem), even if they marry Israeli citizens or residents. Given the sharp rise in Christian emigration over the past few decades, this law is a dire 'existential question' (Ramon 2021: 182) that has disproportionately affected Christian communities. To marry someone from elsewhere (and then reside together in Israel) is becoming an increasing necessity. This has been a particular problem for Orthodox communities, since the Orthodox population has historically been more dominant in the West Bank and Gaza than within the State of Israel (where they constitute perhaps 30% of the Christian Arab population). Because of a political deadlock in the wake of a new government, the law failed to be renewed in July 2021, but the Ministry of Interior, headed by Ayelet Shaked (who has previously argued that Israel's identity as a Jewish state must be maintained, even at 'the expense of equality' [*Haaretz*, February 13, 2018]), stalled the processing of applications for reunification. Nine months later, in March 2022, the law was renewed and subsequently praised by Shaked as a 'Zionist law' that entailed the victory of a 'Jewish and democratic state' over a 'state of all its citizens' (*Jerusalem Post*, March 10, 2022; *Haaretz*, March 10, 2022).

There have been several cooperative ventures between the Patriarchate's leadership and people over the past few decades. These, together with the fact that the Patriarchate's synod now includes three Arab bishops and others who speak Arabic fluently, including Patriarch Theophilos himself, indicate that the Greek–Arab divide is not what it used to be. Nonetheless, that divide is still sometimes there and is typically reinvigorated whenever Patriarchate land is transferred into Israeli hands (even when it is not clear who is entirely responsible). Most recently this has been seen over the land of Mar Elias Monastery in southern East Jerusalem, the possession of which would enable Jerusalem authorities to better connect and expand the ring of settlements around the city. This is, perhaps, an especially poignant case, not only because of what it would mean for nearby Palestinian communities, but also because Mar Elias is one of only two Arabic-speaking churches still regularly serving Jerusalem's Orthodox Christians.

Even when moments of hope between the Greek leadership and Arab faithful arise, the Israeli government frequently seems to work against them, reminding both, directly and indirectly, that Israel is a *Jewish* state. In the 1990s, the Patriarchate donated land in Beit Sahour for an Orthodox housing project, but, early in its construction in 2002, Israeli authorities issued demolition orders that temporarily froze the project. Then, in 2003, Israeli authorities seized land around the project 'for military purposes', eventually constructing a road around it that forced its residents to come and go through an Israeli-controlled gate (*Reuters*, April 11, 2009). This project began around the same time as the settlement of Har Homa, in whose shadow it now sits, and which now includes tens of thousands of Jewish residents. The size of the Greek Orthodox project, meanwhile, pales in comparison. It is always clear on the hills outside of Jerusalem whose immigration and whose emigration the State of Israel's discriminatory policies continually favor.

The worrying results of recent surveys of Jewish Israeli views of Christians (Ramon 2021: 278–98), particularly in Jerusalem, and the dismal way that prejudicial Zionist narratives and historical anti-Christian Jewish sentiment continue to shape Israeli state education on Christians and Christianity (Hirt-Ramon, Gabel & Wasserman 2020) do not lead one to expect that Israeli policies will change any time soon. Yet, some of the most effective advocates for the well-being of local Christian communities in recent years have been Israeli Jews. By such advocacy, one hopes that Israel will be inclined eventually to abandon its deeply discriminatory policies in favor of an actual policy that not merely tolerates for the sake of international reputation, but contributes actively and equally to local Christian (and other minority) flourishing. It is unclear how long the local Christian community can wait.

BIBLIOGRAPHY

Bertram A., & J. W. A. Young. 1926. *The Orthodox Patriarchate of Jerusalem: Report of the Commission Appointed by the Government of Palestine to Inquire and Report upon Certain Controversies between the Orthodox Patriarchate of Jerusalem and the Arab Orthodox Community*. Oxford.

Betts R. B. 2009. *The Southern Portals of Byzantium: A Concise Political, Historical and Demographic Survey of the Greek Orthodox Patriarchates of Antioch and Jerusalem*. London: Musical Times.

Bialer U. 2005. 'Horse Trading: Israel and the Greek Orthodox Ecclesiastical Property, 1948–1952'. *Journal of Israeli History* 24: 203–13.

Hirt-Ramon O., I. Gabel, & V. Wasserman. 2020. *'Jesus Was a Jew': Presenting Christians and Christianity in Israeli State Education*. Lanham: Lexington Books.

Isodoros, Archbishop of Nazareth. 1971. 'Israel and the State of Israel [Greek]'. *Theologia* 42: 407–15.

Katz I., & R. Kark. 2007. 'The Church and Landed Property: The Greek Orthodox Patriarchate of Jerusalem'. *Middle Eastern Studies* 43: 383–408.

Kildani H. 2010. *Modern Christianity in the Holy Land*, trans. G. Musleh. Bloomington, IN: Author House.

Panchenko C. A. 2021. *Orthodoxy and Islam in the Middle East: The Seventh to the Sixteenth Century*, trans. B. P. Noble and S. Noble. Jordanville, NY: Holy Trinity Seminary Press.

Papastathis Konstantinos. 2013. 'Religious Politics and Sacred Space: The Orthodox Strategy on the Holy Places Question in Palestine, 1917–1922.' *Journal of Eastern Christian Studies* 65: 67–96.

PSR: Palestinian Center for Policy and Survey Research. 2020. 'Migration of Palestinian Christians: Drivers and Means of Combating It'. Ramallah.

Ramon, A. 2021. *Christians and Christianity in the Jewish State: Israeli Policy toward the Churches and Christian Communities (1948–2018)*, trans. S. Vardi. Jerusalem: Jerusalem Institute for Policy Research.

Robson L. 2011. 'Communalism and Nationalism in the Mandate: The Greek Orthodox Controversy and the National Movement.' *Journal of Palestine Studies* 41: 6–23.

Roussos S. 2005. 'Eastern Orthodox Perspectives on Church–State Relations and Religion and Politics in Modern Jerusalem'. *International Journal for the Study of the Christian Church* 5: 103–22.

Seidemann Daniel. 2017. *The Israeli Settlement Enterprise in East Jerusalem, 1967–2017*. Jerusalem.

Tamari S. 2014. 'Issa al Issa's Unorthodox Orthodoxy: Banned in Jerusalem, Permitted in Jaffa'. *Jerusalem Quarterly* 59: 16–36.

Theophilos III, Patriarch. 2018. 'Christians Are at Risk of Being Driven Out of the Holy Land'. *The Guardian*, January 7.

Tsimhoni D. 1993. *Christian Communities in Jerusalem and the West Bank since 1948: An Historical, Social, and Political Study*. Westport, CT: Praeger.

Chapter 6

Women in the Synagogue

Miri Freud-Kandel

In the summer of 2021, an outcry broke out in British Jewry following a ruling by the Chief Rabbi, Ephraim Mirvis, to remove the title of Research Fellow at the London School of Jewish Studies (LSJS) from Dr Lindsey Taylor-Guthartz. Although she had served as a highly skilled and popular teacher at this institution for sixteen years, the Chief Rabbi's intervention, in his capacity as president of LSJS, came in response to Taylor-Guthartz's forthcoming ordination as an Orthodox woman rabbi, following her completion of the training programme offered by the innovative American women's rabbinical seminary, Yeshivat Maharat. According to the chief rabbi's statement, this move placed her 'beyond the boundaries of mainstream Orthodoxy and would have sent a misleading message about what LSJS stands for' (Frot 2021).

The battle over women's ordination has a long history in a number of religious traditions. In Orthodox Judaism, as these events highlight, this battle still has some way to go. The contribution of British Jewry to this battle is somewhat limited. In many respects, the two dominant centres of contemporary Jewish life, Israel and America, are the primary locales where the debates are playing out. Indeed, the issue of Orthodox women's ordination in Britain materialised courtesy of American rather than homegrown innovation. Yet this issue fits into a broader feminist critique of Judaism that in many ways encapsulates the challenge that modernity as a whole represents for Orthodoxy, questioning the fundamentals of religious authority. By drawing attention to the androcentrism of Jewish teachings – what could be viewed as the time-bound biases evident in the *mitzvot* (religious commandments), and male hegemony in interpretation – feminism helps highlight the role of human influence in religious interpretation, over and against claims that religious laws are direct commands from God. This chapter considers some

54 *Miri Freud-Kandel*

of the feminist efforts, including Orthodox ordination programmes, which endeavour to challenge received rabbinic wisdom and demonstrate the scope Judaism contains to accommodate women's changing religious needs while respecting the halakhic (legal) system upon which the religion is built.

In relation to women in the synagogue there are two primary interrelated challenges to examine: access to leadership roles and to ritual participation in general. These are by no means the only concerns for Orthodox feminists. Personal status issues, especially the plight of *agunot* – so-called 'chained women' who are stuck in dead marriages as rabbis refuse to innovate to free them – function as a central concern for many. Yet since the advent of modernity, synagogue services have often served as the physical spaces in which debates about communal boundaries in Judaism have been performed. The synagogue functions as a central location for modern Jewish identity construction. Women's marginalisation in prayer can consequently be felt more keenly. Hence the synagogue has become a central battleground for Orthodox feminists as they seek to defend the right for women's greater participation in Orthodox synagogue ritual.

Arguments are increasingly being developed, drawn from in-depth study of received Jewish sources, to defend women's active involvement in the synagogue and in Jewish life more broadly. As Chief Rabbi Mirvis's intervention demonstrates, these initiatives frequently incite a backlash. This highlights how the maintenance of traditional gender roles has acquired the status of a symbolic boundary marker, not just within Orthodox Judaism but for many conservative religious groups who want to demonstrate their broader rejection of secular modern values. By vociferously rejecting feminist efforts to introduce change, conservative religious authorities seek to set themselves up as defenders of some constructed account of tradition. Feminist influences are often approached as threatening subversions of divine teachings that challenge religion as a whole. In some Orthodox quarters, feminism is viewed as a polluting force, seeking to import alien ideas into Jewish life, thought, and practice. Rabbi Hershel Schachter compared Orthodox Jewish feminism with classic heretical models seeking to destroy Judaism (Ferziger 2009). Yet Orthodox feminists argue that a concern for certain forms of equality and certainly an interest in ameliorating the status of women, at least in some contexts, has been a long-standing feature of rabbinic thought and can be drawn from biblical sources too. In Taylor-Guthartz's sermon marking the UK celebrations of her ordination she referenced the biblical account of the daughters of Zelophehad, in Numbers 27, who fight for their inheritance rights, albeit in order to uphold a patriarchal system in which their land can be passed on to their sons (Taylor-Guthartz 2021). On this reading, the modern efforts to exclude feminist influences can themselves be viewed as alien innovations. They reflect wider defensive concerns within Orthodoxy that result in women too often bearing the consequences. The classic Talmudic statement often invoked by those arguing for change claims: 'both these and those are the words of the living God' (Babylonian Talmud, *Eruvin* 13b). Efforts to bring about change are driven by a yearning to enhance women's religious life. Yet when it comes to Orthodox feminism it appears that this principle is challenged. The battle lines that have emerged capture the opposing approaches to interpreting religious authority and thereby point to some of the challenges that lie ahead for those seeking to defend Orthodox Judaism.

Yeshivat Maharat was established in 2009 by Rabbi Avi Weiss and Rabba Sara Hurwitz, the first woman he ordained in a private ceremony alongside Rabbi Daniel Sperber. Hurwitz was not the first Orthodox woman to receive *semikha* (rabbinic ordination). Three women in Israel – Mimi Feigelson, Eveline Goodman-Thau, and Haviva Ner-David – had independently received private *semikha* from supportive Orthodox rabbis between 1998 and 2006. Dr Dina Najman was appointed Rosh Kehillah (head of community) of Kehillat Orach Eliezer in New York in 2006, although she was not formally ordained as a rabbi. Ordination of women rabbis outside Orthodoxy can be dated back to 1935, when Regina Jonas was privately ordained in Berlin. The creation of a formal rabbinical training institute for women was, though, a first for Orthodoxy. The rather unwieldy title of Maharat is a construct that was developed in an effort to overcome Orthodox opposition to the idea of women rabbis. It is an acronym for *Manhigut Halakhah Ruchaniyut Torah* – leadership, Jewish law, spirituality, and Torah. The opposition this institution has faced since its inception indicates how its efforts at gaining acceptance have, so far, been broadly unsuccessful. In 2013, responding to the first ordination of graduates of Yeshivat Maharat, the Orthodox Rabbinical Council of America (RCA) issued a statement explaining: 'The RCA views this event as a violation of our *mesorah* (tradition) and regrets that the leadership of the school has chosen a path that contradicts the norms of our community' (RCA 2013). Notwithstanding this opposition to its programme and policies, by 2021, as Yeshivat Maharat celebrated its Bat Mitzva year, Taylor-Guthartz joined forty-eight other women who have so far been ordained under its auspices. Its graduates have been appointed to a variety of different roles, including some successful appointments to leadership roles in synagogues. Responding to broader currents in which gender-based rabbinic decisions are increasingly being questioned, as the biases informing these rulings are recognised, the graduates of Yeshivat Maharat are entering a growing job market that values what these halakhically trained women can bring to disparate communities.

Weiss's involvement in this initiative is consonant with the principles of the Open Orthodox Judaism he championed in a pivotal journal article, 'Open Orthodoxy! A Modern Orthodox Rabbi's Creed' (Weiss 1997). In this article, while expressing his unabashed commitment to Orthodox Judaism and its halakhic system, Weiss argued that *halakhah* (Jewish law) contains more flexibility than some within Orthodoxy are willing to countenance. This reflects how Orthodoxy encompasses a spectrum of religious positions. In seeking to defend Orthodox interpretations of Judaism against the twin threats of non-Orthodox forms of Judaism and modern thought more broadly, with its assault on religious authority, a tendency has developed to focus on boundary-marking – demarcating what is and is not acceptable under the Orthodox umbrella. Open Orthodoxy, as its name indicates, argues for the possibility of accommodating a more inclusive approach. Concerns about gender are explicitly identified as one of the central issues for which more creative halakhic solutions are sought.

The feminist scholar Ronit Irshai has identified a growing emphasis in certain sectors of Orthodoxy on what she terms 'Akeda theology'. Drawn from the Abrahamic model of the binding of Isaac in Genesis 22, this involves a suspension of the ethical in favour of submission to what is thought to be the divine will. Irshai argues that this model disproportionately penalises women and other minority groups. It encourages enablers to put aside their own values in order to serve others; so women are encouraged to serve God by helping their husbands and sons, rather than focusing on their own religious needs. When it comes to halakhic issues facing women, the influence of Akeda theology can encourage halakhic decisors to throw up their hands and argue that they are bound by legal precedent, even as they acknowledge the challenge of certain ethically problematic aspects of *halakhah*. Notwithstanding evidence of far-reaching halakhic innovation in certain issues, the willingness to tackle the types of thorny halakhic questions that impair women's religious experiences are all too often driven by subjective concerns.

By way of contrast, Irshai argues that an alternative model for halakhic decision-making can be identified within received Jewish sources. Michel Foucault distinguishes between legal decisors, who interpret the law, and the community observing these laws, whose norms help to define the tools applied in the task of interpretation. The implication of Irshai's analysis is that communal pushback against legal decisions has the potential to shift how laws are interpreted. One example is the rabbinic prohibition on men hearing a woman's voice, which is used as one of the grounds for marginalising women in public prayer. In Babylonian Talmud, *Berakhot* 24a, it is stated that the voice of a woman is '*ervah*'. Literally this term could be translated as 'nakedness'; more broadly it symbolises something immodest and sexually provocative about men hearing women's voices. As the Orthodox feminist philosopher Tamar Ross notes: 'the limitations placed upon women's voices are now understood as merely another tactic intended to preserve the familiar and comfortable atmosphere of what has traditionally functioned

Women in the Synagogue

as the proverbial men's club' (Ross 2010). Ross champions a move towards 'stripping halakhic discourse of unfounded metaphysical claims regarding the eternal nature of men and women'. Such a shift, she suggests, has the potential to offer 'some measure of acknowledgment to the notion that halakhic issues relating to the women of our day can no longer be measured in exclusively male terms'. The combination of Weiss's theological model of Open Orthodoxy and the feminist legal theory Irshai sets out in contrast to Akeda theology indicates the possibility of developing distinctive approaches that could still claim to fit under an Orthodox umbrella.

When interviewed on BBC Radio's *Woman's Hour* programme, Taylor-Guthartz was asked why, given the backlash, she chose to stay within Orthodoxy: could she not find willing acceptance in other religious streams of Judaism? Tova Hartman, another Orthodox feminist innovator, based in Israel, recounts facing similar challenges (Hartman 2007). Hartman is a founding member of Shira Hadasha, the first so-called Partnership Minyan (prayer group). Established in Jerusalem in 2002, Shira Hadasha was designed to try to introduce greater egalitarianism into Orthodox prayer while remaining committed to *halakhah*. This is achieved by offering women opportunities to lead certain parts of the prayer service and participate in the Torah reading by drawing on alternative halakhic interpretations of rules that had previously restricted women in these areas. The development of Partnership Minyanim responds to the challenge experienced by women as they are marginalised and attributed second class status in communal prayer. As the opportunities for women in wider society grow, this marginalisation can be experienced as ever more jarring. Women in Jewish law are often placed in the same category as minors and slaves. These latter two groups both have the potential to progress from their status; *halakhah* keeps women trapped. Blu Greenberg, in a seminal text for Orthodox feminism, had already argued in 1981 that 'where there is a rabbinic will, there is a halakhic way' (Greenberg 1981). A founding member of JOFA, the Jewish Orthodox Feminist Alliance, a representative body founded in America in 1997, preceding Kolech, the Orthodox Women's Forum, the Israeli equivalent which was created in 1998, Greenberg insisted that feminism and *halakhah* were far from incompatible; it should not be necessary for feminists to exit Orthodoxy in order to find an accommodating Jewish home. What is required is a willingness to seek out the halakhic flexibility contained within the sources of tradition. This is where access to the types of halakhic training offered to Taylor-Guthartz by Yeshivat Maharat can help empower Orthodox Jewish women to look with fresh eyes at Jewish legal sources. For both Taylor-Guthartz and Hartman, exiting Orthodoxy, leaving male rabbis to interpret the sources without considering the shifting communal norms of some of the communities observing these laws, would entail abrogating opportunities to demonstrate the availability of alternative approaches. Commenting on the growth of women's Torah study within Orthodoxy, which represents a veritable revolution in women's access to the sources, Irshai contends: 'While Orthodox feminism has focused in the last three decades on alternative interpretations of halakhah that challenge the traditional hegemonic male interpretation and pursue greater gender equality in ritual and halakhic life. . . . So long as gender equality is perceived as part of an invalid, Western worldview rather than an intrinsically Jewish moral stance, no such change is possible' (Irshai 2014). Orthodox feminists are seeking to drive this type of change from within.

Facing what was evidently an unanticipated level of opposition to his ruling seeking to oust Taylor-Guthartz from LSJS once she became a *rabba* (the feminine form of *rav*, a male rabbi), Chief Rabbi Mirvis felt compelled to offer a clarification of his position, which many viewed as backtracking. In a statement issued by LSJS, the compromise position that was reached recognised that 'our academic fellows are not religious appointments – and therefore should be made on the basis of academic merit'. Excluding a teacher for seeking to extend the learning they can transmit went against the values of 'academic freedom' (Frazer 2021). What this about-turn seems to indicate is how rabbinic authority is shifting. As women's learning increases, growing engagement with the sources helps draw attention to the possibility of constructing alternative interpretations. By challenging received views it becomes possible to respond better to changing communal norms that seek an increased role for women's voices and an appreciation of their different experiences of Jewish life and practice.

Mirvis's struggle to assert his religious authority had already been evident earlier in his chief rabbinate, when he failed in his attempt to shut down the Partnership Minyan model that had been transplanted onto British shores. At the time of writing, there are at least five Partnership Minyanim active in Greater London. The JOFA website lists over fifty communities worldwide offering Partnership Minyanim. In 2013, soon after he acceded to the chief rabbinate, and again in 2016, Mirvis spoke out against these prayer groups: 'they are contrary to halacha and should not take place under the auspices of any of our United Hebrew Congregations' (Rocker 2016). He had to acknowledge, nonetheless, that 'many of those participating in partnership minyanim are among our most engaged and valued congregants'. As such, it was not possible wholly to marginalise active participants in Partnership Minyanim from involvement in the mainstream Orthodox synagogues under the auspices of the chief rabbi without significantly undermining those communities. Highlighted here is how Partnership Minyanim have been attracting a number of the more Jewishly literate members of mainstream Orthodox communities in Britain, the lay members who are most active in their communities. These individuals, who are equipped with the skills to study the relevant halakhic sources and question rabbinic interpretations of these texts, feel empowered to defend alternative positions. In this sense, the growth of Partnership Minyanim reflects the impact of the Jewish educational revolution that has occurred in recent times since this has laid the groundwork for examining the relevant textual sources with new eyes, bringing alternative perspectives (Fuchs 2013).

In Britain, an outlier in world Jewry, generally following rather than setting trends, the active participants in Partnership Minyanim have often pursued their learning in the variety of advanced educational institutions that have been established in Israel for both women and men. A number of these institutions have started to develop their own form of women's *semikhah* programming, offering an alternative to the initiatives developed at Yeshivat Maharat. The Israeli models are distinctive, being less concerned with preparing women for communal leadership positions. This reflects the more marginal role that synagogues generally play in constructions of Jewish identity in Israel. In these contexts, ordination instead confers recognition of the level of learning that graduates of these programmes have achieved. In this sense it indicates how the growth of access to learning can create expectations that the knowledge acquired should be put to use. In certain respects this highlights why feminist innovations are opposed by those who set themselves up as defenders of tradition. Once women gain access to the tools of halakhic interpretation, they gain the means of trying to effect change from within. Institutions offering these training programmes include Rabbi Herzl Hefter's Beit Midrash Har'el, Beit Morasha, and Midreshet Lindenbaum. The *haredi*-dominated State rabbinate still retains much control in Israel, limiting the appointment of more moderate religious Zionist male rabbis, let alone women. Nonetheless, a range of new qualifications are becoming available to women, not just in terms of ordination programmes but other educational initiatives too. These include training to serve as advocates in Jewish law courts, or as *yoatzot halakhah*, advisers on family purity laws. In 2015, Rabbi Shlomo Riskin appointed Jennie Rosenfeld as a communal spiritual leader in the town of Efrat. In 2021, again in Efrat, Shira Mirvis (a niece of British Chief Rabbi Ephraim Mirvis) was appointed rabbinic leader of a community that seeks to encourage more egalitarian prayer. According to Mirvis, this appointment also came at the encouragement of Riskin. Noting that she had already been performing this role in an informal manner while completing her training at Midreshet Lindenbaum, he suggested, in an approach that seems to tap into Irshai's analysis on the importance of formalising shifting communal norms, that 'it would be a good idea to make it official' (Maltz 2021).

The mushrooming of educational initiatives in Israel exerts an impact not just on those directly able to take advantage. While British innovators have often spent time in Israeli institutions, an additional critical factor in shifting

60   *Miri Freud-Kandel*

communal norms is the role of the internet and social media in disseminating new ideas. The internet circumvents geographic borders and religious boundaries. It helps draw attention to the existence of alternative models for Jewish life. In this way it can help challenge what individuals experience in their own communities. Through online interactions, rather than feeling an outsider for seeking change, an individual can encounter the innovative possibilities that are available, and seek out other like-minded individuals in their own locations in order to introduce similar changes. The textual resources for learning about how change can be justified can easily be made accessible through the internet. The availability of this source material on the internet also helps to democratise the entire halakhic process, further challenging rabbinic efforts to defend an unchanged approach to religious authority. An example is the halakhic debate regarding Partnership Minyanim. Women's marginalisation in prayer is a consequence of a number of halakhic factors. We have already considered arguments relating to female modesty and the perceived threat associated with women's voices. Other concerns include the ruling in Mishna, *Kiddushin* 1:7, which states that women are subject to a general exemption from the category of time-bound positive *mitzvot*. This includes the obligation to pray at fixed times in a quorum, and since women have a lesser level of obligation in this *mitzvah*, it is argued that women can neither count towards the necessary quorum, nor lead prayers on behalf of men. Another halakhic impediment is the ruling in Babylonian Talmud, *Megilla* 23a which states: 'All may be included among the seven [called to the Torah on Shabbat], even a minor and a woman, but the Sages said that a woman should not read in the Torah because of the dignity of the congregation.' Two different halakhic arguments have been set out, by Rabbis Mendel Shapiro and Daniel Sperber, to justify an emphasis on the permissive first part of this text, rather than the more restrictive qualification that follows. Widely shared via the web-based *Edah* journal, the grounds for constructing an innovative halakhic interpretation that could permit women to read from the Torah on the Sabbath became readily available. Although subjected to equally detailed online rebuttals, the internet was used in some quarters to help defend the alternative halakhic opinions justifying women's greater involvement in public worship. When combined with the internet's ability to demonstrate the growth of physical communities applying these halakhic arguments to legitimise the creation of Partnership Minyanim, this makes it easier to understand why Chief Rabbi Mirvis struggled to have his opposition to these services accepted. Equally, it helps explain why those who have set themselves up as defenders of Orthodoxy are so concerned about the potential impact on religious authority of feminism in combination with the internet.

In a new epilogue written for the second edition of her book *Expanding the Palace of Torah*, Tamar Ross noted how the changes that have been wrought

Women in the Synagogue   61

by Orthodox feminists over the last twenty or so years have been astonishing, proceeding at a wholly unanticipated pace. She nonetheless warned that 'the trend to individualism radically decimates the transformative power of grassroots initiative' (Ross 2021: 274). The danger in challenging rabbinic authority and encouraging innovation based on a democratised access to the sources is that the shift towards independent, non- or postdenominational prayer groups leads to religious innovations that are harder to connect to the chain of tradition that Orthodoxy claims to defend and uphold. As Ross equally acknowledges, it is disingenuous to claim that this chain of tradition has not already been subject to considerable change. Indeed, the very concept of ordination and interpretations of the rabbinic role have themselves been subject to enormous change. The perception that change can be rooted in tradition has nonetheless been critical to the evolutions that have been facilitated in the development of Orthodox Judaism. The challenge for Orthodox feminists, then, is to try to bring about halakhic innovation without bringing down the entire edifice of *halakhah*.

What Irshai and Ross in their different ways both seek to argue is that there is a duality to *halakhah* that 'is embodied in the tension between nomos and narrative; between the regulative function of gatekeepers and the transformative potential of the law's practitioners, who establish the meaning of these laws' (Ross 2021: 273). The imperative for those Ross terms halakhic feminists is to bring about practical change on the ground, from the grassroots up, which in turn can incite a willingness to implement the innovative halakhic interpretations that are possible. As Irshai argues, the scope for achieving meaningful change in this direction will only come when feminist principles shape the halakhic process itself. The possibility for achieving this goal is enhanced by the role of the internet in transmitting ideas and transforming the very means of accessing, studying, and interpreting halakhic texts. As Ross expresses it, 'As connected critics we struggle mightily to honor our commitment to a system that we revere, lest something invaluable be lost if we do not play by the established rules. . . . At the same time, as feminists we take into account the historical development of the halakhic system and the pervasive obstacles that its deep-seated patriarchal roots pose to current notions of justice' (Ross 2021: 259).

As one interviewee in a study of gender and Judaism explained, 'To be an Orthodox woman and a feminist can feel very lonely' (Israel-Cohen 2012: 87). The two components can each confer outsider status on the other. Orthodox critics insist that efforts to introduce feminist innovations, when not simply dismissed outright as heresy, risk destroying the parameters of the halakhic system as a whole. Meanwhile, the limits that some Orthodox feminists impose on the changes they seek within Judaism – in an effort to preserve the underlying halakhic system – can contribute to feminist critiques that view many religions as irredeemably patriarchal. Increasing efforts are being made to emphasise the value of feminists applying an intersectional lens, recognising the varieties of marginalisation different women experience in varied contexts, beyond those of white, westernised women. Relatedly, such intersectional analysis helps draw attention to how some religious women may consciously choose to use their personal sense of agency to embrace religious acts that others may view as limiting women's rights.

Although the challenge for Orthodox feminists can come from all sides, the signs of change nonetheless remain hard to ignore. Where it will lead is far harder to predict. The backlash against innovation in some sectors of Orthodoxy indicates, on one level, how efforts are forcefully being made to reassert and entrench rabbinic authority, removing even legitimate grounds for halakhic innovation. This perpetuates the damaging model of Akeda theology that limits the types of religious expression Jewish women and men can access. On another level, the growing limits to this authority are also displayed as defenders of change refuse to be cowed into accepting halakhic arguments they believe through their own learning there is good cause to challenge.

One by-product of the opposition to feminist innovations like women rabbis and partnership minyanim is the growing willingness to promote alternative practices that are deemed to be acceptable within Orthodox synagogues. So the idea of women's prayer groups is increasingly now encouraged, although it was previously opposed. The same applies to alternative opportunities – for example, for women to give sermons in mainstream Orthodox synagogues, to be appointed as *yoatzot halakhah*, or to participate in women's readings of the Scroll of Esther on the festival of Purim. While these innovations are deemed more acceptable, they capture the underlying challenge for Orthodox Jewish feminists in the synagogue: how to carve out a path that can envoice women, empowering them to feel present, heard, and part of the community, able to forge a connection to their religion, without this being interpreted and experienced through a wholly male prism. The partnership minyan model creates a space in which Orthodox feminist women are empowered to reclaim the power of their voices. A key feature of these services is their commitment to partnership between men and women; it is an inclusive model that builds from a strategy of envoicing all participants. However, it is predicated on a male willingness, first, to participate in these services, to create the necessary male quorum for reciting many of the prayers, and second, to rescind their claims to lead certain parts of the service thereby enabling women to take them on instead. As long as women require permission from men in order to have their voices and their experiences heard and considered, the scope for real inclusivism will remain limited. This is why women's ordination is so important. And also why it remains so challenging for Orthodoxy. Only by

Women in the Synagogue 63

incorporating female voices, perspectives, and experiences into the halakhic process itself is there any chance for women to engage with their Judaism as independent subjects, moving beyond a subjectification in which they are primarily expected to serve men, so that men can be the ones to serve God. This is the challenge that remains: for women to influence both nomos and narrative, how Jewish ritual is interpreted and observed.

BIBLIOGRAPHY

Ferziger A. S. 2009. 'Feminism and Heresy: The Construction of a Jewish Metanarrative', *Journal of the American Academy of Religion*, 77, 3: 494–546.

Ferziger A. S. 2018. 'Female Clergy in Male Space: The Sacralization of the Orthodox Rabbinate', *The Journal of Religion*, 98, 4: 490–516.

Frazer J. 2021. 'Female rabbi given back her research role at London School of Jewish Studies', *Jewish Chronicle*, July 6.

Frot M. 2021. 'Rabbis attack "glass ceiling of Torah" after female lecturer dropped from Jewish studies role', *Jewish Chronicle*, June 16.

Fuchs I. 2013. *Jewish Women's Torah Study: Orthodox Religious Education and Modernity*. Oxford: Routledge.

Greenberg B. 1981. *On Women and Judaism, A View from Tradition*. Philadelphia: Jewish Publication Society.

Hartman T. 2007. *Feminism Encounters Traditional Judaism*. Waltham, MA: Brandeis University Press.

Irshai R. 2010. 'Toward a Gender Critical Approach to the Philosophy of Jewish Law (Halakhah)', *Journal of Feminist Studies in Religion*, 26, 2, 55–77.

Irshai R. 2014. '"And I Find a Wife More Bitter than Death." Feminist Hermeneutics, Women's Midrashim, and the Boundaries of Acceptance in Modern Orthodox Judaism', *Journal of Feminist Studies in Religion*, 69–84.

Irshai R. 2017. 'Religion and Morality: Akedah Theology and Cumulative Revelation as Contradictory Theologies in Jewish Modern-Orthodox Feminism', *Journal of Modern Jewish Studies*, 219–35.

Israel-Cohen Y. 2012. *Between Feminism and Orthodox Judaism: Resistance, Identity, and Religious Change in Israel*. Leiden & Boston: Brill.

Maltz J. 2021. 'Orthodox, Female and Running Their Own Shuls – Just Don't Call Them Rabbis', *Ha'aretz*, July 12.

RCA. 2013. 'RCA Statement Regarding Yeshivat Maharat', https://rabbis.org/rca-statement-regarding-recent-developments-at-yeshivat-maharat. Accessed 19/9/21.

Rocker S. 2016. '"Excluded" for running partnership minyanim', *Jewish Chronicle*, November 17.

Ross T. 2010. 'The Contribution of Feminism to Halakhic Discourse: Kol be-Isha Ervah as a Test Case', *Emor* 1 (January), 37–70.

Ross T. 2021. *Expanding the Palace of Torah: Orthodoxy and Feminism*, 2nd edition. Waltham, MA: Brandeis University Press.

Shapiro M. 2001. 'Qeri'at ha-Torah by Women: A Halakhic Analysis', *The Edah Journal*, 1:2.

Sperber D. 2002. 'Congregational Dignity and Human Dignity: Women and Public Torah Reading', *The Edah Journal*, 3:2.

Taylor-Guthartz L. 2021. 'UK Smicha Celebration', https://www.youtube.com/watch?v=jXQFVOoHgdk, accessed 19/9/21.

Weiss A. 1997. 'Open Orthodoxy! A Modern Orthodox Rabbi's Creed', *Judaism* 46.4, 409–21.

Chapter 7

Women in the Orthodox Churches
Modernity and Change

Mary B. Cunningham

The role of women in Orthodox churches around the world today presents a paradox. Whereas patristic tradition and modern theology uphold women's equality with men, since both sexes were created according to the image and likeness of God (Genesis 1:26), they are barred from certain important roles – most noticeably the ordained priesthood. Although other Christian churches, especially the Protestant denominations, have moved towards allowing women to administer the sacraments and preach, the Orthodox churches have not yet reached a stage even of discussing this question in official settings. Nevertheless, women play increasingly important and varied roles in parishes and dioceses around the world. Many are highly educated and offer their expertise to the administrative and pastoral activities of local churches. Such contributions are not usually sanctioned by means of ritual sacraments or blessings, but they are welcomed and acknowledged in the wider Orthodox community. A volume of essays that was compiled in response to the Great and Holy Council (held in 2016 on the Greek island of Crete) draws on the expertise of female theologians, historians, scientists, choir leaders, iconographers, and others. Nevertheless, as the editor, Carrie Frederick Frost, notes in her Introduction, only four women attended that Council – in contrast to over 250 male (mainly clerical) delegates who represented many of the separate patriarchates and dioceses of the Orthodox Christian world (Frost 2018: iv–v; https://www.holycouncil.org/delegations). What occurred at this ecclesial gathering demonstrates that preventing women from being members of the ordained clergy (even at the level of the diaconate) also excludes them from participating in official discussion of doctrine and practice. Nevertheless, as Elizabeth Theokritoff has pointed out, 'being a full, and fully responsible, member of the Church has nothing to do with ordination' (Theokritoff 2007: 256). Orthodox tradition sets great store by the biblical passage, 'But you are a chosen race, a royal priesthood, a holy nation' (1 Pet 2:9). All lay and ordained people represent members of the body of Christ (Rom 12:5; 1 Cor 12:27, etc.) to use the metaphor which the apostle Paul used in various epistles. Each has his or her part to play, with that of the ordained priesthood being only one function of what creates the conciliarity (Russian *sobornost*) of the church.

The Orthodox Christian churches that are covered in this chapter include those patriarchates or autocephalous dioceses which adhere to the fourth ecumenical Council of Chalcedon (451 CE) and which are located historically in Greece, the Balkans, and Russia but which also flourish in diaspora or native communities around the world. The non-Chalcedonian churches that belong especially to Near Eastern and North African countries such as Egypt, Iraq, Lebanon, and Syria, as well as the Armenian church, are equally important but are excluded from this chapter for reasons of space. Not only the Chalcedonian and non-Chalcedonian Orthodox churches, but also the Catholic and Protestant ones, are rooted in a common tradition that developed during the first centuries of the Common Era. The history of women's role within Christianity is significant for each of these churches although later doctrinal schisms caused them to develop – and interpret that early tradition – in different ways. The first part of this chapter deals with the theological and ecclesiological background of the early church since this continues to exert a significant influence on Orthodox Christianity. The second part turns to the practical working out of this tradition in the modern world. As stated above, this is a story of frustratingly slow progress, as regards the representation of women at important councils and their ordination to the diaconate (or conceivably even the priesthood), but also of their increasing involvement in nonclerical ecclesial roles.

The traditional, or patristic, view of women in Christianity, as in Judaism, is based on scripture. According to Genesis 1:26–27, God created humankind according to his image and likeness, 'male and female he made them' (Pietersma & Wright 2007: 6–7). The early fathers of the church, including especially the fourth-century Cappadocian brothers Basil of Caesarea and Gregory of Nyssa, understood this verse to mean that both women and men are destined for salvation, provided that they are baptised and practise virtuous lives (Harrison 1990). Although women were regarded as the weaker sex, as witnessed especially in Eve's role in the original fall from grace, they were believed to be capable of overcoming the deficiencies of their gender and becoming 'like men' (Thomas 2019: 79–80). Such a view, which associates character traits such as courage or weakness with gender rather than with biological identity, was characteristic not only of Late Antique but also

Byzantine Christian culture (Neville 2019: 33–58). It means that the hagiographical convention of describing holy women as 'manly' in their character and behaviour succeeds in transcending, rather than reaffirming, a 'culturally entrenched misogyny' (Harrison 1990: 447). The fathers in any case viewed human sexuality and gender as aspects of creation that would become less important – or even disappear – after the final resurrection. God, according to the philosophical traditions that early leaders of the church inherited and adapted to Christian theology, is genderless although 'he' may be described by means of gendered language. Human beings are differentiated as male and female at birth but may grow into greater likeness to God in accordance with Paul's statement in Galatians 3:28: 'There is no longer Jew or Greek, there is no longer slave or free, there is no longer male and female; for all of you are one in Christ Jesus.'

Women played an active role in the earliest church, according to the Pauline Epistles and other sources. It is possible that they acted as priests and preached or prophesied in some of the Gnostic and Montanist communities that were declared heretical by mainstream followers of Jesus Christ. The official church, which adopted a hierarchical threefold clerical structure (bishops, presbyters, and deacons) during the late first and second centuries, gradually suppressed such tendencies. Women could dedicate themselves formally to the roles of widow or virgin and, perhaps from an early period, might be ordained as deaconesses (FitzGerald 1998: 1–17; Kateusz 2019: 49–65; Wijngaards 2002). Although they were thus barred from the more powerful clerical positions in the early church, women acted in a variety of pastoral and spiritual roles. The order of deaconess, which had the practical function of helping to baptise adult women and looking after other female members both inside and outside the church, survived until about the twelfth century in the Eastern Roman church. The abandonment of the order occurred for a variety of reasons, including the shift from adult to infant baptism and influence from the Western church (FitzGerald 1998: 134–47). Lay women, including those who chose the monastic life, nevertheless continued to play significant roles within the Byzantine church: they could participate as fully as men in liturgical celebrations, act informally as spiritual guides or confessors, and achieve a level of spiritual perfection that qualified them to be saints. The list of female as well as male martyrs and ascetic saints that appears in hagiographical compilations such as the *Synaxarion of Constantinople* is striking (Delehaye 1902); it suggests that equality of the sexes existed as an ideal concept, if not as a reality, in Byzantium.

The Virgin Mary, or 'Mother of God' as she is called in both Byzantine and modern Orthodox communities, represents an exception among women. Mary is held to be 'greater in honour than the Cherubim and beyond compare more glorious than the Seraphim' (Lash 2011: 47). In other words, she occupies a rank that precedes even that of the highest angelic powers because she gave birth to Christ, the Word of God. The Virgin Mary is celebrated in hymns, sermons, and hagiographical texts that continue to be sung or read in Orthodox churches today (Cunningham 2015). Although the Orthodox church has not endorsed doctrines such as the Immaculate Conception, on the grounds that this diminishes Mary's ties with the rest of humanity, it does celebrate her as a model of purity and virtue. Whereas the Mother of God might thus be viewed as an example of 'ideal womanhood', especially in her role as the 'Second Eve', who reversed the disobedient act of her first female ancestor by accepting the incarnation of Christ, some scholars argue that she stands for all of humanity, female and male, in her relationship with God (Behr-Sigel 1991: 206–9; Cunningham 2021: 33–34). The Virgin manifests both masculine and feminine qualities, according to Byzantine and modern Orthodox liturgical narratives (Cunningham 2021: 25–34). For example, according to the famous *Akathistos Hymn*, she acts as 'leader in battle and defender' for Christians while at the same time being 'the womb of the divine Incarnation' (Peltomaa 2001: 3–5). Mary is thus an ambiguous figure according to Orthodox Christian tradition: she transcends both men and women in her power and holiness but remains anchored to the created world and its temporal problems. As Byzantine preachers and hymnographers repeatedly remind their audiences, the Mother of God is an antitype of Jacob's ladder between heaven and earth (Gen 28:10–17), helping to draw humanity closer to its intended genderless, or angelic, state (Ladouceur 2006: 15–19).

Turning now to the position of women in the modern Orthodox churches, one of the first questions that is usually asked by outsiders is why this tradition is so slow to follow the Protestant churches (and perhaps eventually the Catholic church) in ordaining women to the priesthood. Although the question remains for the most part dormant in official ecclesiastical circles, it has been discussed in academic and less formal contexts in recent years (Behr-Sigel 1987; Behr-Sigel 1991; Hopko 1983; Hopko 1999; Thomas & Narinskaya 2020). Those who oppose change cite two main arguments, referring first to 'holy tradition', that is, the beliefs and practices (some of which remain unwritten) that have been passed down through generations of Orthodox parish and monastic life. This is believed to be inspired by the Holy Spirit and it should not be confused 'with cultural stereotypes' or 'social convention' (Kallistos of Diokleia 1999: 10). Considerations that relate to tradition include what we know about Jesus Christ's appointment of mainly male apostles to spread the good news about Christianity and to baptize converts, the wisdom of church leaders during subsequent centuries in ordaining only men as bishops and priests, and the acceptance of this situation by most Christians. The second argument is more theological: this deals with the 'iconic' nature of the priesthood, arguing that since Christ was male, the priests who represent him as mediators between God and humanity should also be of that gender. This argument stresses the importance of the incarnation as the basis for human interaction with God. Those individuals who stand at the altar represent, or image, the human and divine high priest, Christ; they should thus reflect the reality of his gendered personhood in their own human nature and masculinity (Kallistos of Diokleia 1999: 40–52).

One of the most influential thinkers to counter such arguments against the ordination of women to the priesthood has been the French theologian Elisabeth Behr-Sigel. In a wide-ranging study, which covers biblical, cultural, and theological aspects of women's place in the Christian church, Behr-Sigel argues that this is a community made up of equal, albeit different, members from its origins in the first century CE. Even if the ecclesial body has not always manifested such high principles during its sojourn in a fallen and imperfect world, the vision of an ideal community persists (Behr-Sigel 1991: 93–102). Behr-Sigel also addresses the 'iconic' argument against the ordination of women to the priesthood. She starts by asking exactly what is meant by the concept of the priest's iconic representation of Christ at the altar. Is it Christ's 'maleness' or his *humanity* that he represents when imitating the former's actions at the Last Supper and distributing the Eucharist to the faithful? Behr-Sigel notes in this context that the priest not only represents Christ in carrying out this liturgical action, but he also stands for the church. In other words, he stands for the High Priest who both 'offers' and 'is offered'. The words of the Divine Liturgy according to an Orthodox rite that dates (at least in parts) to the fourth century say little about the gender either of Christ or the priest; rather, it is their humanity, which stands in a loving relationship with God, that is important (Behr-Sigel 1991: 177–79).

Bishops including Metropolitans Anthony of Sourozh (who wrote a preface to the French version of Behr-Sigel's book) and Kallistos of Diokleia have engaged seriously with Behr-Sigel's arguments concerning the ordination of women (Anthony of Sourozh 1991; Kallistos of Diokleia 2020). Metropolitan Anthony, for example, agrees that God revealed himself in Christ as 'the perfect Man (*anthropos*) who contains and reveals the totality of the human being and not just the "virile" side'. He compares the sacramental service of priests to the sacrifice of the Mother of God when she allowed her Son, Jesus Christ, to be crucified (Anthony of Sourozh 1991). The bishop also agrees with Behr-Sigel that the ordination of women represents an important theological issue. It demands prayerful discussion and reflection on the part of all Orthodox Christians.

Nevertheless, the fact remains that most Orthodox hierarchs, along with their flocks, oppose changes to holy tradition. They see the ordination of women to the priesthood as something that has been presented by the Western churches and their surrounding culture, arguing that is not an issue that arose naturally within the Orthodox church (Kallistos of Diokleia 1999: 5–7). Again, Metropolitan Anthony contests this view, stating that the ordination of women 'must become for us a question that is asked "from the inside"' (Anthony of Sourozh 1991: xiv). In general, the appeal to 'tradition', which is sometimes described as a 'mystery', prevails among the opponents of reform since the 'iconic' argument fails to stand up to scrutiny. Most Orthodox Christians are accustomed to seeing priests and bishops celebrating church services and sacraments in a 'patriarchal' guise: they display long beards and other unmistakable signs of age and masculinity. For many lay and clerical members of the church, it is thus difficult to imagine female ministers serving at the altar or in other sacred contexts.

One aspect of the ordination question does show signs of development. This is the question of the ordination of women to the diaconate. This order, as we saw above, was active in the early and Byzantine churches until about the twelfth century CE (Madigan & Osiek 2011: 25–140). A rite of ordination, called *cheirotonia*, which was equivalent to that of male deacons, appears in early service books. Deaconesses played important sacramental and pastoral roles during the first millennium of Eastern Christianity, helping with baptisms, keeping order in the ranks of women during services, visiting them in their homes (perhaps also delivering the Eucharist to those who were ill), and offering instruction to female catechumens. Although these duties reflect the segregated nature of early Christian and Byzantine societies, they fulfilled an important service to the community (FitzGerald 1998; Kallistos of Diokleia 1999: 15–17; Karras 2004). Discussions concerning the reinstitution of the female diaconate have occurred during the twentieth and early twenty-first centuries at various formal assemblies. A Consultation of Orthodox Women, held at Agapia, Romania, in 1976 resulted in a plea for the 're-activation' of this order; the conference described the ministry as 'a lifetime commitment to full vocational service in the church . . . and extension of the sacramental life of the church into the life of society' (Tarasar & Kirillova 1976: 40). An Inter-Orthodox Symposium, held in Rhodes in 1988, also advocated the revival of the order of deaconesses (Kallistos of Diokleia 1999: 18). Despite these initiatives, progress has been slow. Since no official pronouncement has been made on the subject – for example, at the Great and Holy Council of Crete 2016 – it has depended on individual synods or bishops to ordain women to the diaconate. For example, the Synod of Alexandria voted to revive the female diaconate in November 2016 and followed this up with the ordination of five women in the Democratic Republic of Congo on 17 February 2017 (Frost 2017). It may well be that practical, rather than ecclesiological, considerations will dictate whether this move is replicated in other jurisdictions of the Orthodox church.

Women in the Orthodox Churches 71

There are several reasons for what may appear to be a lack of impetus for the ordination of women to the priesthood in Orthodox Christianity. The first has to do with the concept of priesthood itself (Louth 2020). Unlike the Catholic and Protestant churches, the ecclesiastical hierarchy, which includes both bishops and priests, is understood (at least in theory) as a vehicle for service rather than for wielding power. The structure can be visualised as an upside-down pyramid, with the clergy supporting, or ministering to, the wider body of lay Christians. At a practical level, the sacramental and pastoral service that priests perform can be gruelling, especially in parishes that place all responsibility in the hands of their clergy. Although there are numerous exceptions to this rule in the modern world, many priests, according to Byzantine and modern traditions, still receive no pay for their services; they often work at a day job, such as school or university teaching, in order to support themselves and their families. Another reason for the absence of debate on the subject of ordination was mentioned at the beginning of this chapter: the Orthodox Christian tradition upholds the idea that all lay members of the church belong to the 'royal priesthood' that is described in 1 Peter 2:9. Lay Orthodox Christians are reminded of this vocation in sermons, catechesis and other forms of instruction, especially in those jurisdictions or episcopal sees that aspire to a less clerical and more democratic ecclesial structure. Following the Pauline idea that each member of the church has particular gifts to offer (Romans 12:6, 1 Corinthians 12), both women and men perform a variety of functions within their parishes and in the wider church community. It is possibly also for this reason that female candidates for the priesthood are scarce and that debate on the subject currently remains more abstract than practical.

Women, although for the most part not ordained even as deaconesses, nevertheless play important roles in Orthodox jurisdictions throughout the world. Patricia Fan Bouteneff recently carried out a survey which established that women perform a wide variety of leadership roles within the Orthodox church, even if they do not 'wear cassocks, beards, and pectoral crosses'. Such roles include pastoral care, chaplaincy, spiritual direction (especially on the part of women who have dedicated themselves to a monastic life), diplomacy within the church, administration, acting as trustees, directors, or treasurers of theological seminaries or parishes, organising music and serving as choir directors, teaching, serving as librarians or archivists, painting icons, embroidering church vestments, teaching Sunday school, engaging in public speaking and academic writing, blogging, translating, and many others (Bouteneff 2016). Although this list of roles is incomplete, it provides a strong indication of women's importance in the daily running of the church – both at official and local levels. Bouteneff notes, however, that such activity remains largely unacknowledged and unrewarded by the official church hierarchies (Bouteneff 2016; Bouteneff 2018: 2–3). To counter this somewhat pessimistic conclusion, it is worth noting some promising signs of change. Bouteneff has since founded an organisation called 'Axia', which celebrates the achievements of individual Orthodox women (Axia Women ongoing). She and other prominent Orthodox women continue to create networks for discussion and mutual support between female members of the church who contribute so much to its mission and pastoral service throughout the world.

The experience of ordinary women in Orthodox churches around the world is also beginning to be documented and analysed. Nadieszda Kizenko provides a wide-ranging assessment of the position of women in the post-Soviet Orthodox church in Russia, based on internet sources and personal contacts (Kizenko 2013). Concerning religious life during the period of atheist Communist rule before 1990, Kizenko notes that women – especially over the age of fifty-five – upheld the persecuted church. 'They were the ones who attended services, who secretly brought children to be baptized, and who kept up domestic religious rituals for the life transitions of birth, marriage, and death. They were the ones who were willing to take to the streets in defence of their churches and priests' (Kizenko 2013: 597). There are parallels here with other Orthodox nations, such as Greece and Cyprus, where it is often the *giagiades* ('grandmothers') who make up the bulk of the congregation. The situation changed in Russia, however, after the end of Communism at the beginning of the 1990s. Kizenko describes a body which she calls the 'virtuosi', that is, men and women of all ages who strive 'for perfection within an existing tradition' or 'to fulfil to the utmost the demands of his or her religious tradition' (Kizenko 2013: 600). In the case of women, this often includes (in addition to attending church regularly, fasting, confessing, and adhering to other canonical rules) wearing modest clothing, head coverings, and attempting to abide by 'patriarchal' ideas about gender roles. It has also led, however, to a number of female-led initiatives, such as the publication of magazines, blogs, films, and other media that are aimed specifically at women (Kizenko 2013: 601–5). The commitment to religious life that manifests itself especially in women is a subject that would benefit from further study, not only with regard to post-Soviet Russia, but also in other Orthodox Christian nations and communities.

Women do continue to encounter obstacles, however, which may cause either discouragement or anger. Because the various jurisdictions of the Chalcedonian Orthodox church continue (at least in theory) to adhere to canons that were established during the first millennium of the Common Era, rules about purity – especially in relation to the holiest aspects of religious worship – persist. Many local churches continue to 'church' women forty days after childbirth: that is, they are invited to attend church with their newborn babies where they are 'purified' of any 'sin' or 'uncleanness' that is associated with childbirth (Hapgood 1975: 268). After the churching ceremony, many priests carry male infants into the sanctuary but, in the case of female ones, only go as far as the Holy Doors that separate the nave from the sanctuary (Hapgood 1975: 270). Another aspect of such purity laws, which has been abandoned in many modern parishes, is the denial of the sacraments of Confession or the Eucharist to menstruating girls and women. Such practices are often attributed to the influence of Judaism on early Christianity. It is possible that dialogue between the two religions, especially with regard to the theological meaning of rules about female purity, would help both to understand their history and meaning – and perhaps eventually to abandon them in modern practice.

In conclusion, the paradoxical position of women in the modern Orthodox church offers an opportunity for hope and further action. That women play an important role in the church is undeniable: from flower arranging, church cleaning, and preparing coffee to leading parish councils, teaching, directing choirs, and many other important functions, women support the community in innumerable ways. The impetus to reward such efforts by ordination to the diaconate – or at least by formal blessings – is growing, even if the path towards women's ordination to the priesthood or even episcopacy remains uncertain. The Christian view that every person in the church is an essential member of the whole body – and belongs to 'a royal priesthood' (1 Pet 2: 9) – undermines to some extent the need for women, as well as men, to be ordained. However, the absence of women from official synods or councils is a problem that needs to be rectified. It is likely, following the published interventions of women following the recent pan-Orthodox Council in Crete (2016), that this situation will change (Frost 2018). In the meantime, women continue to write, speak, interact, and otherwise make their presence felt in Orthodox jurisdictions throughout the modern world.

Acknowledgment: I would like to acknowledge the generosity of Carrie Frederick Frost in helping me to compile the following bibliography.

BIBLIOGRAPHY

Anthony of Sourozh. 1991. 'Preface' in Behr-Sigel 1991, xiii–xiv.
Axia Women. Ongoing. Online at: https://www.axiawomen.org/.
Behr-Sigel E. 1987. *Le ministère de la femme dans l'église.* Paris.
Behr-Sigel E. 1991. *The Ministry of Women in the Church*, trans. S. Bigham. Redondo Beach, CA: Oakwood Publications.

74 *Mary B. Cunningham*

Bouteneff P. F. 2016. 'Invisible Leaders in the Orthodox Church', *Aphaia Resources*, posted 5 September, online at: https://www.aphaiaresources.com/2016/09/05/invisible-leaders-in-the-orthodox-church/.

Bouteneff P. F. 2018. 'The Changeless Church in the Age of Change.org', in Frost 2018, 1–5.

Cunningham M. B. 2015. *Gateway of Life. Orthodox Thinking on the Mother of God.* Yonkers, NY: St. Vladimir's Seminary Press.

Cunningham M. B. 2021. *The Virgin Mary in Byzantium, c. 400–1000 CE. Hymns, Homilies and Hagiography.* Cambridge: Cambridge University Press.

Delehaye H., ed. 1902. *Synaxarium Constantinopolitanum. Propylaeum ad AS Novembris.* Brussels.

FitzGerald K. K. 1998. *Women Deacons in the Orthodox Church. Called to Holiness and Ministry.* Brookline, MA: Holy Cross Orthodox Press.

Frost C. F. 2017. 'Women Deacons in Africa; Not in America', posted in Women in the Church, Orthodox Christian Studies Center, online at: https://publicorthodoxy.org/2017/03/02/alexandria-deaconesses/.

Frost C. F. ed. 2018. *The Reception of the Holy and Great Council. Reflections of Orthodox Women.* New York: Greek Orthodox Archdiocese of America Department of Inter-Orthodox, Ecumenical & Interfaith Relations.

Hapgood I. F. 1975. *Service Book of the Holy Orthodox-Catholic Apostolic Church.* Englewood, NJ: Antiochian Orthodox Christian Archdiocese.

Harrison N. V. 1990. 'Male and Female in Cappadocian Theology', *Journal of Theological Studies* 41, n.s., 441–71.

Hopko T., ed. 1983. *Women and the Priesthood.* Crestwood, NY: St. Vladimir's Seminary Press.

Hopko T., ed. 1999. *Women and the Priesthood,* rev. ed. Crestwood, NY: St. Vladimir's Seminary Press.

Kallistos of Diokleia. 1999. 'Man, Woman and the Priesthood of Christ', in Hopko 1999, 5–53.

Kallistos of Diokleia. 2020. '"Why I Have Changed My Mind." Revisiting the Ordination of Women', in Thomas & Narinskaya 2020, 79–84.

Karras V. 2004. 'Female Deacons in the Byzantine Church', *Church History* 73, no. 2 (June), 272–316.

Kateusz A. 2019. *Mary and Early Christian Women: Hidden Leadership.* New York: Springer.

Kizenko N. 2013. 'Feminized Patriarchy? Orthodoxy and Gender in Post-Soviet Russia', *Signs* 38, no. 3 (Spring), 595–621.

Ladouceur P. 2006. 'Old Testament Prefigurations of the Mother of God', *St Vladimir's Theological Quarterly* 50, nos. 1–2, 5–57.

Lash E. 2011. *The Divine Liturgy of Our Father among the Saints, John Chrysostom* (rev. ed.). Oxford: The Greek Orthodox Archdiocese of Thyateira and Great Britain.

Louth A. 2020. 'Revisiting an Orthodox Theology of Priesthood', in Thomas and Narinskaya, 85–98.

Madigan K. & C. Osiek, eds. 2011. *Ordained Women in the Early Church. A Documentary History.* Baltimore, MD: Johns Hopkins University Press.

Neville L. 2019. *Byzantine Gender*. Leeds: ARC Humanities Press.

Peltomaa L. M. 2001. *The Image of the Virgin Mary in the Akathistos Hymn*. Leiden, Boston and Cologne: Brill.

Pietersma A. & B. Wright, eds. 2007. *A New English Translation of the Septuagint and the Other Greek Translations Traditionally Included under That Title*. Oxford and New York: Oxford University Press.

Tarasar C. J. & I. Kirillova, eds. 1976. *Orthodox Women. Their Role and Participation in the Orthodox Church*. Geneva: World Council of Churches.

Theokritoff E. 2007. 'We "Being Many Are One Body": The Conciliarity of the Church as Exemplified in Lay Women,' in *Orthodox and Wesleyan Ecclesiology*, ed. S. T. Kimbrough, Jr. Crestwood, NY, 255–68.

Thomas G. 2019. *The Image of God in the Theology of Gregory of Nazianzus*. Cambridge: Cambridge University Press.

Thomas G. & E. Narinskaya, eds. 2020. *Women and Ordination in the Orthodox Church. Explorations in Theology and Practice*. Eugene, OR: Cascade Books.

Wijngaards J. 2002. *No Women in Holy Orders? The Women Deacons of the Early Church*. Norwich: Canterbury.

SUGGESTIONS FOR FURTHER READING

Belonick D. 1983. *Feminism in Christianity: An Orthodox Christian Response*. Syosset, NY: Department of Religious Education, Orthodox Church of America.

Breaban C., S. Deicha, & E. Kasselouri-Hatzivassiliadi, eds. 2006. *Women's Voices and Visions of the Church: Reflections of Orthodox Women*. Geneva: World Council of Churches.

Evdokimov P. 1994. *Women and the Salvation of the World. A Christian Anthropology on the Charisms of Women*, trans. A. P. Gythiel. Crestwood, NY: St. Vladimir's Seminary Press.

Farley L. R. 2012. *Feminism and Tradition: Quiet Reflections on Ordination and Communion*. Yonkers, NY: St. Vladimir's Seminary Press.

FitzGerald K. K., ed. 1999. *Orthodox Women Speak. Discerning the 'Signs of the Times'*. Geneva: WCC Publications.

Frost C. F. 2019. *Maternal Body: A Theology of Incarnation for the Christian East*. Mahwah, NJ: Paulist Press.

Harrison N. V. 2001. 'Women, Human Identity and the Image of God: Antiochene Interpretations', *Journal of Early Christian Studies* 9, 205–49.

Karras V. 2002. 'Eschatology', in *The Cambridge Companion to Feminist Theology*, ed. Susan Parsons. Cambridge, 243–61.

Liveris L. B. 2005. *Ancient Taboos and Gender Prejudice: Challenges for Orthodox Women and the Church*. Aldershot and Burlington, VT: Ashgate.

Chapter 8

Orthodoxia and Orthopraxia
On the Issue of Blood

Elena Narinskaya

This presentation looks at the issue of ritual purity/impurity with regard to menstrual blood, from various perspectives. Firstly, it looks at the earliest canonical evidence from the Christian sources and examines the biblical foundation of the arguments in them, starting from the Leviticus regulations about ritual impurity. A further excursion via a short selection of transitional elements – i.e., early Christian texts – shows the appropriation of the Leviticus laws and also the discussion about the question of obedience to Leviticus legislation in the context of the Christian communities. A final part of this study offers a brief commentary on the current practices of obedience to the Leviticus laws of ritual impurity in contemporary Christianity. We shall offer a historical, textual, theological and practical overview of a certain religious legislation which was received across the religious spectrum of the Jewish–Christian milieu.

The aim of this study is to consider the levels of appreciation of the impurity laws in the practical aspects of the contemporary lives of some Orthodox Christian communities. The limited selection of Christian sources only schematically points to various contrasting argumentations of the developing Christian tradition in approaching the laws of ritual impurity. The study may open the door for further studies that will need to explore the contextual/historical/canonical developments in Christianity, and to consider these developments with closer scrutiny and attention.

The first early Christian document we shall consider is Canon II of Dionysius of Alexandria, a pope and patriarch of Alexandria from 248 to 264. He wrote this document in 262 in Egypt, reflecting concerns of the early Christian community with the issues of ritual impurity for women, and it was received as a Church legislative Canon. In the following quotation Dionysius writes instructions as to how he thinks his church is to address the issue of menstruating women partaking in the communion:

> Concerning menstruating women, whether they ought to enter the temple of God while in such a state, I think it superfluous even to put the question. For, I think, not even themselves, being faithful and pious, would dare when in this state either to approach the Holy Table or to touch the body and blood of Christ. For not even the woman with a twelve years' issue would come into actual contact with Him, but only with the edge of His garment, to be cured. There is no objection to one's praying no matter how he may be or to one's remembering the Lord at any time and in any state whatever, and petitioning to receive help; but if one is not wholly clean both in soul and in body, he shall be prevented from coming up to the Holy of Holies. (Feltoe 1904, 102–3)

Dionysius evokes the Gospel story of a woman described in Matthew 9:20–22 and in Mark 5:25–34, and also reflects on Leviticus laws of ritual impurity of a menstruating woman (Lev. 15:19, 25, 33).

The biblical references in this document lead us into the biblical context and its guidance as to where the Jewish and Christian scripture stands on the issue of blood.

> Lev. 15:1–3: The Lord said to Moses and Aaron, 'Say to the people of Israel, When any man has a discharge from his body, his discharge is unclean. And this is the law of his uncleanness. . . .'
>
> Lev. 15:19: When a woman has a discharge of blood which is her regular discharge from her body, she shall be in her impurity for seven days, and whoever touches her shall be unclean until the evening.

The Hebrew of the verses uses the same word referring to the 'issue' at hand, in relation to the blood discharge of a woman and the discharge of a man. The difference lies in Hebrew words describing male and female impurity. The feminine noun form for 'impurity' can be understood as abhorrent, shunned with a much clearer element of shunning, exclusion being present in the Hebrew word addressing female impurity. Another distinction is that a menstruating woman is perceived as being sick with her impurity (Lev. 15:33).

The affliction of women with pain and unwellness could be initially traced to the curse of 'unwellness' to the woman after the Fall, as described in Genesis 3:16: To the woman he said, 'I will greatly multiply your pain in childbearing; in pain you shall bring forth children, yet your desire shall be for your husband, and he shall rule over you.'

Orthodoxia and Orthopraxia 79

To the man the curse of sorrow is distributed, but not the curse of unwellness, as in Genesis 3:17: 'in toil you shall eat of it all the days of your life.' A similar curse of labours of sorrow is mentioned as a 'wave of Adam's curse' in Noah in Genesis 5:29: 'Out of the ground that the Lord has cursed this one shall bring us relief from our work and from the toil of our hands.'

The above excursion into the biblical stories of sorrows and impurities is undertaken in order to show that there is an etymological distinction between male and female impurities, and that there are different consequential outcomes of these impurities for men and for women. Although the difference is minor, it is still worth mentioning here as a practical application of the laws of the impurity in religious communities. Schematically, female impurity led to excluding a woman from the community for the seven-day period of her menstrual cycle, while male impurity applied for a much shorter time and was obliterated straight after performing ritual cleansing.

The overarching biblical purpose of the Leviticus laws is to strive for the holiness of Israel, as clearly indicated in the verse of Leviticus 20:26. The goal for the chosen people of God is to obtain holiness. They are to imitate God in his attribute of holiness. This could bear resemblance to the Christian concept of deification, the striving of a human person to become like God. According to the biblical verse, such a state is projected onto the people by God, and He did so by speaking to them directly.

In the instances of direct speech of God to people, a twofold goal or the task is set between the people and their God. On the one hand, by their obedience to the law people keep their holiness, and consequently keep themselves away from any state of uncleanness. On the other hand, there is a need for a synergetic collaboration with God in following the general guidelines of the laws and in continuously maintaining the living tradition of these legislative norms relevant, contemporary, comprehensive and alive. In other words, the main commandment of keeping the people holy has to be contextually implemented in the everyday lives of these very people and in historical contexts where they find themselves. One can identify at least two driving forces or elements in ritual purity legislation: general divine guidance, which is supplemented, as the second stem, by its human implementation.

Once received and reflected in the scriptural canon, divine guidance acquires the definitions of being flawless, timeless, transcendent, constant and continuous throughout the history of God–human collaboration. Human collaboration is essential in order to understand, implement and carry on fulfilling the scriptural guidance throughout the historical development of the God–human relationship. In describing this very human element one has to allow a possibility to change, evolve, be updated in accordance with a new revelation of God or a new era in the history of humanity. When God offers new revelations, human synergistic collaboration assumes a continuous

80   *Elena Narinskaya*

process of change on the part of an individual human person or a human community of believers, or the whole of humanity in its relationship with the Creator.

The Christian perception of a Christ event as being that new revelation of God for humanity had an impact on human ability to process the path leading to holiness and deification. Christian tradition claims to have received a new revelation from God in the Incarnation and it consequently developed a new understanding of the Old Testament Law. The relationship of the New Testament with the Leviticus laws is rather complicated. On the one hand, the New Testament could be interpreted as abrogating some of the Old Testament laws and stipulations, while, on the other hand, such one-sided conclusions contradict some of the New Testament verses.

For example, Hebrews 9:22 reaffirms the Old Testament perception about sacrificial blood as cleansing and purifying. The verse confirms the Old Testament law to be a requirement for the New Testament revelation, and affirms that nearly everything is cleansed with blood, and without the shedding of blood there is no forgiveness. This stipulation of the Old Testament law is brought in support of Jesus' sacrifice, and later is transformed into the understanding of the eucharistic sacrifice (which is called a bloodless sacrifice in Christian eucharistic theology). In further describing Christ's sacrifice, the Jewish concepts of High Priest, Holy of Holies, and sacrificial purification through blood are very much part of the New Testament's theological arsenal. The Jewish concepts are used to amplify the significance of Christ's ministry in obtaining 'eternal redemption' for the people (Heb 9:11–12).

Exploring the New Testament understanding of the Law further, one notices that the same letter to Hebrews describes Jesus as a mediator of a new covenant of God with the people, demonstrating that his blood gives better word/witness/testimony than the blood of Abel (Heb 12:24). It is important to emphasise that the New Testament understanding of the continuous nature of the God–human relationship sees the Christ event as a sign of a new step in it. There is an attempt to contextualise the New Testament revelation into the existing legislative norms and convictions. In order to do so, parallels are drawn between the temple sacrifice and the sacrifice of Jesus 'to make the people holy through his own blood' (Heb 13:11).

The change to the guidance of the Old Testament law in the New Testament could be seen in the institution of the Eucharist, when the eating of the flesh and the drinking of the blood is required. This could be seen in opposition to the doubly-repeated prohibition against eating/drinking of blood in Leviticus 17:10–14. The New Testament can be taken here as an abrogation of Old Testament law. Looking in the context of these verses one can see that in the episode of the Last Supper, which is taken as a blueprint for the Eucharistic prayers of Anaphora, Jesus's words 'this is my flesh, this is my blood. . . . eat/

Orthodoxia and Orthopraxia

drink it in remembrance of me' (Lk 22:19–20, Mt 26:26–28, Mk 14:22–24) are said within the context of a Jewish meal/practice/ritual, when Jesus was sharing a meal as a Jew and among his Jewish followers. In this sense one cannot simply disengage the New Testament eucharistic beginnings from Jewish tradition, Jewish legislative norms and so on. On the contrary, the following claim of Jesus could be understood in direct relationship with Leviticus 17:11, and referring to Jesus' blood as 'the blood on the altar to purify you, making you right with the Lord. It is the blood, given in exchange for a life that makes purification possible.'

Jesus himself talks about his blood as the blood of the covenant, which clearly refers to the Jewish tradition and people's covenantal relationship with their God. In Matthew 26:28 Jesus says: 'This is my blood of the covenant, which is poured out for many for the forgiveness of sins.' The same formula is used in the other two Gospels (Mk 14:24, Lk 22:20). The verses of the three canonical Gospel writers are clearly associating the Christ event with the new covenant between God and the people, and also confirm this new covenant with Jesus' blood, which is again done in close relation to the Jewish tradition of covenantal relationship with God. The Gospel of John, in reflecting on the reality of the new Covenant with God through the Christ event, amplifies the reality of it to the extent of the necessity of partaking in the flesh and blood of Christ as a way of accessing eternal life, raising of the dead, and the intimate relationship with Christ (Jn 6:53–56).

A completely new reality emerges here: the cup of the new covenant. However, this new reality is not a disengagement from the reality of the Jewish traditions of sacrificial and redemptive rituals, but to some extent a continuation of them in the light of the new revelation of the Christ event. If one looks at it from the legislative norm of Leviticus, it is very hard to reconcile. However, this reconciliation is necessary if one is to consider the following saying of Christ, which cannot be ignored, in relationship to his ministry and the Old Testament law: 'Do not think that I came to abolish the Law and the Prophets; I have not come to abolish them but to fulfil them' (Mt 15:17). Therefore, much more understanding is needed of the relation between Old Testament law and New Testament revelation. The early church tried various avenues to resolve the problematics.

The letter to the Corinthians quotes Jesus' saying that the new covenant is sealed by his blood, and he also advises his followers to repeat the ritual of breaking the bread and drinking the wine in his remembrance (1 Cor 11:25, also 10:16 about the blessing of the communion of the body and blood of Christ). The letter to the Ephesians brings about the concept of redemption that is achieved through the blood of Jesus, as well as the forgiveness of sins as a sign of divine initiative and God's grace (Eph 1:7). Another important consequence of the Christ event and his sharing his blood, according to the letter to the Ephesians, is the next step in the relationship between God and the people. Ephesians 2:13 indicates that the next step was made towards a more intimate and more personal mode of this relationship, the closeness that has occurred between people and God 'through the blood of Christ'.

The verses from the Christian scriptures are developing the reality of the Christ event and Jesus sharing or offering his blood for the people within the context of Jewish traditions. In order to understand the relationship of these verses of the Christian scripture and the verses of Leviticus, it is important to find what questions to ask. An emerging reality of the tradition of eucharistic communion of the body and blood of Jesus has developed across the Christian scriptures and a Christian tradition. There is also a reality of Leviticus laws, especially Leviticus 17 which imposes a strict prohibition of eating flesh and drinking blood. In considering the Leviticus prohibitions and emerging Christian practices one is naturally concerned about defining the relationship of Christian scriptures/traditions and the Jewish Leviticus laws. How does one define the nature of the relationship between two scriptures, or between two traditions? What is it that the Christian scriptures, based on their understanding of the Christ event, are trying to convey? If it is not the way of abrogating or abolishing the Old Testament Law then how do they claim to fulfil it? As a direct illustration, in relation to the issue of menstrual blood, the following question has to be posed: if Jesus reinterpreted the Leviticus 17 ritual impurity laws with Christological understanding, then how do we deal with the Leviticus 15 prohibition of drinking blood?

Throughout his earthly mission Jesus places himself within the Jewish tradition, and he applies Jewish scriptures to his ministry every step of the way. But the way he does it is often unorthodox, thought-provoking and asking searching questions. The Gospel of Mark 12:18 reports that the Jewish religious leaders were at a loss what to make of Jesus and his teachings, or they went after him to destroy him, as the same verse suggests. However, if we look at Jesus as offering his interpretations of Jewish scriptures, he cannot be considered as standing out of the patterns of rabbinical exegesis, which often offer polar-opposite arguments as a way of resolving the biblical complexity. The following part of the study will look at how the followers of Jesus attempted to decide between the Mosaic law and the revelation of Jesus.

Among the followers of Jesus after his crucifixion there were many of Jewish persuasion and also many gentiles. The most important question that they faced was whether the gentiles had to be converted to Judaism so as to be followers of Jesus. During Jesus's lifetime this was not a problem, as most of his close followers were Jews. However, with numbers of followers increasing there was a need for an Apostolic Decree in Jerusalem. The outcome of this decree was that gentile converts to Christianity were not obligated to keep most of the law of Moses, including the rules concerning circumcision.

Orthodoxia and Orthopraxia 83

This clearly indicated that gentile conversion to Judaism was not necessary. However, certain prohibitions on eating blood were retained, as well as the one on eating meat of animals not properly slain, and on fornication and idolatry. The conclusion of the apostolic decree is reported in Acts of the Apostles 15:28–29: 'For it has seemed good to the Holy Spirit and to us to impose on you no further burden than these essentials: that you abstain from what has been sacrificed to idols and from blood and from what is strangled and from fornication. If you keep yourselves from these, you will do well. Farewell.'

Paul in his letter to the Galatians (2:1–10) provides his theology behind the above Council's decision, in clearly advocating the freedom from the Law that was obtained through Christ event, which Paul applied in his ministry to the gentiles. In both cases this freedom from the Mosaic law was selectively applied. Summarising all of the above one can assume that in its relationship with the Old Testament law Christianity brought its emphasis on obtaining holiness through obedience to Christ over obedience to the Old Testament law, while still allowing selective application of Old Testament legislative postulates.

In the following part of the study, the case study of the Leviticus laws of menstrual impurity and their different ways of appropriation in the Christian communities will be discussed.

Early Christian communities demonstrate different approaches to the Leviticus laws of ritual impurity. Some canonical sources support Leviticus laws, while others, of noncanonical nature, do not. The variety of opinions with regards to the ritual impurity laws of Leviticus was demonstratively present in early Christian sources and practices, and remains so in the contemporary expressions of Christian thought and practice.

We will now look at a direct contradiction between opinions/practices/theologies in Canon II of Dionysius of Alexandria and in the *Didascalia* (third century CE, Syria/Antioch). Both sources are from the same period, and they also discuss the same issue which must have been relevant for the Christian communities in Syria/Antioch and Egypt, and which the churches there faced at the time.

Two respectful and important early Christian documents, *Didascalia* and Letter/Canon II of Dionysius, in their arguments for or against Leviticus laws of ritual impurity, refer to the same Gospel story in support of their contrary conclusions. These documents suggest that the menstruating woman either 'can' or 'cannot' receive communion. The texts of the *Didascalia* clearly do not support the Leviticus laws of ritual impurity, and thus contradict Canon II. One can even push the argument further in suggesting that the *Didascalia* forbids Christians to observe the Leviticus law, with the following statement:

84 *Elena Narinskaya*

> If you think, woman, that you are stripped of the Holy Spirit during the seven days of your menstruation, then if you die at this time, you will depart thence empty and without hope. Now think about it and recognize that prayer is heard through the Holy Spirit; and the Eucharist is received and consecrated through the Holy Spirit; and the Scriptures are words of the Holy Spirit and holy. Therefore if the Holy Spirit is within you, why do you isolate your soul and not approach the works of the Holy Spirit?
>
> You shall not separate those who have their period, for even the woman with the issue of blood was not reprimanded when she touched the edge of our Saviour's garment; she was rather deemed worthy to receive forgiveness of all her sins. (Didascalia 26)

The Gospel story of the woman with the issue of blood also features in Canon II, both sources referring to the gospel story of a woman who had been subject to bleeding for twelve years, and who was healed by Jesus by touching the edge of his cloak (Mt 9:20–22). Two points are important to emphasise here. Firstly, the woman was courageous or desperate enough to go against the laws of impurity, and all other cultural norms, when she touched a man, Jesus. Secondly, the fact that her belief was appraised openly by Jesus, and as the reward her healing was granted. The same story in the Gospel of Mark 5:25–34 gives a more detailed account of the event, putting greater emphasis on the immediate healing of the woman from her suffering. Jesus states in the Gospel that the woman's faith has healed her and he freed her from her suffering. The lesson could be seen here in faith overruling the Law, and also in Jesus' ability to free women from the suffering (perhaps a parallel could be drawn here to Eve's curse in Genesis 3:16).

Two early Christian sources understood the Gospel parable differently. Can one look at it from another level of complex relationship, namely the relationship between Orthodoxia and Orthopraxia? The conflicting recommendations about upholding Leviticus laws of ritual impurity in early Christian documents at hand were drawing their conclusions on the same Gospel illustrations.

Below is another important early Christian document, the *Apostolic Constitutions* (375 to 380 CE), from the same geographical area as Didascalia. This document is in alliance with the *Didascalia* in its didactics about the Leviticus law and its relevance to the Christian community at the time (*Apostolic Constitutions*, 3158–69). The argumentation of the *Apostolic Constitutions* is based on counterposing Christian anthropology and ritual impurity laws. The grounds for the Christian anthropological argument are derived from trinitarian dogma of the Christian tradition, and supported by the conclusion that the nature of a person in whom the Holy Spirit dwells cannot be defiled. Hence, the laws of ritual impurity of Leviticus 15 cannot be

Orthodoxia and Orthopraxia 85

applicable, as they do not adequately reflect on the Trinitarian/Christological reality. This new Christological reality advocates that the Leviticus legislation does not have the authority to separate a person from the purifying state of the Holy Spirit. According to the *Apostolic Constitutions*, only impiety and idolatry defiles and separates. (One has to point out here that the Leviticus legislation uses similar concepts of defilement and separation in relation to the ritual impurity defiling aspect of Lev. 15:19).

The reality of the God–human synergistic relationship could be seen as an ongoing process in which God initiates the dialogue and then steps into the relationship, and expects humanity to respond with their active participation in that relationship. Considering the obstacle of sin and the bondage of sin in the relationship between God and the people the mediation of the Mosaic law was afforded to help the people in their continued striving for purity and holiness. Hence, the Mosaic law could be seen as an aid to maintaining the God–human relationship, inasmuch as it was helping people to stay away from the defilement of sin, or rather to control the effect of this defilement. The Mosaic law was able to prevent people from increasing their sinful state, but it was not able to free people completely from sin. In that sense, it was never going to bring people to holiness and perfection, but was training people in the ways of God's law and in obedience to God through fulfilling the commandments and prescribed legislative norms. The Christ event, according to the Christian sources considered in this study, granted this long-awaited and needed freedom from sin. The curse of sin and the defilement of sin was lifted through Christ's sacrifice. This was a divine contribution, divine aid to the God–human synergetic collaboration. Freedom from sin also gave freedom of choice to humanity.

The reality of the church post–Christ-event is such that the church is granted the path of freedom from the defilement of sin through the gift of Christ-revelation of God. And yet, the church has to uphold its legacy of following the Old Testament law. There is another reality that can be noticed, that is, the reality of people continuing to be the followers of the divine Law without being slaves of the letter of the law (e.g., Rom. 7:1–6). What is crucial in this problematic is a clear understanding about the law and its purpose or relevance to the progress of humanity in reaching the state of deification. Christian sources advocate the path of imitating the sacrificial nature of Christ's love alongside the continuous experiential process of appreciating the Old Testament law.

Theologically speaking, and bringing the New Testament verses consulted in this paper together, a serious challenge could be posed to the reality of ritual impurity in Christ's revelation. If one is to relate defilement solely to sin, then it is eliminated together with sin, which is washed and cleansed with Christ's blood via his sacrificial death on the cross and his resurrection. More so, the eucharistic participation in his body and blood relives, revives and re-enacts Christ's sacrifice bringing it at the very core, the very foundation of the Christian church, the life of the Christian communities, and the lives of its members.

However, when sin is eliminated on the ontological level, it is brought back by the people's continuous contribution to the synergetic collaboration with God. The sinful path of humanity remains constant throughout its history. The conflict of Orthodoxia (Christology) and Orthopraxia (human sinful inclination) jeopardises the fullness of Christological experience in the church. The church reverts to its obedience to Mosaic law in its canonical guidance in order to guard its people from further defilement. Whether excommunicating menstruating women from taking part in the sacramental life of the church does this remains rather questionable.

In conclusion, we must emphasise that the conversations of the early Christian communities with Old Testament law continue in modern times. On the basis of the textual evidence considered in this study, it reaches its open-ended conclusion, allowing space for further and more detailed historical analysis of sources outside those selected. This analysis, however, considers the ritual impurity arguments significantly weakened by the Christological argument. Therefore, further studies of the relationship between the Leviticus law of impurity and its reception in the Christian tradition have to be envisaged.

This study attempted to enter into the process of creative struggle/contradictions or further appreciation of Leviticus by the Gospel, and also by early Christian documents upholding opposing arguments. Each of the early Christian documents had certain implications for the practice of Christian communities, as each document was issued in a way of didactic instructions to its respective communities. The practice of the early Christian communities could be seen as upholding two alternative ways of dealing with Levitical purity laws. One way is to uphold Leviticus, and another is to reinterpret it, as in the particular case of the issue of menstrual blood. It may be added that the 'creative struggle' between Leviticus and Christology continues into modern times and into the modern practices of Orthodox Christian communities.

Christian tradition adopted, inherited or organically evolved from the Jewish tradition. In this sense, there are some overlapping elements in both. The experience of the living traditions of both Christianity and Judaism presupposes their active engagement and responses to the challenges of modernity, of which one is their respective appreciation of the Leviticus laws of ritual impurity in relation to twenty-first-century realities. Perhaps this could be seen as a common Jewish–Christian path of dialogue and mutual learning as a way of resolving certain stumbling blocks of modernity, on which ritual impurity laws could be seen as a good starting point.

BIBLIOGRAPHY

Feltoe C. L. (ed.). 1904. *The Letters and Other Remains of Dionysius of Alexandria.* Cambridge.

SUGGESTIONS FOR FURTHER READING

Frederick Frost C. 2012. 'Purify Her Uncleanness', First Things Online, December (https://www.firstthings.com/web-exclusives/2012/12/purify-her-uncleanness).

Frederick Frost C. 2016. 'Churching: The Orthodox Rite of Churching the Mother and Child after Childbirth', *Saint Phoebe Center for the Deaconess,* April (https://orthodoxdeaconess.org/resources/women-church-praxis/).

Frederick Frost C. 2017. 'Childbirth Is a Blessing, Not an Occasion for Impurity', Public Orthodoxy, April 26 (https://publicorthodoxy.org/2017/04/26/childbirth-a-blessing-not-impurity/).

Grahn J. 1993. *Blood, Bread, and Roses: How Menstruation Created the World.* Boston: Beacon Press.

Larin V. 2008. 'What Is Ritual Impurity and Why', *St Vladimir's Theological Quarterly* 52:3–4, 275–92.

Neusner J. 1973. *The Idea of Purity in Ancient Judaism.* Leiden: Brill.

Chapter 9

Kashrut—Niddah—Milah
On the Issue of Blood

Sybil Sheridan

'At the head of all death am I, Blood. At the head of all life am I, Wine.' This inscription, carved over a gateway, caused Rabbi Bana'ah to object and suggest instead, 'At the head of all sickness am I, Blood. At the head of all medicine am I, Wine' (Babylonian Talmud, *Baba Batra* 58b Soncino translation). Either way, the passage from the Talmud sums up neatly the association of blood with death.

But this is only half the story, for blood pervades Judaism and is associated with life as well as with death; with purification as well as putrefaction. Its presence is felt at every transformative ritual and often it is not opposed to, but synonymous with wine. Killing is shedding blood because blood is life. Joshua explains to Rahab his responsibility in the words: 'If a hand is laid upon anyone who remains in the house with you, his blood shall be on our heads' (Josh 2:19 [JPS]).

In the ancient ritual, blood was used for acts of purification. On Yom Kippur, the sprinkling of blood on the altar cleansed the area of ritual impurities. Blood was used in purifying the leper also, where the blood of a bird brought for sacrifice was sprinkled over the one who had been afflicted (Lev 14:4–6, 18–29, 49–53). Blood was used in the consecration of a priest (Lev 29:21). Blood kills, but it also saves. It saves Moses from the wrath of God when he becomes 'bridegroom of blood' on his return from Midian (Ex 4:24–26). It saves the Israelites from the plague of God when painted on the doorposts and lintels of their homes (Ex 12:7, 22–23).

There are three areas that impact on the practice of Judaism today where blood is key: *kashrut*, the laws pertaining to the eating of meat; *niddah*, the

90   *Sybil Sheridan*

rules associated with menstruation and childbirth; and *milah*, the ceremony of circumcision.

Regarding *kashrut,* we read in Leviticus 17:10–14:

> And if anyone of the house of Israel or of the strangers who reside among them partakes any kind of blood, I will set my face against the person who partakes of the blood, and I will cut him off from among his kin. For the life of the flesh is in the blood, and I have assigned it to you for making expiation for your lives upon the altar; it is the blood, as life, that effects expiation. Therefore I have said to the Israelite people: No person among you shall partake of blood, nor shall the stranger who resides among you partake of the blood. And any Israelite or any stranger who resides among them hunts down an animal or a bird that may be eaten, he shall pour out its blood, and cover it with earth. For the life of all flesh – its blood is its life. Therefore I say to the Israelite people: You shall not partake of the blood of any flesh; for the life of all flesh is its blood. Anyone who partakes of it shall be cut off.

This passage occurs just after the detailed description of the sacrificial ritual associated with Yom Kippur, the Day of Atonement. Together they describe two different situations where meat is eaten; the first is sacrificial meat, the second the more secular practice of hunting game for food. In both, blood is forbidden; the commandment extends to non-Israelites and the fact that the blood contains the life of the animal is emphasised. According to the Bible commentator Rabbi Simon ben Isaac (Rashi) life is identical to blood, while Moses Nachmanides (Ramban) suggests life and blood are mixed together like 'wine when diluted with water, in which case the water is in the wine and the wine is in the water and each one is "in" the other' (Commentary on Leviticus 17:11).

The universality of the command to avoid eating blood is matched by only one other commandment: that of murder. God commands Noah after the flood, 'You must not, however, eat flesh with its life-blood in it. But for your own life-blood I will require a reckoning: I will require it of every beast; of man, too, will I require a reckoning for human life, of every man for that of his fellow man! Whoever sheds the blood of man, by man shall his blood be shed; for in His image did God make man' (Gen 9:4–6).

Here again the association of blood with life is made. The two are closely linked. Killing animals for food is also murder. The initial world created in Genesis did not include the consumption of meat and it is only when Noah offers his sacrifice that the eating of animal flesh is mentioned for the first time. It has been interpreted as a concession to the violent nature of all creatures that prompted the flood in the first place. Meat is now permitted, but the blood must be offered to God as an act of atonement.

The blood of animals that are hunted for food is covered with earth. This is not a sacrifice, but either to render the blood unfit for consumption, or recognising blood as life requires its burial as you would bury a body in recognition that 'from dust the animals were created and to dust they return' (Gen 3:19). Punishment for failing to observe this is *karet* – the most serious punishment meted out by God, that the soul is cut off from among the people. The reason for the prohibition, according to mediaeval commentators, has to do with the practices of local idolaters, or that the ingestion of animal blood creates a more bestial nature within ourselves.

Samson Raphael Hirsch, the nineteenth-century German commentator, however, sees the prohibition as far more symbolic. 'The ever-present blood is the ever-present visible messenger in the body of the ever-present invisible directing soul. Hence it is the visible representative of the soul and hence is most suitable to be the symbolic expression in offerings of elevating and devoting the soul to God as well as of its faithful remaining with God' (Commentary on Leviticus 17:10–14). Thus it is the soul that is in the blood. The Hebrew word *nefesh* is used to mean both 'soul' and 'life' in the Genesis passage.

The laws of *kashrut*, of eating only what is 'fit' meat, have been scrupulously observed, defining how to slaughter an animal in such a way as to ensure the greatest possible blood loss. This is followed by rules for making it *kasher* – soaking, salting and soaking meat again to remove residual blood, while the liver, heart and lungs, which contain a greater density of blood, cannot be salted but must be grilled to remove it. It is a bitter irony, therefore, that the mediaeval blood libel may have found its source precisely in the scrupulous attention to detail regarding the removal of blood. In the Talmud passage *Keritot* 20b, after the Mishnah has listed many types of blood that are forbidden, the question is asked about 'those that walk on two legs,' which after discussion appears to be allowed. Human blood is permitted, so that if you cut your finger you can suck it clean. But quoted out of context this passage has sinister overtones totally at odds with the truth. Jews who eat kosher today are a long way from the notions of blood libel, blood as life, or blood as atonement. Buying meat in the butcher, where it has not only been slaughtered for you, but made *kasher* for you, means living at a distance from the process and one rarely sees any blood to speak of. But the fact that observant Jews will examine each and every egg they cook for the tiniest speck shows that the horror of consuming blood remains deep in the psyche.

When examining the subject of *niddah*, the key text is Leviticus 15:19–24: 'When a woman has a discharge, her discharge being blood from her body, she shall remain in her impurity seven days; and whoever touches her shall be unclean until evening. Anything that she lies on during her impurity shall be unclean; and anything that she sits on shall be unclean.'

92   *Sybil Sheridan*

The laws regarding ritual purity and impurity are probably among the hardest for us to understand today. Purity – *tohar* – and impurity – *tum'a* – are states that bear no moral judgement: the body is not at fault and the state of *tum'a* can be reversed through time and water. But the state is contagious and can defile sacred objects. Therefore, those that contract such impurity cannot enter the sanctuary, or engage in any form of sacrifice. The passage quoted is part of Leviticus chapter 15, which deals with the ritual purity and impurity that comes from our bodies, either naturally – semen emission, menstruation – or through illness, *tzara'at*, traditionally translated as leprosy. Further sources of impurity include contact with a corpse – human or animal – and fungal growth on houses and clothes. All forms of impurity, it seems, relate to death and procreation. *Tzara'at* points to the decomposition of our flesh, the fungal growth to inevitable disintegration of every human-made artefact. Genital discharges, related to procreation, demonstrate a loss of potential life.

We are dealing here with a woman's menstruation, that renders her *tame* – impure – for seven days. She must refrain from physical contact with others, and the place she sits and the bed upon which she lies contract a secondary form of impurity which can be transferred to others. For them, this lasts a day. The recipient must wash their clothes and themselves and are *tahor* – pure – from the evening onwards. That the woman is considered 'impure' at this time makes a certain sense in the context. But while the male who has a semen emission is required to separate himself till the evening, the woman must remain isolated for a full seven days, not just the days of her period. This suggests that blood has some sort of greater power of impurity that requires further care. In this context we should also refer to the laws surrounding childbirth. Leviticus 12 details how after the birth of a boy a mother must count seven days of *tum'a* and then a further thirty-three days, at which point she is able to go to the sanctuary and offer a sacrifice. However, if the child is a girl, her impurity lasts for fourteen days and she must wait a further sixty-six before coming to the sanctuary. Why the difference? Is it because a girl child contains blood that will issue forth in the years to come? The mother it would seem is keeping the laws of purity for the both of them.

The term for a menstruating woman in Hebrew is *niddah* – from the verb which means to put away, or exclude. It suggests a state of isolation and uncleanness and with it a repulsion and a whiff of harlotry and idolatry that is reflected in some of the biblical texts. Jerusalem is likened to a menstruating woman after her destruction – all keep away in Lamentations 1:9, 17. Idols are likened to a 'menstrual cloth' in Isaiah 30:22, and in Ezekiel 36:17 the sinful actions of Israel are like the uncleanness of a menstruating woman. This suggests that impurity is not all that morally neutral – and in Rabbinic literature it gets worse.

'Adam was the blood of the Holy One Blessed be He and Eve came and spilled it' (*Avot de Rabbi Natan* 8:9). The linguistic connection in the Hebrew between *Adam* – the man – and *dam* – blood – suggests a close relationship between the two which Eve, through her act of disobedience, interrupts in some way, and so, measure for measure, blood becomes part of her punishment. Menstruation becomes 'the curse' – the result of that disobedience. Since it involves the expulsion of unfertilized eggs, the loss of potential life each month is the equivalent of a death. We have here both bloodshed and blood loss; the monthly shedding of blood of a human being in addition to the blood of menstruation. The association of women's blood with death goes further in rabbinic literature. While the biblical punishment for disobeying God in Eden was *karet* – the expulsion of both parties from the Garden which would ultimately lead to the death of both, in the Mishnah the punishment falls exclusively on the woman, in that failure to obey the laws of *niddah* will result in death in childbirth (Mishnah, *Shabbat* 2:6).

Once the Temple was destroyed the *raison d'être* for the whole structure of purity and impurity lost its relevance. Over time, it all fell away, with the exception of a few instructions regarding priests and corpses. But while impurity regarding *tzara'at* and the impurity of men was no longer a requirement, that for women grew and multiplied and developed into a series of intricate laws that cover a whole tractate in the Mishnah and Talmud, and endless books and responsa since. The seven days of isolation were extended to the days of the period itself plus a further seven days. Fears of inadvertent contact just as the menses began led to an obsessive system of checking and rechecking. Intercourse became forbidden from the time menstruation was expected even if no blood was detected. This meant that in a cycle of twenty-eight days in at least twelve of them the husband and wife would be separated. At the end of this period of separation, after seven clean days the woman must go to the *mikvah* – a pool of natural water – and immerse herself, otherwise her state of impurity continues (Babylonian Talmud, *Shabbat* 64b).

Why should this be? The original injunctions were really for the men. They could not sleep with their wives for fear of rendering themselves unclean. Once the Temple was destroyed the practice had lost its point. Why continue the system, when the rest of the impurity laws were more or less put into abeyance? For many writers today, the continuation of the laws of *niddah* demonstrates a deep misogyny within the rabbinic texts. So much of rabbinic literature is written about women, but without their consultation, or involvement. They remain outsiders – only referred to when their lives impinge on the men. For this school of thought, the persistence of the laws of *niddah* is a way of men controlling women, of punishing them for their wayward, free-flowing, bloody bodies.

94   *Sybil Sheridan*

But there is another way of looking at this. The continuation of what became known as *taharat ha-mishpachah* – family purity – actually helped women. It gave them an autonomy over their own bodies that was not the norm in the early Middle Ages, where women belonged to their husbands, and had no say in when, or how, or how often they would be required for sex. The Jewish practice gave women space, and it gave them control. I do not think it fanciful to suggest that it was the women who were responsible for continuing the practice after the Temple's destruction, and that the Rabbis *ex post facto* legislated for it (Sheridan 2000, 26).

Finally, we turn to *milah* and Genesis 17:11–14: 'And you shall circumcise the flesh of your foreskin; and it shall be a sign of the covenant between me and you. And he who is eight days old shall be circumcised among you, every male child in your generations, he who is born in the house, or bought with money from any stranger, who is not of your seed.'

This is the covenant of Abraham. God promised numerous descendants and, in return, those descendants would be circumcised on the eighth day after birth, a *mitzvah* (commandment) observed to this day by religious Jew and secular Jew alike. Once 'an indispensable act of national consecration and purification' (Kohler 1916, 92), it has become a badge of identity and an act of defiance over the centuries, when circumcision was forbidden, or when the sign of it could condemn you to death. Baruch Spinoza was probably quite right when he said, 'The practice of circumcision alone is sufficient to ensure the survival of Jewish people' (Tractatus Theologico-Politicus 1679).

It seems on the face of it a fertility symbol. God promises Abram children, and marks the sign of that promise on the object of procreation. 'And when Abram was ninety-nine years old, the Lord appeared to Abram, and said to him I am the Almighty God; walk before me, and be perfect' (Gen 17:1). God made Abram perfect through circumcision. Each male, it implies, is born physically defective and this act rights the wrong. It is God and humanity working in partnership. God creates the child, but he is not 'finished' till, in common parlance, he has his *brit.*

But where is the blood? The removal of the foreskin will evoke blood loss, but this passage does not seem to be interested in that aspect. We must turn to Moses and Zipporah returning to Egypt to free the Israelites (Ex 4:26), where God comes to kill Moses. He is saved by Zipporah circumcising his youngest son. She flings the foreskin at Moses' feet saying: 'Surely a bridegroom of blood are you to me.' A bridegroom of blood because of the circumcision. Blood is the point. *Milah* in this case is not to do with fertility. The circumcision of their son saves Moses' life – but specifically it is the blood of the circumcision that does so. For the Rabbis, this harked back to an age of child-sacrifice. God had every right to take the child for his own, but would be appeased with a part instead of the whole – the foreskin rather than the infant.

The salvific role of blood is read back into the story of Abraham in mediaeval midrash: 'On Yom Kippur, Abraham was circumcised. Every year [on the Day of Atonement] God looks at the blood of Abraham our forefather's circumcision which atones for our sins' (*Pirkei de Rabbi Eliezer* 29:2).

Jacob's sons circumcised themselves and then they circumcised their children. They passed the custom down as an eternally binding precept until Pharaoh ordained stringent measures, forbidding the covenant of circumcision. But the day they left Egypt, all of them, from the old to the young, were circumcised, as it says, 'All the people who left Egypt were circumcised' (Josh 5:5). They took the blood of their circumcision and the blood of the paschal lamb and put it on the doorposts of their homes. When God passed by to smite the Egyptians, He saw the circumcision blood and the paschal lamb's blood and was filled with compassion for Israel as it is said, 'By your blood live, By your blood live' (*Pirkei de Rabbi Eliezer* 29:11).

The last quotation, from Ezekiel 16:6, is quoted many times in this context: 'I passed by you and saw you wallowing in your blood and I said to you: in your blood live; I said to you: in your blood live.'

Two bloods. The Rabbis of the Mishnah added to the ceremony of circumcision. After removing the foreskin, the mucous membrane is split and rolled down to expose the head of the penis. More blood. So added to the blood of *mila* is the blood of *peria*. While it is not required in the biblical injunction, it is the blood that flows as a result of the operation that becomes the key element rather than the foreskin. Thus a child born circumcised, or a circumcised adult who wishes to convert, must undergo *hatafat dam brit* – the shedding of the blood of circumcision – for, it is said, there is no circumcision without blood.

'Were it not for the blood of the covenant, heaven and earth would not exist' (Babylonian Talmud, *Shabbat* 137b).

Once the operation is completed, the child, like Abraham, is named. A prayer dating back to mediaeval times says:

Our God and God of our fathers, preserve this child to his father and to his mother and let his name be called in Israel ___ son of ___. Let the father rejoice in him that came forth from his loins and let the mother be glad with the fruit of the womb; as it is written, 'Let your father and your mother rejoice and let her that bore you be glad' (Prov 23:25). And it is said: 'I passed by you and saw you wallowing in your blood and I said to you: in your blood live; I said to you: in your blood live' (Ezek 16:6).

96 *Sybil Sheridan*

But the Ezekiel passage in its context refers to Jerusalem, and the blood that is being wallowed in is menstrual blood, not that of circumcision. Several scholars today, such as Daniel Boyarin and Lawrence Hoffman, posit the theory that the ceremony of circumcision has become a second 'birthing' ritual for boys – birth into the covenant of men:

> The creation of the collective tribal brotherhood based on circumcision ensures the continuity of the patriarchal lineage and acculturates the baby boy into maleness while publicly diminishing the female birthing role; some see it as a ritual of male empowerment that bonds men in a phallic way . . . not only in procreative activity but also as the source of cultural and intellectual creativity. (Hoffman 1996)

Childbirth is merely 'birth into a state of nature' while circumcision sees man's birth into his cultural state. Women's blood is free-flowing and uncontrolled. Men's blood is deliberate. Women represent nature – wild and intuitive. Men represent culture – considered and educated. Circumcision sanctifies the human body, while menstruation exposes its weakness. Circumcision saves, menstruation pollutes. One can go further – if circumcision demonstrates how Abraham walked and became perfect, ensuring the eternal continuation of his line, menstruation is a permanent reminder of the disobedience of Eve who brought death into the world.

The construction presented here makes it impossible for any religious meeting-point between the sexes. Circumcision excludes women. Does that mean they are not, and never were, part of the covenant? Kabbalistic Judaism suggests they join it at marriage, when they 'receive' the circumcision from their husbands. But that only makes it worse. It suggests a girl has no part in the *brit* in her own right, and if she does not marry is condemned to remain forever outside that special relationship with the Divine.

Modern Jewish life cycle rituals attempt to reconcile the sexes. But they do so at the expense of the centrality of blood. Eighth-Day covenant rituals have been developed over the last two decades, for girls, principally, but also for some boys where parents have made the decision not to circumcise. Immersion in the *mikvah* has experienced something of a revival, not just for *taharat ha-mishpachah*, but for new rituals of healing.

'Many are using mikvah to purify themselves,' writes Rachel Adler, 'of events that threatened their lives, or left them feeling wounded, or bereft or sullied as sexual beings: ovarian tumours, hysterectomies, mastectomies, miscarriages, incest, rape' (Adler 1997, 204). The focus is on the healing waters, not the blood.

Adler eschews the cult of perfection presented by the traditional view of circumcision, and presents instead a revision of a theology of purity:

If purity is the mirroring of God's oneness in human wholeness, it is not less fragile and transitory than humankind itself. Our flesh is gnawed by disease, eroded by age . . . we keep breaking or being breached. We keep knitting our-selves together, restoring ourselves, so we can once again reflect God's completeness. . . . Human is not whole. Human is full of holes. Human bleeds. Human births its worlds in agonies or blood and bellyaches. . . . Beneath even the woman hating words of Ezekiel I hear You breathing 'in your blood live'. (Adler 1997, 206)

While life in modern times has conspired to distance us from the reality of blood as actually present in the food that we eat and in the ceremonies we enact, nevertheless it retains its power as a residual presence in the rituals, both old and new, that we observe today.

BIBLIOGRAPHY

Adler R. 1997. '"In Your Blood Live": Re-Visions of a Theology of Purity', *Life Cycles* vol. 2, ed. D. Ornstein & J. R. Litman, 197–206. Woodstock.

Hoffman L. 1996. *Covenant of Blood: Circumcision and Gender in Rabbinic Judaism.* Chicago: University of Chicago Press.

Kohler K. 1916. 'Circumcision', *The Jewish Encyclopedia,* ed. Isidore Singer, 92–96. New York & London.

Sheridan S. 2000. 'Discovering Hannah: Women's Rituals in Second Century Palestine', *Taking up the Timbrel,* ed. Sylvia Rothschild & Sybil Sheridan, 24–30. London: SCM Press.

SUGGESTED FURTHER READING

Baskin J. R. 2002. *Midrashic Women: Formations of the Feminine in Rabbinic Literature.* Hanover and London: Brandeis University Press.

Milgrom J. 1963. 'The Biblical Diet Laws as an Ethical System', *Interpretation 17*(3), 288–301.

Milgrom J. 1997. 'The Blood Taboo', *Bible Review 13*(4), 21, 46.

Chapter 10

Judaism and Homosexuality

René Pfertzel

The question of sexuality and gender concerns human beings, how they identify themselves, how they see their place in the larger world, and how they are welcomed – or not – by society. Some people feel a romantic and sexual attraction towards people of the same gender, which in most cases puts them at odds with the larger narrative of the society in which they live. Homosexuality has always existed, but, at least in Western civilizations strongly influenced by the Bible, it has been rejected, and homosexuals have been subjected to discrimination or more. Indeed, homosexuality is a challenge for a society. The working assumption of this exploration of homosexuality within Judaism is that people do not have the choice to be gay, lesbian, bisexual, or heterosexual. The word homosexuality is understood here in its etymological definition as an attraction between people of the same gender, namely, gay men and lesbian women.

In order to understand the dynamics between Judaism and homosexuality, a survey of the sources is necessary. The Torah contains two verses that have often created despair among Jewish homosexuals. The rabbinic literature has expanded on this question and largely reinforced the prohibition against male homosexuality (the sources are mostly silent about lesbianism). Modern Judaism has a plurivocal attitude to traditional sources: the responses of contemporary Jewish movements vary greatly, and a survey of the different attitudes towards homosexuality will be necessary. This study would not be complete without an attempt to understand the reasons behind the prohibition of homosexuality. Why has male and female homosexuality been forbidden, and what are the arguments that enable acceptance of gays and lesbians in the Jewish community?

The Book of Leviticus sits at the centre of what Jewish tradition calls Written Torah, the first five books of the Bible. At the centre of Leviticus,

100 René Pfertzel

Biblical scholarship has identified the 'Holiness Code', named so after the repeated use of the word 'holy' (chapters 17 to 26). In its middle, chapters 18 to 20 stray away from purely sacrificial regulations to address moral issues. Chapter 18 verse 3 sets the tone: 'You must not act as they do in Egypt, where you used to live, and you must not act as they do in the land of Canaan, where I am bringing you. Do not follow their practices.' The Children of Israel are in a liminal space, between two lands and two cultures, and they need to find their own voice. Chapter 18 lists a series of prohibited relationships, known as the *arayot* (literally 'nakedness' it describes a list of forbidden sexual relationships), sins so serious that it is permitted to sacrifice one's life rather than commit them (Steinsaltz 2014: 285). Leviticus 18:22 says, 'Do not lie with a man as one does with a woman (*mishkevei ishah*). It is an abomination (*to'evah*).' Leviticus 20:13 repeats this prohibition and specifies the punishment: 'it is an abomination they both did; they are to be put to death, their blood is upon their heads'. The Hebrew expression *mishkevei ishah*, the 'lyings of a woman', has called for many commentaries: why the plural form? What does it really mean? The Spanish commentator Abraham Ibn Ezra (d. 1164 or 1167) explains that the plural form indicates two types of intercourse, anal and vaginal, both prohibited with a man because, said Ibn Ezra, 'since the male was created to make (i.e. to penetrate) and the woman to be made (i.e. to be penetrated), Scriptures notes than one should not reverse the words of God.' Another Spanish commentator, Moses ben Nachman, (Nachmanides, d. 1270), uses the same argument and adds: 'The reason for this prohibition is well known, as it is an abominable act for the preservation of the human species because it . . . will not beget offspring'. Commenting on Leviticus 20:13, Ibn Ezra says that if both partners had a consensual relationship they are both liable to death, whereas if one raped the other only the perpetrator is to be punished by death. Rabbeinu Chananel, a Tunisian scholar of the eleventh century, explains that some men may deceive others by attracting them into such behaviour. Babylonian Talmud, *Keritot* 5a explains that the punishment is death by stoning. Interestingly, the vision of sexuality in these sources is functional, to beget offspring, and hierarchical, male penetrative sex. There is no allusion to romantic involvement. The sexual act is about power and prohibited between men, but as Rabbi Steven Greenberg suggests, sexual desire is acknowledged and accepted:

> First, there are a variety of ways that men can pleasure each other sexually. If the prohibition is defined by anal penetration, then a whole array of sexual engagements between two men . . . would not be formally prohibited. [. . .] Third, homosexuality, that is, same–sex emotional and physical desire, is not prohibited in Scripture. Actions are prohibited, not psychological states or

Judaism and Homosexuality 101

sexual desires. Fourth, there is an enormous omission in the text: the Torah does not prohibit lesbian relationships.' (Greenberg 2004: 85)

So far, we have analysed Biblical texts that belong to the category of *halakhah*, Jewish law. *Halakhah* is not concerned with emotions or sentiments, and its focus is to define the law, the norms that a society must follow to obey the *Metzaveh,* the 'God Who Commands'. Biblical literature knows another literary genre, *aggadah*, that tells stories, and that narrates the life of biblical characters. There is a tension between these two genres. *Halakhah* is not detached from the life of people: a law responds to real circumstances. *Aggadah* is the framework of *halakhah.* Conversely, stories interpret the law, and sometimes break away from the letter of the law.

Immediately after they announced the birth of Isaac to Abraham and Sarah, three divine messengers 'gazed down upon Sodom' (Gen 18:16). God says to Abraham, 'the outcry of Sodom and Gomorrah, how great it is! And their crime, how grave it is!' (Gen 18:20). For their crime they must be punished, and their cities destroyed. Abraham tries to appease the divine anger and argues with God: 'Will you sweep away the innocent with the wicked? . . . Must not the Judge of all the earth do justly?' (Gen 18:23, 25). Abraham tries to bargain, but they were so wicked that no innocent person was to be found, apart from Lot and his family who happened to be there. Both cities are destroyed. What was their crime? The Bible tells us that when the three emissaries went to Lot's home in Sodom, a mob gathered around the house and asked, 'Where are the men who came to you tonight? Bring them out so we can have them' (Gen 19:5). For the traditional commentators, they wanted to have sex with these three men, and from this line of interpretation emerged the notion of *sodomy*, anal sex. Their motive was domination by penetrative sex, rape, and certainly not a romantic relationship. Lot's response was shocking. He offered them his virgin daughters instead, to protect his guests. Nachmanides commented that this shows 'an evil heart', because Lot was ready to abandon his daughters to prostitution. Both attitudes are repugnant, but only sex between men has passed to posterity. The Rabbis in the Talmud and the Midrash explained that the crimes of Sodom and Gomorrah were much more serious. They lived in the Jordan valley, a land of plenty, 'well–watered everywhere' (Gen 13:10), and their wealth made them selfish. Rabbi Nathaniel commented that the people of Sodom refused to give food to the stranger or traveller; they even constructed fences above their gardens so that no bird flying by could eat from their trees. Rabbi Yehudah said, 'The leaders of Sodom made a proclamation in which they declared, anyone who gives even a loaf of bread to the poor or the needy shall be put to death by fire' (*Pirkei deRabbi Eliezer*, 25). They wanted to keep everything for themselves and were also stealing from any person who happened to pass by. The greatest

102   *René Pfertzel*

evil of Sodom and Gomorrah was that cruelty became the social norm. It was a place of lawlessness.

Later, in the time of the Judges, in the land of Judah, a widow named Naomi has just lost both her sons and her husband. She advises her daughters-in-law Orpah and Ruth to return to their mothers' homes to find security and the prospect of a new husband. They cry, kiss farewell, but Ruth does not want to leave Naomi. 'Do not push me to leave you and to turn back. For wherever you go, I will go; wherever you dwell, I will dwell. Your people shall be my people, and your God my God' (Ruth 1:16). Ruth is considered by the Jewish tradition as the first convert. When they return to Bethlehem, Ruth marries Boaz, and their child, Obed, 'was the father of Jesse, father of David' (Ruth 4:17).

On the face of it, nothing indicates any romantic relationship between Ruth and Naomi. However, there are some 'who advocate a queer reading of the text. Such a reading inevitably focuses on the relationship between Ruth and Naomi . . . the two women are regarded as having formed a bond that transcended age, nationality, and religious tradition. The oath of loyalty uttered by Ruth to her mother-in-law is regarded as a declaration of deep and abiding love and friendship' (Davis 2016: 526). Both were married, and Ruth will later marry another man, and give birth to a lineage that includes King David, and even Jesus Christ according to the opening chapter of the Gospel of Matthew. However, their bond was unique, and transcended the traditional role ascribed to women. In a society where women could only be mothers and wives, the Book of Ruth told a different story. Women were constrained by the overarching patriarchal narrative. Their sexuality was purely reproductive, and very little is said about their emotional life. And yet, this book, which is read during the festival of Shavuot, the celebration of the gift of Torah, addresses the possibility of different relationships for women.

The biblical text, whether in its purely legalistic aspects or in its story-telling nature, is male-centred. The sexual act is purely seen as a means to ensure the reproduction of a generation, and between men it is an abomination, because anal sex is perceived as the subjugation of the receiving partner to the giving actor. The relationship between Ruth and Naomi opens the possibility of same-sex attraction, but it is buried under the heterosexual context of these two women as wives.

However, another biblical story is more explicit. The young shepherd David has just defeated the Philistine giant Goliath. He is taken to King Saul, who asks his name: 'Who are you?' David responds, 'I am the son of Jesse the Bethlehemite' (1 Sam 18). Jonathan, Saul's son, witnesses the scene. The text says: 'When David finished speaking with Saul, Jonathan's soul became bound up with the soul of David. Jonathan loved David as himself. Saul took David into his service, that day, and would not let him return to his father's house. Jonathan and David made a pact because Jonathan loved him as himself' (1 Sam 18: 1–3). As David's star rises, his relationship with Saul sours, and Jonathan helps him to escape his father's clutches. But David and Jonathan are in competition for the throne of Israel, and the latter dies in a battle that opposes Saul's supporters to David's. When Jonathan falls, David expresses his grief with these poignant words, 'I grieve for you, my brother Jonathan. You were most dear to me. Your love was wonderful to me, more than the love of women' (2 Sam 1: 25–26). Much has been written about them. What was the nature of their love? Were they lovers in a physical and romantic way? For Jonathan, it was clearly love at first sight, but did David respond to his love? As in the story of Ruth and Naomi, the Bible gives a hint that a strong bond can exist between people of the same sex. These homosocial relationships that are based on equality and emotional connection resemble the experience of many gays and lesbians today. The prohibition in Leviticus does not exclude sexual intercourse *per se*, but it strongly condemns penetrative sex between men, perceived as an act of violence and domination.

Unsurprisingly, the rabbis in the Talmud and Midrash upheld the prohibition of anal sex. David Brodsky quotes a debate in the Talmud about how many forms of penetrative sex are forbidden according to Torah. Its conclusion is clear: 'Women and female animals each have two orifices the penetration of which constitutes sex. This leaves the vagina and the anus as the obvious two orifices. Since men do not have vaginas, it means men having only one forbidden orifice, and thus the sole prohibition of anal penetration' (Brodsky 2009: 161). The purpose of this Talmudic *sugya* (literary unit) is to make explicit the prohibition of anal sex in Leviticus 18 and 20 by defining two forms of penetrative sex: *kedarko*, literally 'the normal way', and *she–lo kedarko*, literally 'not the normal way', that is, anal sex. The second category is forbidden, whereas the first, that can apply only to women, is permitted. There is no judgment, no emotion, just the blunt legal language of the Talmud.

Another source in the same tractate explains that it is worse for a male than for a female to be raped (Babylonian Talmud, *Sanhedrin* 73a). The medieval French commentator Rashi explains that the rape of a man will bring disgrace and embarrassment upon him. Once again, sexuality is understood here as a means to exert power over another human being. Rape is condemned on multiple occasions in Talmudic literature, and in that passage, a man will suffer an additional opprobrium.

The Rabbinic world was male-centred and hierarchical. The rabbis created legal categories having different rights and duties towards the law: men, women, minors, and slaves. Depending on their position in the social order, individuals had certain rights and obligations, more or less freedom of choice. Men were in a dominant position, which was translated in sexual terms by the

104 René Pfertzel

fact that men penetrate, and women are penetrated. If a man is penetrated, he breaks the order of things. The perpetuation of this prejudice was probably due to proximity with Roman culture, which was the environment for much of the first centuries of Rabbinic Judaism. A freeborn Roman man could have sex with a woman or another man as long as he was in the penetrative position (Richlin 1992: 25). In the Roman patriarchal society, being penetrated meant to be in an inferior position. And the Midrash tells us, 'Master of all universes, is it not enough for us that we are subjugated by the seventy nations? Must we also be subjugated by this one [Rome] who is penetrated like women?' (*Bereshit Rabbah* 63:10). There was a clear desire to set themselves apart from the pagan Roman majority, as an echo to the injunction, 'You must not act as they do in Egypt, where you used to live, and you must not act as they do in the land of Canaan, where I am bringing you. Do not follow their practices' (Lev 18:3). And yet, there is a discrepancy between the idealised world of Torah as dreamed by the Rabbis and the reality of their daily lives. In Mishnah, *Avodah Zarah* 4:3, we read the story of a conversation between a Gentile, Proklos ben Flosfos, a Greek philosopher, and Rabban Gamliel, who can be identified either with the grandson of Hillel the Elder in the first century, or Rabban Gamliel II, the grandson of the former. In either case, Rabban Gamliel was a leading figure of the first–second-century Jewish community in the land of Israel. Rabbi and philosopher are both in a bathhouse in Akko, near modern-day Haifa, and are debating the presence of the statue of the Greek goddess Aphrodite. Does being in the same place as a statue constitute idolatry? asks Proklos. Rabban Gamliel responds that if the statue is considered as a work of art, it is not idolatry, because it is not worshipped. The text does not comment on the environment. And yet, they are both in a bathhouse, a place where people are naked, the epitome of Greco-Roman culture, and Rabban Gamliel does not seem to be anxious about this. The only caveat is, according to the Sage, that we do not talk about Torah matters in the bath itself, and they carry on their conversation outside. Two men can be together, probably naked, or lightly-dressed, in a place that may also lead to some promiscuity, without any issue. There is a risk to reading the old texts of religious traditions with modern eyes, and to seeing in them confirmation – or invalidation – of current values or prejudices. Context and intention, however difficult they may be to fathom, are paramount to keeping the relevance of these old texts for today.

To summarize what the Jewish tradition says about this issue: its textual sources, whether Biblical or Rabbinic, were written in a patriarchal and hierarchical world, where women have less space than men. In these texts, sexuality is considered in terms of penetration, giver and receiver, for the sake of reproduction. Amorous relationships are alluded to in narratives, and their prohibition is less palpable. It is impossible to legislate on emotions, therefore the legal parts deal only with the practicalities of sexual intercourse.

The Enlightenment and the advent of Modernity in eighteenth- and nineteenth-century Western Europe and North America profoundly transformed the lives and the perspectives of the Jews who lived in those lands. The values upheld by modern societies have helped Jews to reassess their place in the wider society, and to articulate their responses to new challenges. In the wake of the gay liberation movement that emerged in the late 1960s and early 1970s, alongside feminist movements, Western society had to respond to the claim and the need for more equality. To a large extent, all the movements described below are a response to Modernity. As far as homosexuality is concerned, Jewish movements have provided a wide range of answers, from a total rejection, an odd response like 'we love the sinners but hate the sin', to a certain acceptance, as long as homosexuals refrain from homoerotic practices, and lastly, total acceptance.

Orthodox Judaism posits a strict and traditional adherence to Jewish law, seen as revealed by God to Moses, and therefore untouchable and sacrosanct. Orthodox Jewish movements and synagogues do not condone homosexuality as a valid way of life. Rabbi Chaim Rapoport, an Orthodox British rabbi, published in 2004 the '*authentic Orthodox view*'. His aim was to allow 'those of homosexual orientation to be able to reach a *modus vivendi* with themselves, their parents, their communities, and, above all, their Father in Heaven' (Rapoport 2004: 134). Rabbi Rapoport explains that 'Jewish Law clearly proscribes homosexual activity for both males and females'. However, homosexuals should not be rejected because of their sexual orientation, because, he says, they have no choice in the matter. 'Homosexuals are essentially no different to any other Jew' (Rapoport 2004: 135), and they can take part in any aspect of community life. However, they should refrain from engaging in homosexual activities, and study Torah and observe the *mitzvot* (commandments) to control their disposition. Sadly, in other circles, homosexuality is still described as a reversible condition (Moss & Kern Ulmer 2008: 87). Rabbi Rapoport's book demonstrates an Orthodox trend for a more compassionate approach to homosexuals, but in other circles the rejection is stronger, and gays and lesbians can either stay in the closet or leave their communities. In Haredi communities the homosexual narrative is simply nonexistent. Rabbi Steven Greenberg is the first Orthodox rabbi to come out of the closet. In the first chapters of his book *Trembling Before God* he explains the pain suffered by a young man who feels attracted by other men, the tension between the values of his milieu and his inner world. He described his journey in a film released in 2001, *Trembling Before G–d*. Many lesbian and gay Orthodox Jews have started to challenge the accepted Orthodox norm. In May 2017, Rabbi Joseph Dweck, the Senior Rabbi of the Sephardi Community in London, gave a lecture in which he said that Jewish law does not legislate against the feelings involved in a same-sex relationship. A lengthy controversy arose among Orthodox rabbis, and Rabbi Dweck agreed to step down as a Dayan (Judge) of the Sephardi community. However, he retained his position as Senior Rabbi of the community. These few examples show that the boundaries are slowly shifting in the Orthodox world towards a more compassionate approach to this issue.

The two main non-Orthodox movements in Europe, North America and Israel are the Conservative/Masorti and the Progressive/Liberal/Reform. It is beyond the scope of this article to highlight their differences, but these movements have responded in their time to some overarching issues: discrimination against homosexuals, acceptance of homosexuals in community life and in community leadership, and same-sex commitment ceremonies. The first step was to proclaim that discriminations against gays and lesbians had no place in these movements any more, which was achieved by the early 1980s. Once this statement of principles was agreed, LGBT students were accepted in rabbinic programmes. The last step was dependent on the evolution of the law in the various countries about legalizing same-sex marriage.

Reconstructionist Judaism, a small but very influential movement in North America (about 4% of affiliated Jews), was the first to open its rabbinical school to lesbian and gay students in 1984, and to endorse same-sex ceremonies in 1993. It was quickly followed by the Reform movement in North America (about 40% of affiliated Jews), which invited lesbian and gay students to apply to its rabbinical schools in 1990 and allowed its rabbis to perform same-sex blessings in 2000. The Conservative movement in North America wrestled longer – and is still wrestling – with this question. In January 2007, the Committee on Jewish Law and Standards (CJLS) adopted five resolutions on this issue, two taking a conservative stand, considering that Jewish law cannot be changed on this matter, two adopting a more liberal approach, recognising that science on sexual orientation has shown that being gay or lesbian is not a choice, and one proposing a middle way, accepting homosexuality, but upholding the biblical prohibition of anal sex for male homosexuals. Conservative rabbis and rabbinical schools make their own decisions based on these resolutions. As a result, the Jewish Theological Seminary in New York opened its doors to LGBT students in 2007, but the Conservative seminary in South America did not.

In Europe, Leo Baeck College in London accepted its first lesbian students in 1984. Rabbi Elli Tikvah Sarah and Rabbi Sheila Shulman were ordained five years later, paving the way for acceptance of LGBT rabbis in the United Kingdom and in Europe. The other progressive European rabbinical schools (Berlin, Amsterdam and Paris) have an open policy for LGBT applicants. As of 2021, 20% of the British Progressive rabbinate are Rainbow rabbis. On the continent, LGBT rabbis are serving communities in many countries. To a large extent, the inclusion of Rainbow rabbis has had a similar impact on the rabbinic world to the advent of female rabbis. The Progressive religious leadership echoes the evolution of society in terms of equality and inclusion. It has offered estranged Jews a safe space to live their Judaism.

Same-sex weddings became a possibility when the law started to change in some countries. Once the law was passed, the movements had to decide whether they would allow rabbis to perform such ceremonies or not. In 2004 in the United Kingdom, the *Civil Partnership Act* created civil partnership for people of the same sex. Liberal Judaism UK, which had campaigned in favour of it, created a specific liturgy and enabled its rabbis to perform same-sex civil partnerships if they wished to. Rabbis were allowed to perform same-sex marriages when the law was adopted in 2014. In France, same-sex marriage has been legal since 2013. The French Progressive Rabbinical Assembly, KEREM, left it to the conscience of individual rabbis and communities whether to perform same-sex ceremonies. Rabbi Pauline Bebe in Paris was the first to introduce a *Brit Ahavah* (Covenant of Love) liturgy, echoing Rabbi Rachel Adler's ground-breaking work in her book *Engendering Judaism* (1998), particularly chapter 5, where she drafted a new liturgy for same-sex couples, *Brit Ahuvim* (Covenant of Lovers). The situation is far from being the same in all countries, and in some it is still illegal to marry people of the same sex. Over seventy countries in the world have legislation that criminalizes homosexuality, and recently in Poland, Hungary and Russia laws were passed to 'counter the gay agenda'.

The biblical and rabbinic prohibition of homosexuality reflects a worldview where sexuality is first and foremost a means to ensure the reproduction of the generations. This prohibition also reflects patriarchy. The laws and social norms are defined by men, and when two men engage in sexual intercourse they are disrupting this order. When a man is penetrated by another, he relinquishes his position of power. Sodomy is akin to male violence and rape. Emotions, sentiments and love seem to be absent from the conversation, and Jewish sources are rather silent when it comes to an amorous relationship. Scarcity of sources regarding lesbianism makes perfect sense in a patriarchal society. To a large extent, female sexuality is reduced to procreation. As long as women are wives and mothers, the legislator does not take much interest in the rest of their lives.

The fundamental question is essentially how modern religious people relate to ancient texts, born in a very different *Zeitgeist.* Should one follow the letter of these texts, or is there scope for an evolving interpretation? Already in the Talmud the rabbis questioned some of the written Torah texts to render them more acceptable. According to a saying attributed to Rabbi Mordecai Kaplan (d. 1983), cofounder of Reconstructionist Judaism, 'The tradition has a vote,

108 *René Pfertzel*

not a veto'. Science has shown us that gender identification is not a matter of choice, or, more accurately, the only choice is to accept who we are. Nobody decides to become gay, lesbian, transgender, and so on, but how one decides to respond to these inner challenges is a choice. Humankind is diverse, and diversity is part of God's plan. Binary modes of thinking were useful to distinguish truth and untruth, good and evil, and even to a large extent male and female. However, there is more, and the new challenges ahead of us in this first part of the twenty-first century are to understand the difference between sex and gender, how different people identify their gender, the role that societies play in defining roles and places, and the necessity of accepting the variety of human expression of the self, and to create an inclusive society where all have a safe space.

BIBLIOGRAPHY

Adler R. 1998. *Engendering Judaism. An Inclusive Theology and Ethics*. Philadelphia, Jerusalem: Jewish Publication Society.

Bethmont R. & M. Gross, eds. 2017. *Homosexualité et traditions monothéistes: vers la fin d'un antagonisme?* Geneva: Labor et Fides.

Brodsky D. 2009. 'Sex in the Talmud: How to Understand Leviticus 18 and 20: Parashat Kedoshim (Leviticus 19:1–20:27)', in *Torah Queeries. Weekly Commentary on the Hebrew Bible,* G. Drinkwater, J. Lesser & D. Shneer, 157–69. New York: New York University Press.

Davis E. W. 2016. 'Political and Advocacy Approaches', in *The Hebrew Bible. A Critical Companion,* ed. J. Barton, 507–31. Princeton: Princeton University Press.

Dorff E. N., D. Novak & A. L. Mackler. 2008. 'Homosexuality: A Case Study in Jewish Ethics', *Journal of the Society of Christian Ethics*, 28/1 (Spring/Summer 2008), 225–35.

Drinkwater G., J. Lesser & D. Shneer. 2009. *Torah Queeries. Weekly Commentary on the Hebrew Bible.* New York: New York University Press.

Greenberg S. 2004. *Wrestling with Men and God. Homosexuality in the Jewish Tradition*. Madison: University of Wisconsin Press.

Magonet J., ed. 1995. *Jewish Explorations of Sexuality.* Oxford: Berghahn Books.

Moss J. A. & R. B. Kern Ulmer. 2008. '"Two Men Under One Cloak" – The Sages Permit It: Homosexual Marriage in Judaism', *Journal of Homosexuality*, 55/1, 71–105.

Rapoport C. 2004. *Judaism and Homosexuality: An Authentic Orthodox View.* London: Vallentine Mitchell.

Richlin A. 1992. *The Garden of Priapus: Sexuality and Aggression in Roman Humor*. New York & Oxford: Oxford University Press.

Steinsaltz, A. E.-I. 2014. *Reference Guide to the Talmud.* Jerusalem: The Toby Press.

Chapter 11

Orthodoxy and Homosexuality
Mapping the Vectors

Misza Czerniak

In the ecumenical movement, and even in interfaith dialogue, it is common knowledge that the Orthodox church is one of the most conservative religious bodies, focused on preserving the ways of the past and hardly prone to adopt any emerging trends or discourses. That presumption is strong not only outside the Orthodox church but also within it. The sacred role of tradition, crucial for the Orthodox belief system, has been used as grounds for legitimising a rather reductivist perception of history and progress, according to which the golden age of Orthodoxy is history, and all challenges of modernity are nothing more than temptations.

Within such a framework, the stance of the Orthodox church towards the issue of homosexuality and homosexual persons seems to be clear: as the Basis of the Social Concept of the Russian Orthodox Church claims, 'Holy Scriptures and the teaching of the Church unequivocally deplore homosexual relations, seeing in them a vicious distortion of the God-created human nature' (The Basis of the Social Concept of the Russian Orthodox Church 2000: XII.9). In fact, the document, adopted by the Moscow Patriarchate in 2000, presents such a clear and concise picture from that corner of the debate that we will have to include the whole section:

'If a man lie with mankind, as he lieth with a woman, both of them have committed an abomination' (Lev 20:13). The Bibles relates a story about a heavy punishment to which God subjected the people of Sodom (Gen 19:1–19) precisely for the sin of sodomy. St Paul, describing the moral condition of the Gentiles, names homosexual relations among the most 'vile affections' and 'fornications' defiling the human body: 'Their women did change the natural use into that which is against nature: and likewise the men, leaving the natural use of women, burned in their lust one towards another; men with men working that which is unseemly, and receiving in themselves that recompense of their error which was meet' (Rom 1:26–27). 'Be not deceived: neither effeminate, nor abusers of themselves with mankind . . . shall inherit the kingdom of God,' wrote the apostle to the people of corrupted Corinth (1 Cor 6:9–10).

The patristic tradition equally clearly and definitely denounces any manifestation of homosexuality. *The Teaching of the Twelve Apostles*, the works of Saints Basil the Great, John Chrysostom, Gregory of Nyssa and Blessed Augustine and the canon of St John the Faster all express the unchangeable teaching of the Church that homosexual relations are sinful and should be condemned. People involved in them have no right to be members of the clergy (Gregory the Great, Canon 7; Gregory of Nyssa, Canon 4; John the Faster, Canon 30). Addressing those who stained themselves with the sin of sodomy, St Maxim the Greek made this appeal: 'See for yourselves, damned ones, what a foul pleasure you indulge in! Try to give up as soon as possible this most nasty and stinking pleasure of yours, to hate it and to fulminate eternally those who argue that it is innocent as enemies of the Gospel of Jesus Christ and corrupters of His teaching. Cleanse yourselves of this blight by repentance, ardent tears, alms-giving as much as you can and pure prayer. . . . Hate this unrighteousness with all your heart, so that you may not be sons of damnation and eternal death.'

The debate on the status of the so-called sexual minorities in contemporary society tends to recognise homosexuality not as a sexual perversion but only one of the 'sexual orientations' which have the equal right to public manifestation and respect. It is also argued that the homosexual drive is caused by the individual inborn predisposition. The Orthodox Church proceeds from the invariable conviction that the divinely established marital union of man and woman cannot be compared to the perverted manifestations of sexuality. She believes homosexuality to be a sinful distortion of human nature, which is overcome by spiritual effort leading to the healing and personal growth of the individual. Homosexual desires, just as other passions torturing fallen man, are healed by the sacraments, prayer, fasting, repentance, reading of Holy Scriptures and patristic writings, as well as Christian fellowship with believers who are ready to give spiritual support.

While treating people with homosexual inclinations with pastoral responsibility, the Church is resolutely against the attempts to present this sinful tendency as a 'norm' and even something to be proud of and emulate. This is why the Church denounces any propaganda of homosexuality. Without denying anybody the fundamental rights to life, respect for personal dignity and participation in public affairs, the Church, however, believes that those who propagate the homosexual way of life should not be admitted to educational and other work with children and youth, nor to occupy superior posts in the army and reformatories. (The Basis of the Social Concept of the Russian Orthodox Church 2000: XII.9)

For some, this would be everything that can be said on the subject. Yet, as the personal experiences of hundreds of people (the faith journey experience of the author of this piece and other LGBT+ persons of faith, the pastoral experience of many Orthodox priests, the theological experience of many scholars, and the crying out experience of psychologists working with religious trauma) show, there is much more that can and must be said, which could place the approach outlined above in serious question, based on its complete disregard of the new evidence that the world has accumulated over the centuries since the culture forming these norms has ceased to exist.

As Volodymyr Bureha, professor at Kyiv Theological Academy, reminds us in his excellent paper titled *Attitudes to Homosexuality in Christianity* (Bureha 2014), which I recommend to anyone wishing to explore the history of the subject, homosexuality as a term did not appear until the late nineteenth century. And the language we can use today to express the reality of persons with homosexual orientation, along with the very opportunity to freely use it, is such a new and game-changing factor that it warrants that the Orthodox church not only defines its pastoral approach to homosexual persons but also looks honestly at its system of beliefs, for what is the worth of a belief if, for centuries, it was not being adopted in freedom, but was defined with significant parts of the picture missing?

One of the arguments put forward by those who advocate a revision of the church's position on homosexuality is the so-called Gentile Analogy (Perry 2010): gentiles were considered impure in the early church but then God himself revealed to the apostles that His Kingdom was open to those whom they had previously excluded based on the cultural paradigm of their tradition (cf. Acts 11). I would like to extend this argument even further: I propose we look at the very history of the church as that of the clash of the two vectors, one of *ex*clusion and one of *in*clusion. One of law and one of mercy. One of re(gu)lations and one of personal re(ve)lation.

Although for the traditional mind-set boundaries and limitations (such as sticking with ritual purity rules of the past and not trusting personal conscience choices as leading to alleged abuse of freedom and impunity) are an instrument of protection of what we hold dear and sacred, this is not the only possible take on it. It is psychologically explainable as an attempt to bring order to the uncontrollable and frightening living chaos of the reality, but it does not hold water theologically, as God has shown again and again throughout the sacred history how He does not need our protection and how He cannot be contained in boxes, an idea that is deeply coherent for the apophatic nature of the Orthodox theology.

In twentieth-century Western theology, the notion of radical inclusion as the core Christian message has come to the front. And while it is rejected by some in the Orthodox world as being too 'worldly' or 'social', it is nevertheless profoundly grounded in the scriptures and tradition. As St Paul puts it in his letter to the Ephesians:

> But now in Christ Jesus you who once were far away have been brought near through the blood of Christ. For he himself is our peace, who has made the two one and has destroyed the barrier, the dividing wall of hostility, by abolishing in his flesh the law with its commandments and regulations. His purpose was to create in himself one new man out of the two, thus making peace, and in this one body to reconcile both of them to God through the cross, by which he put to death their hostility (Eph 2:13–16).

It is my deepest conviction – and something that has kept me *in*side the church despite all the troubles and pain experienced throughout the years – that taking care of the dividing walls is the very essence of what our Lord Jesus Christ wants his church to do.

The early church initially put a requirement on gentiles wishing to join it: they first had to agree that there is something inherently wrong with them that can only be undone by the symbolic means of circumcision, by renouncing the part of their identity that may have never been their choice and by becoming someone else. Yet, the Holy Spirit led the church away from viewing the gentiles as unclean and inherently unable to enter communion with God. God's only requirement for them was their faith: 'God has granted even the Gentiles repentance unto life' (Acts 11:18). 'If God gave them the same gift as he gave us, who believed in the Lord Jesus Christ, who was I to think that I could oppose God?' (Acts 11:17). 'Whoever is not against us is for us' (Mk 9:40).

This mind-shift from exclusion to inclusion has allowed the church to spread all over the world and fulfil its missionary calling. Instead of exterminating all diversity with the fire of ritual purity, the church was able to grow by including whatever was good and divinely inspired in encountered cultures and by translating its core message into the terms and languages of people it included.

What might have happened had the church ignored the divine suggestion of this expansion of horizons? We can only guess. The history of the church has always been a cycle of missing the signs, making mistakes, and then learning to grow out of them. Some time after the gentiles' issue, emerging monasticism had to balance out the 'diffusion' of Christianity that had become a state religion. Throughout the centuries, new waves of 'washing out' of faith and the church's serving the interests of elites led to new rebellions of daring holy women and men. When even that was not enough, the collapse of all social and political systems upholding Christianity as a religion brought back the purifying and humbling experience of a persecuted church, without which

Orthodoxy and Homosexuality   113

it would not have learned how to speak to a secular human being, rooted in science and culture more than in faith.

Similarly, I believe that the key challenge of modernity for the Orthodox church is to learn to see the 'modern issues' (gender, sexual diversity, race, etc.) not as a threat but as yet another divine lesson. In some sense, it is the 'language' of human rights and dignity that the church has now to process and engage with by making yet another inclusion choice.

And there are signs that this is already happening all over the globe. First, there are a growing number of spaces, offline and online, where Orthodox persons who also happen to be homosexual gather for prayer, mutual support, and advocacy work. These are courageous persons who believe in Jesus Christ, value the Orthodox tradition (theirs by birth or choice) and believe that they are not out, but inside the church. Back in 1980, the very first group of homosexual Orthodox Christian persons in the United States chose to be called AXIOS (Greek for 'worthy'): I like to see it as an Orthodox 'translation' of the word 'pride' (associated globally with the LGBT+ movement) as opposed to shame (which besides upholding social norms can also be an induced feeling that serves as an instrument to control individuals and whole groups).

Instead of the destructive (excluding) vision of a homosexual person as inherently wrong and having to be ashamed of themselves in general, groups of LGBT+ Orthodox Christians propose an including and healing narrative of being worthy and precious in God's eyes. They believe that, whatever the origin of gender and sexual diversity in the world, the *theosis* (Greek for 'deification') calling of all human beings is a requirement for qualitative change and renouncing of egoism rather than a demand of forcing oneself into a heterosexual frame. In simple terms, they claim that 'God cares more for *how* we love than *whom* we love.' This leads them to abolish the imposed dichotomy of being either Orthodox or LGBT+: they make the daring decision not to make this unnecessary choice and to take the risk of answering for that to the Almighty and All-Merciful One.

Along with the AXIOS group existing in a few countries of the West, there are several groups of LGBT+ Christians sharing this discourse and active in Eastern European countries with a predominant Orthodox presence: for example, *Nuntiare et Recreare* (Latin for 'herald and strengthen') in St Petersburg, Light of the World in Moscow, Russian-speaking online worship community *My Tut Ryadom* (Russian for 'we are right here'). There are also Orthodox LGBT+ persons scattered around other ecumenical groups of LGBT+ Christians all over Europe. Among the online spaces, one could name the Orthodoxy in Dialogue site and Facebook community led by Giacomo Sanfilippo, a Canadian scholar focusing on same-sex desire and Orthodox theology.

Acknowledging the fact of growing visibility of Orthodox LGBT+ persons and issues, the European Forum of LGBT Christian Groups, a pan-European networking and advocacy ecumenical association, organized a series of workshops on Orthodoxy and inclusion of LGBT+ persons in 2015 and 2018 in Finland. Besides gathering a great constellation of activists and theologians, lay and ordained, LGBT+ persons and allies, for a first such open discussion, this process bore two important fruits. The papers presented at the first workshop, along with the transcript of some of its sessions and key additional documents, were published as an anthology of texts on Orthodoxy and inclusion under the title 'For I Am Wonderfully Made' (Cherniak, Gerassimenko & Brinkschroeder 2016). It was the very first attempt to build a coherent narrative around the possibility of inclusion and affirmation of LGBT+ persons in the Orthodox church.

Another public initiative that followed the workshops of the European Forum was the Open Letter from Orthodox LGBT+ Persons to the Holy and Great Council of the Orthodox Church (Cherniak, Sommers & Elhorst 2016) that gathered in Crete in June 2016. As one of the letter's authors, it would be immodest of me to praise it, yet it seems to have been the largest and loudest endeavour in history to put the words LGBT+ and Orthodox into one sentence in the debate within the Orthodox world. The letter was written using the church's vocabulary (as opposed to secular, rights-based language) and spoke of the everyday reality of Orthodox LGBT+ persons who are ostracized, expelled from their communities, barred from the sacraments, forced into heterosexual marriages or monastic life, driven away from the church and from God, and, in an alarming number of instances, pushed to take their own life in an attempt to resolve the conflict tearing them apart. The authors of the letter urged the bishops gathered in Crete to put an end to the potentially life-giving tradition of the church being abused to harm and even kill people and to create spaces of dialogue and common prayer for the church hierarchy and Orthodox LGBT+ persons. And while the text, distributed in the Council halls by allies of the cause, did not affect the agenda or proceedings, it nevertheless can be considered an important historical point when a question is asked so loudly for the first time that it cannot and will not be ignored. The authors have received numerous responses from all over the globe: from an Orthodox lesbian woman in Africa who cannot put her questions to anyone without the risk of being caned by her community, from another Orthodox lesbian from the Netherlands who was asked by her priest to not share her story in church and in effect was pushed back into the framework of shame, from an Orthodox dignitary living in diaspora who considered this letter to be a wake-up call, and many others. The letter was met with support and gratitude from many LGBT+ allies in Orthodox parishes and affirmative priests who strive for justice and inclusion for everyone in Orthodox communities.

The choice of Finland as the place for the two above-mentioned workshops was deliberate, and this leads us to a second important sign of the *in*clusion mind-shift taking place. As recent research (d'Alo, Stockdale, Brouwer & Zorgdrager 2021) into the inclusivity of the official policies and practices of European churches has shown, the situation of LGBT+ persons in Orthodox churches varies significantly from country to country. The leader among Orthodox churches is the Church of Finland, scoring 32% (15 points out of 47 possible). Among other interesting observations, the researchers show that the level of inclusion of LGBT+ persons in Orthodox churches is higher in those contexts where the churches are less entangled in worldly power games and do not play the role of state or quasi-state religion. The more the church learns to accept its position in a secular state and the freedom this gives it, and the more it is engaged with the modern world while being true to its core, the wider are the spaces in church communities where LGBT+ believers can feel at home and nourished. The lowest scores among the Orthodox churches in Europe belong to the Russian Orthodox Church. This does not come as much of a surprise, given the current disposition in the relations between the church and the state there and the fact that Russia perceives itself as one of the last strongholds of traditional Christian values in the world, which is an artificial and contentless concept intentionally promoted by the regime to advance Russian geopolitical interests on the global arena. There are numerous reports on how Russian state actors cooperate with other ultraconservative figures and groups globally to push back against the progress in human rights, especially women's rights and rights of LGBT+ persons. Using the same allegedly Christian discourse and following Russia's example, other countries, such as Poland and Hungary, are actively working on introducing anti-LGBT+ legislation and policies. And though the church in Russia sees itself as a partner of the state in this crusade, all signs indicate that the state just uses the church to build its narrative but does not really care for the matters of faith.

Interestingly, in the RICE research the Church of Serbia scored above the average level for Orthodox churches in Europe, which the researchers interpret as a consequence of the prodemocratic changes in Serbian society, aspiring to join the community of EU nations. The Serbian Patriarch Porfirje even spoke in favour of the civil partnerships law in one of his interviews in 2021: 'I can understand people with this type of sexual orientation, their countless administrative problems, the challenges and pressures, and their need to regularize their situation' (Anđelković 2021). Even though this declaration does not seem to come from a place of genuine inclusion and affirmation, it nevertheless stands out against the general background of the Orthodox world.

Incidentally, since the research only included 'national' churches, the views of the diaspora churches were not taken into consideration. Yet, there is at least one document of interest for this discussion, coming from Germany.

It is the Letter from the Bishops of the Orthodox Church in Germany to Young People concerning Love, Sexuality, and Marriage, published in 2017 and adopted by the representatives of seven local Orthodox churches present in Germany. Written in a language fitting extremely well the addressees of the letter, it says explicitly: 'A burning issue today is the question of homosexuality and homosexual partnerships. That this topic is discussed openly in our society can in principle be seen as a good thing. For homosexual men and women were ignored for centuries, and even oppressed and persecuted, as for instance in the time of National Socialism' (Augoustinos 2017). It then discusses how 'we are largely in ignorance about how homosexuality arises' (Augoustinos 2017), how homosexual inclinations can be overcome with ascetism and restraint, and how frank questions relating to homosexual persons are a matter of spiritual welfare and tactful guidance from the church. Again, this is hardly an affirmative statement as such, but it constitutes a strong departure from the rhetoric of such documents as the Basis of the Social Concept of the Russian Orthodox Church from 2000.

The RICE research unfortunately could not consider the views of the Ecumenical Patriarchate, with its seat in Constantinople and presence chiefly in diaspora. It is even more unfortunate given that the church that exists mostly in exile has found itself actively looking for answers to the questions of the modern world in the Western, secular context. In 2019, the Ecumenical Patriarchate summarised its existing discourse on social issues (including referring to the letter of German bishops) and published an outstanding document called 'For the Life of the World. Towards a Social Ethos of the Orthodox Church.' Its paragraph on homosexuality deserves to be quoted in full:

§19. We live in an age in which sexuality has come more and more to be understood as a personal fate, and even a private matter. A great many political and social debates in the modern world turn upon the distinct demands and needs of heterosexual, homosexual, bisexual, and other sexual 'identities'. It is true, as a simple physiological and psychological fact, that the nature of individual sexual longing is not simply a consequence of private choice regarding such matters; many of the inclinations and longings of the flesh and the heart to a great extent come into the world with us, and are nourished or thwarted – accepted or obstructed – in us at an early age. It must be accounted, moreover, a basic right of any person – which no state or civil authority may presume to violate – to remain free from persecution or legal disadvantage as a result of his or her sexual orientation. But the Church understands human identity as residing primarily not in one's sexuality or in any other private quality, but rather in the image and likeness of God present in all of us. All Christians are called always to seek the image and likeness of God in each other, and to resist all forms of discrimination against their neighbors, regardless of sexual orientation. Christians are called to lives of sexual continence, both inside and outside of marriage, precisely on account of the sanctity of sexual life in the created order. But Christians are never called to hatred or disdain for anyone. (Hart & Chryssavgis 2020)

This comprehensive document, created by the theologians of the Church of Constantinople in the aftermath of the Holy and Great Council of 2016, for the very first time speaks of homosexuality not being a result of personal (sinful) choices. It also leaves no place for religiously framed discrimination or hatred. It is clearly polemicising with the Basis of the Social Concept of the Russian Orthodox Church of 2000 that insisted on banning 'those who propagate the homosexual way of life' from certain professions. The 2019 text devoted to the social ethos of the Orthodox church is not looking for loopholes and remains focused on spiritual matters of likeness of God or renouncing hatred.

Along with the persons affected directly (LGBT+ persons of faith) and the hierarchy with its official positions, there is another layer of Orthodox reality that should be mentioned explicitly: academia. Orthodox academic theologians have gathered to deliberate on issues of sexuality and, more specifically, homosexuality on a number of occasions in the past five years. From 2016 to 2018, the University of Oslo and its Coalition on Freedom of Religion or Belief gathered Orthodox theologians from around the globe for three *New Directions in Orthodox Christian Thought and Practice* workshops to discuss issues of gender, sexuality, and pastoral care. The proceedings of the workshops were published recently (Arentzen et al. 2022). In 2017, the Amsterdam Centre for Orthodox Theology at the Vrije Universiteit hosted a *Symposium on Orthodox pastoral care and sexuality*. In 2019, numerous participants of those two series, along with other theologians, clergy and a few activists (representing the European Forum process), met in Oxford for the conference *Bridging Voices. Contemporary Eastern Orthodox Identity and the Challenges of Pluralism and Sexual Diversity in a Secular Age*, which de facto was the most representative event on the topic in history in terms both of the number of participants and of the breadth of approaches and attitudes represented. While a significant number of Orthodox theologians participating in these discussions express their (personal) view on the need for wider inclusion of LGBT+ persons in the Orthodox church, there is a serious gap between the academics and the policymakers within the church. Yet what is most remarkable is that the process was conducted in a respectful and gracious manner despite the common level of complexity and emotions that normally accompany such discussions. That fact in itself carries hope that the openings of the last few years will not be shut down. More and more important theological publications are coming up (e.g., Rich 2023).

Last but not least, I would like to mention the role of parish communities. Numerous Orthodox theologians and writers from across the Orthodox globe have been reminding us of the importance of the Eucharist and of the royal priesthood of all faithful for years. While the process is still ongoing, it has already raised the level of self-awareness of many Orthodox believers. They realise that they have an active role to play both in the Eucharist itself, as well as in the building of the community, and through both those ways, mystically and practically, contributing to the life and growth of the church. Those parish communities where members receive such formation (along with being instructed on matters of personal relations with and responsibility to God) see not only a rise in social ministry and mission, but also a greater openness to the *Other*. Higher level of involvement and self-awareness of parishioners allows them to see the *Other* not as a challenge or threat to their faith, but as a neighbour, a fellow believer, or even as Christ himself, persecuted and crucified. For this reason, many of such communities have also proved to be a place of greater concern for racial/ethnic/gender equality and inclusion for 'marginal cases' such as LGBT+ believers. Parishioners get to know each other, and they share each other's burdens. Trust allows the LGBT+ members of the community to come out and, thanks to this closeness and sharing of lives, personal stories bear fruits. The same trust then allows the community members to make brave decisions to embrace such exceptions even though this may contradict the letter of the church law. The number of such communities is obviously still small, but it is growing by the day. And observations show that in most cases this process follows the process of overall renewal of Eucharistic and parish life, which is definitely a sign of God's plan for the church in our times.

Instead of growing in resources or power or numbers, the church is growing deeper into its roots and into the relations between its members. This process of reconciliation, that our Lord Jesus Christ started on the Cross two thousand years ago, is continuing – tearing down new walls and healing new wounds. As a Russian Orthodox priest murdered in 1990, Fr Alexander Men, put it, 'Christianity is only just beginning.' And if we look at its past and future through the hermeneutic lenses of the '*ex*' and '*in*' vectors, it is only by accepting this Divine Pedagogy of going forward through such '*in*' leaps of faith that Christianity can both extend into the future and grow in strength by being increasingly true to its essence of reconciliation and radical *in*clusion.

BIBLIOGRAPHY

Anđelković N. 2021. 'Srpska pravoslavna crkva i Porfirije: Šta je rrekao patrijarh u prvom televizijskom gostovanju – u 100 i 500 reči' [Serbian Orthodox Church and Porphyry: What the patriarch said in the first television appearance – in 100 and 500 words]. *BBC News na srpskom,* Belgrade. https://www.bbc.com/serbian/cyr/srbija-56266813 (accessed 25.10.2021).

Arentzen T. et al., eds. 2022. *Orthodox Tradition and Human Sexuality.* New York: Fordham University Press.

Augoustinos et al. 2017. *Letter from the Bishops of the Orthodox Church in Germany to Young People Concerning Love, Sexuality, and Marriage.* Dortmund. http://www.obkd.de/Texte/Brief%20OBKD%20an%20die%20Jugend-en.pdf (accessed 25.10.2021).

Bureha V. 2014. 'Otnoshenie k probleme gomoseksualizma v sovremennom zapadnom khristianstve' [Attitude to homosexuality issue in modern Christianity], *Gomoseksualnost' i khristianstvo v XXI veke* [Homosexuality and Christianity in the 21st Century], 118–141. St Petersburg. http://www.insight-ukraine.org/uploads/files/gomoseksualnost_i_hristianstvo_v_xxi_veke.pdf (accessed 25.10.2021).

Cherniak M., E. Sommers & W. Elhorst. 2016. *Open Letter to the Holy and Great Council of the Orthodox Church.* Warsaw/Amsterdam/Bristol. https://www.lgbtchristians.eu/media-press/orthodox-churches/223-open-letter-to-the-holy-and-great-council-of-the-orthodox-church (accessed 25.10.2021).

Cherniak M., O. Gerassimenko & M. Brinkschröder, eds. 2016. *'For I Am Wonderfully Made': Texts on Eastern Orthodoxy and LGBT Inclusion.* Warsaw/Amsterdam.

d'Alo P., R. Stockdale, R. Brouwer & H. Zorgdrager. 2021. *RICE 2020: Rainbow Index of Churches in Europe 2020.* Amsterdam. https://inclusive-churches.eu/download/Annual-Review-Full-2021.pdf (accessed 25.10.2021).

Gallaher B. & G. Tucker, eds. 2019. *Eastern Orthodoxy and Sexual Diversity: Perspectives on Challenges from the Modern West. Interim Report of the Exeter-Fordham Bridging Voices Project.* Exeter & New York. https://www.fordham.edu/download/downloads/id/14010/BV_Report.pdf (accessed 25.10.2021).

Gallaher B. & G. Tucker, eds. 2020. *Orthodox Christianity, Sexual Diversity & Public Policy (2020). Final Report of the Exeter-Fordham Bridging Voices Project.* Exeter/New York. https://www.fordham.edu/download/downloads/id/14882/orthodox_christianity_sexual_diversity_and_public_policy.pdf (accessed 25.10.2021).

Hart D. B. & J. Chryssavgis, eds. 2020. *For the Life of the World. Toward a Social Ethos of the Orthodox Church.* Brookline, MA. https://www.goarch.org/social-ethos (accessed 25.10.2021).

Louth A. & G. Tucker, eds. 2018. *The Wheel.* Spring/Summer 2018. Arlington, MA.

Perry J. 2010. 'Gentiles and Homosexuals: A Brief History of an Analogy', *The Journal of Religious Ethics,* June 2010: 321–47.

Rich B. E. 2023. *Gender Essentialism and Orthodoxy: Beyond Male and Female.* New York: Fordham University Press.

Sozaev V., ed. 2014. *Gomoseksualnost' i khristianstvo v XXI veke* [Homosexuality and Christianity in the 21st Century]. St Petersburg. http://www.insight-ukraine.org /uploads/files/gomoseksualnost_i_hristianstvo_v_xxi_veke.pdf

The Basis of the Social Concept of the Russian Orthodox Church. 2000. https://old .mospat.ru/en/documents/social-concepts/ (accessed 25.10.2021).

Chapter 12

Confronting Environmental Crisis

What Do Jewish Traditions Teach about Using the World?

Tanhum Yoreh

Ever since I first heard of the concept of ecological footprints, the idea fascinated me. Developed by scholars William Rees and Mathis Wackernagel, an ecological footprint is a quantitative measure of the amount of productive land we need to support our consumption (1996). Since the 1990s footprint calculators have been created to measure other environmentally related resources such as water and carbon consumption. Footprint calculators ask questions such as how often you fly, drive, or eat animal protein. The footprint calculator then magnifies individual consumption to a global level indicating that if everyone were to consume at a level commensurate to our own, we would require x number of planet Earths to support the world's human population. The calculators hem and haw, but for those with occidental consumption habits the answer is almost always the same: our consumption patterns are either entirely unsustainable or profoundly inequitable, most likely both.

Jewish cosmology traditionally views the world as created for the sake of humans (Mishnah, *Sanhedrin* 4:5). Together with the directive in Genesis 1:28 for humans to have dominion over the rest of the created world, humans possess a privileged place in the world. Indeed, traditionally, humans are considered to have been created in the image of God (Gen 1:26). Scholars such as Lynn White Jr. (1967) pointed to the Judeo–Christian tradition in arguing that that cosmological narrative gave rise to the ecological crisis. White's argument has been critiqued an untold number of times and need not be revisited here (see Yoreh 2010a). Suffice it to say that whether he was correct in his observation or not, humans have relentlessly dominated and (ab)used the Earth's systems to the verge of ecological collapse. Simply put, we must change what and how much we consume if we are to live within the limits of Earth's ability to regenerate, within Earth's carrying capacity. Thankfully, there are many paths to achieve this goal including ones that are distinctly Jewish. Judaism offers two main frameworks to limit consumption: prescriptive and voluntary. The following contents are far from an exhaustive list of what falls into each of these categories but offer an introduction to different approaches Jewish traditions and communities have had to using the world.

The Torah, the foundational text of Judaism, contains among other things narratives, theology, cosmology, history, ethics, national identity, and, of course, law. It is also so much more than that, but we will focus on the legal dimensions of Jewish approaches to using the world. Jewish law, *halakhah*, originated in the Torah, was expanded by the sages in the Mishnah and Talmud, and continues to develop and evolve in our time. The law is broken down into positive commandments (actions that must be undertaken) and negative ones (actions that must be abstained from). This first section will focus on the prohibition against wastefulness, on Sabbath and sabbaticals, and on sumptuary laws.

The prescription most obviously related to consumption is *bal tashḥit* – 'waste not'. This law originated in Deuteronomy 20:19 where warring Israelites were commanded not to cut down the fruit trees belonging to the enemy city upon which they were laying siege. The sages of the Mishnah and Talmud took this prohibition and through various exegetical methods of interpretation expanded it into a general law prohibiting all forms of needless waste or destruction. *Prima facie*, this law would appear to be a useful tool in mitigating wasteful consumption, but, as I have discussed elsewhere in great detail (Yoreh 2019b), the way in which 'waste not' has been conceptualized throughout history limited its effectiveness in achieving this outcome.

As a case in point, one of the most significant developments in the conceptualization of *bal tashḥit* was the creation of the supplemental concept *bal tashḥit degufa adif* – translated as 'not wasting the body takes precedence [over the waste of material goods]'. This concept emerged as part of the process of the rabbinic sages problematizing the relationship between the human body and the rest of the material world. When pitted against each other, the sages inevitably prioritized the well-being of humans above almost all else. This is illustrated in the following text:

> Rav Ḥisda also said: When one can eat barley bread but instead eats wheat bread he transgresses 'waste not'. Rav Papa said: When one can drink beer but instead drinks wine, he transgresses 'waste not'. But this is incorrect: 'Waste not', as applied to one's own body, takes precedence. (Babylonian Talmud, *Shabbat* 140b, modified translation my own)

The presumption was that wine and wheat were considered to offer their consumer greater health benefits than beer and barley (Stein 2000), but at a higher financial cost. Rav Ḥisda and Rav Papa's seemingly ascetic approach was rejected and the dictum of the Talmud was that human well-being is prioritized over suppressing material waste. While this position is consistent with rabbinic notions of human privilege, it does not come with any quantifiable boundaries defining what the limits of this dynamic are. How much waste needs to occur before it is no longer considered reasonable relative to the increase in human well-being? In the Jewish context, Diamond (2002) documented legal decisions that permitted harmful industries to exist despite their violation of Jewish law. The argument for human well-being has also been used to justify the prevalence of single-use plastics in ultra-Orthodox communities (Yoreh 2019a).

To further complicate matters, Maimonides, in his code of law the *Mishneh Torah*, Laws of Kings 6:10, established the criterion that in order to transgress 'waste not' a person would have to undertake an action with destructive intent (*derekh hashhatah*). An action that is wasteful but not intentionally so would not be considered a transgression. Together with the aforementioned prioritization of human well-being, the effectiveness of 'waste not' as governing Jewish use of the world appears to be limited.

Yet, 'waste not' is not an esoteric legal concept: it is an important part of lived religion. Green Course, one of the leading environmental organizations in Israel, led a campaign calling for a reduction in the use of disposable plastic dishes during the festivals of the month of Tishrei (e.g., Rosh Hashanah, the Jewish New Year) and the rest of the year (Krauss 2019). The campaign included a petition signed by over thirty Orthodox rabbis that opened with the statement 'We the undersigned rabbis feel it our religious and moral duty to call on the public to reduce their use of single-use plastics.' They then evoked the concept of 'waste not' in justifying their position.

As can be seen, there is a complexity and richness to 'waste not' that goes far beyond the challenges listed above. 'Waste not' is not simply a law but also an ethic. *Sefer HaḤinukh*, The Book of (Moral) Education, Law 529 describes the rationale behind 'waste not' in the following way: 'This is the way of the righteous and people of deeds who love peace and delight in the goodness of human beings and draw them near to the Torah. They do not waste even a grain of mustard in this world. Their instinct when encountering waste is to try to prevent it with all their strength.' As such, the driver behind how people act in any given situation is not only whether an action is a perceived transgression or not, but also whether it is morally upright.

In my own work (Yoreh 2019b) I argue that one of the earliest ways 'waste not' was conceptualized included within its scope the prohibition against self-harm (wasting oneself). There appears to have been an ethic that harming the

124 *Tanhum Yoreh*

environment was commensurate to harming oneself. This connection was muted by the sages of the Talmud and developed into its own separate prohibition. We see through the concept of *bal tashḥit degufa adif* that the sages considered human life to be the most important element of the prohibition. The sages only ever used this supplementary concept to justify the waste of material. In a time of climate crisis driven by the way we use the world, it has become clear that overconsumption directly compromises human well-being. In other words, we have reached the point where *bal tashḥit degufa adif* should be used to limit consumption instead of permit it.

A unique set of laws controlling consumption consists of those related to the Sabbath and sabbatical years. The Sabbath is designated as a day of rest, on which manual labor is prohibited. The sages defined thirty-nine categories of labor that are prohibited. Theoretically, because people are mandated to rest the environmental impact they cause is extremely limited. Yet, in practice the lessening of environmental impact remains in potential. For instance, to bypass restrictions on electricity use, some people put lights and hotplates on timers or even leave them on the entire duration of the Sabbath. To maximize rest and minimize effort some opt to use single-use plastic dishes. For Abraham Joshua Heschel (a twentieth-century theologian), however, the Sabbath is the ultimate way in which humans can mitigate their domination of the world. For Heschel, the very act of focusing our hearts and minds on the Sabbath allows us to integrate the Sabbath as an ideal we strive for during the rest of the week (2005). Once the Sabbath becomes our central focus, we start to integrate Sabbath values into how we use the world during the mundane days of the week. Although Heschel focused on the Sabbath and not on sabbatical years, we might extrapolate that his approach also holds for sabbaticals.

The sabbatical year (*shemittah*) is conceptually similar to the Sabbath. The Sabbath focuses on rest for humans and animals, and the sabbatical year is a year of rest for the land. Every seventh year the land is mandated to lie fallow (Exod 23:10–11, Lev 25:4–7), allowing it to regain its nutrients. People are released from debts they owed. Fields cannot be worked, and the fences that surround them are mandated to be removed so that there is equal access to the food that does grow. This put humans in direct competition with wild animals, making the sabbatical year extremely difficult to observe. Gerald Blidstein (2001) noted that difficulties in observing the sabbatical year ultimately resulted in its downfall. Sabbatical observance was limited to the land of Israel, and because of exile became moot for much of Jewish history. With a return to the land by the early Zionist pioneers, the legal questions about sabbatical observance emerged anew. Sabbaticals once again proved too difficult to observe and the Chief Rabbi of Palestine, Rabbi Abraham Isaac Kook, established a legal mechanism to bypass the need to let the land lie fallow in 1909 that still holds (1951).

Yet, with the increasing urgency of the climate crisis, Jewish environmentalists are renewing their commitment to the sabbatical year. This renewal is not concentrated on the legal aspects of sabbaticals but rather on the values that it encapsulates. This shift in focus allows *shemittah* to be observed not only in Israel but also in the Jewish diaspora; not only by farmers, but by anyone who connects to these values. For instance, The Shmita Project in the United States uses the sabbatical year as a platform to explore issues such as 'rest and work, relationship to land, relationship to community, relationship to debt and debt relief, definitions of community, and the issue of consumption itself' (The Shmita Project 2021). In Israel, a similar initiative is underway called Shmita Yisraelit, whose vision is to have the sabbatical year be a time of 'social engagement, spiritual and ethical renewal, and of deep environmental reflection; a year of camaraderie, culture, spirit, family and community . . . a year that leaves its impression on the subsequent six years' (Shmita Yisraelit 2021). The spillover effect that Shmita Yisraelit calls for is precisely the Heschelian way of looking at the Sabbath. If we strive for a time of sabbatical values, these values become the ideal for the other six years of the cycle.

After the disintegration of a central Jewish governing body that could make binding legal decisions applicable to all of world Jewry, in eleventh-century Babylonia, the authority shifted to the legal and communal authorities in each individual community. These issued bylaws, known as *taqqanot hakehilah* (community regulations), and applicable only within the community in which they were issued (*Shu"t HaRashb"a* 3:411). Regulations were at times issued to control the consumption of goods, in which case they were known as sumptuary laws. Jewish sumptuary laws were spatially limited and community-specific, but such laws were extremely common throughout the world and well beyond the Jewish context. For instance, sumptuary laws are documented to have existed in China (Bosco 2014), Italy (Adelman 1991), France (Berkovitz 2001, Roth 1928), the Iberian Peninsula (Booker 2021, Caballero-Navas 2008), central and east-central Europe (Aust 2019), India (Chaturvedula 2015), Iran and Russia (Tazmini 2018), the Maghreb (Zafrani & Vale 1999), the Ottoman Empire (Kavas 2015), and Scotland (Gemmill 2020), among many other locations. Joseph Bosco (2014:168) writes: 'All societies seek to control greed in some way.'

The reasons for sumptuary laws, however, are much broader than simply controlling greed. In fact, greed is rarely the driving factor in instituting sumptuary laws, particularly in the Jewish context. One of the most significant factors behind these laws is maintaining social hierarchies (Berkovitz 2001, Bosco 2014, Muzzarelli 2009). In the broader context, the social elites benefited from being able to dress in finery while the rest of society was sartorially restricted. This prevented the merchant class who could afford luxuries previously only attainable by the elites from upward mobility. It also allowed for easy identification of different classes. One of the ways Jews were prevented from mixing with the dominant groups was by requiring them to wear badges, hats, or a particular style of facial hair (Booker 2021, Caballero-Navas 2008, Roth 1928). One of the most common justifications for the existence of sumptuary laws in Jewish communities was to prevent people from ostentatious behavior that could create envy and resentment and raise the ire of the broader gentile society (Adelman 1991, Berkovitz 2001, Caballero-Navas 2008, Roth 1928).

Sumptuary laws were also instituted to protect the community financial burden (Adelman 1991, Aust 2019). Community members who felt they needed to live up to the social norms by displaying wealth could end up in serious debt. This justification lives on in our time. For instance, the Gerer (Gur) Hasidic dynasty has issued sumptuary laws applicable to their community controlling the number of people permitted to attend lifecycle events such as engagement parties, weddings, and circumcisions. One of the justifications for these laws is to save money for community members (Shefer 2019).

Sumptuary laws were often framed in moral terms (Berkovitz 2001, Muzzarelli 2009). Even when sumptuary laws were initiated by secular authorities, they were infused with a moral narrative by religious leaders. One of the challenges to this approach is articulated by Jay Berkovitz, who claims that 'there is no body of rabbinic literature that consistently condemns luxury as immoral' (p. 3). This in itself, however, has not prevented religious leaders appealing to other moral elements related to conspicuous consumption. Religious leaders are considered to be an important driver of pro-environmental behavior (Tsimpo & Wodon 2016, Yoreh 2010b).

Faith communities offer moral framing to environmental challenges that are missing in scientific or technical discourses (Rolston 2006, Smith & Pulver 2009). Faith-based environmental activists view their engagement with environmentalism as derivative of their faith and therefore a moral imperative (Biviano 2012, Bomberg & Hague 2018, Hancock 2018, Koehrsen 2021, Tirosh-Samuelson 2017). As seen above, the prescriptive ways in which consumption is regulated is interwoven with morality. The righteous avoid even a minimal amount of waste. The Sabbath allows not only us to rest, but mandates rest for the people who work for us and our beasts of burden. Sabbatical years forgive debts and break down barriers of access to food. Even some of the rationale for sumptuary laws is to maintain peaceful relations within a community and among broader society. The examples below are also tied into a legal framework, but their relevance to this discourse is governed more by their voluntary and moral nature than their prescriptive force.

One form of a voluntary approach to mitigating consumption is by becoming a Nazirite, a Jewish form of asceticism (Num 6). Nazirites were required to abstain from wine, from cutting their hair, and from becoming ritually impure by exposure to human corpses. This form of asceticism was not normative, and its status under Jewish law was questionable, though a framework for individuals who chose this lifestyle was laid out in the Torah. Upon ending the vow of asceticism, the Nazirite was required to bring a sin offering to the Temple. There are two positions in rabbinic scholarship as to why a sin offering was required. One position maintains that the sin offering is required only if the Nazirite is exposed to a corpse. The other position argues that being a Nazirite and abstaining from things which are permitted by the Torah is in fact the transgression and the sin offering is to atone for being an ascetic. Maimonides strongly critiqued the choice to become a Nazirite, instead championing the path of moderation. In his Laws of Ethical Behavior 3:1 he wrote the following:

> The sages stated that if a Nazirite who did nothing but abstain from wine requires a sin offering, how much more so does anyone who denies themselves anything. In light of this the sages commanded that a person should abstain only from the things that the Torah prohibited, but not prohibit for themselves through oaths and vows that which is permitted.

The key lessons Maimonides imparts when translating this into an approach to using the world, particularly in a time of climate crisis, are twofold. First, humans should make use of the world. They should partake in and enjoy its resources. Second, consumption should be moderate, never rubbing up against excess at either end of the spectrum. Essentially, Maimonides teaches us that if we are excessively ascetic, we are engaging in self-harm, and if we are excessive by overconsuming, we are also engaging in self-harm. For Maimonides the path of moderation is the 'good and straight path', the Godly path (Laws of Ethical Behavior 1:5).

The laws of kashrut (Jewish dietary laws) are one of the best-known prescriptive ways through which the consumption of food is governed in Judaism. There have been moral rationalizations for some of the specific ordinances, such as using razor-sharp knives in ritual slaughter to reduce the suffering of animals, or separating life from death in not mixing meat and dairy. Yet, these prescriptions and their rationalizations do little for the environmental impacts of food consumption. Ecotheologians Zalman Schachter-Shalomi and Arthur Waskow have tried to expand the prescriptive aspect of kashrut to include a moral dimension through the concept 'eco-kosher' (1992). Eco-kashrut asks questions about the process of producing the food and not just whether traditional Jewish law permits or prohibits its consumption. Did

128 *Tanhum Yoreh*

animals suffer in the production process? Were humans exploited? What was the environmental impact of producing and consuming the item? The answers to these questions are the ones that dictate whether a product is eco-kosher or not. Eco-kashrut is by no means limited to food products but is a lens through which to evaluate all the things that we consume. For instance, Waskow (1992) asks: Is the heavy use of pesticides kosher? Are investments in fossil fuel companies kosher? Is a poorly insulated home kosher? Along this vein, Rabbi David Rosen (2017) asks 'If at point Z the animal's throat was cut the right way and its internal organs checked, but from A to Y all injunctions and prohibitions have been ignored and desecrated, how can that product really be called kosher?' In other words, if the way we use the world is not consistent with our ethics, we are not using the world in a kosher way.

To find alternatives to empty consumerism, Waskow (2018) asks 'How do we delight in restraint?' In other words, how can we find the intentional act of consuming less, joyful? This profound question touches upon a key element missing from traditional discourses of limiting consumption: individual benefit. Reducing consumption in a time of perceived plenty is a challenge, particularly when there is a perception that it requires giving something up and not necessarily getting anything tangible back in return. Waskow's approach is refreshing. It focuses on what we stand to gain, and not what we might lose. He asks this as an open-ended question, inviting people to find their own vehicles of delighting in simplicity. Of course, Waskow has his own answer: community. For him, being in community is a way to shift focus from consumerism to relationship-building. For Heschel the answer is the Sabbath. Coveting time instead of space tempers desire for material things. When we covet restraint, our impact on the world of space diminishes. These two ideas connect on the Sabbath, the most common time for Jews to gather as community.

Acknowledgment: I would like to thank Maytal Lazarovic and Freia de Waal for their assistance with parts of the literature review.

BIBLIOGRAPHY

Adelman H. 1991. 'Rabbis and Reality: Public Activities of Jewish Women in Italy during the Renaissance and Catholic Restoration', *Jewish History*, vol. 5, no. 1, 27–40.

Aderet S. B. 1965. *Shu"t HaRashb"a*. Part 3. Bnei Braq.

Aust C. 2019. 'Covering the Female Jewish Body. Dress and Dress Regulations in Early Modern Ashkenaz', *Central Europe*, vol. 17, no. 1, 5–21.

Berkovitz J. R. 'Social and Religious Controls in Pre-Revolutionary France: Rethinking the Beginnings of Modernity', *Jewish History*, vol. 15, no. 1, 1–40.

Biviano E. L. 2012. 'Worldviews on Fire: Understanding the Inspiration for Congregational Religious Environmentalism', *CrossCurrents*, vol. 62, no. 4, 495–511.

Blidstein G. 2001. 'Man and Nature in the Sabbatical Year', in *Judaism and Environmental Ethics: A Reader*, ed. Martin D. Yaffe, 136–42. New York: Lexington Books.

Bomberg E. & A. Hague. 2018. 'Faith-Based Climate Action in the Christian Congregations: Mobilisation and Spiritual Resources', *Local Environment*, vol. 23, no. 5, 582–96.

Booker S. 2021. 'Moustaches, Mantles, and Saffron Shirts: What Motivated Sumptuary Law in Medieval English Ireland?', *Speculum*, vol. 96, no. 3, 726–70.

Bosco J. 2014. 'The Problem of Greed in Economic Anthropology: Sumptuary Laws and New Consumerism in China', *Economic Anthropology*, vol. 1, no. 1, 167–85.

Caballero-Navas C. 2008. 'The Care of Women's Health and Beauty: An Experience Shared by Medieval Jewish and Christian Women', *Journal of Medieval History*, vol. 34, no. 2, 146–63.

Chaturvedula N. 2015. 'On the Precipice of Ruin: Consumption, Sumptuary Laws, and Decadence in Early Modern Portuguese India', *Journal of World History*, vol. 26, no. 2, 355–84.

Diamond E. 2002. 'How Much Is Too Much? Conventional versus Personal Definitions of Pollutions in Rabbinic Sources', in *Judaism and Ecology: Created World and Revealed World*, ed. H. Tirosh-Samuelson, 61–80. Cambridge, MA: Harvard University Press.

Gemmill E. 2020. 'Debt, Distraint, Display and Dead Men's Treasure: Material Culture in Late Medieval Aberdeen', *Journal of Medieval History,* vol. 46, no. 3, 350–72.

Hancock R. 2018. *Islamic Environmentalism: Activism in the United States and Great Britain*. New York: Routledge.

Heschel A. J. 2005. *The Sabbath: Its Meaning for Modern Man*. New York: Farrar, Straus and Giroux.

Kavas S. 2015. '"Wardrobe Modernity": Western Attire as a Tool of Modernization in Turkey', *Middle Eastern Studies,* vol. 51, no. 4, 515–39.

Koehrsen J. 2021. 'Muslims and Climate Change: How Islam, Muslim Organizations, and Religious Leaders Influence Climate Change Perceptions and Mitigation Activities', *Wiley Interdisciplinary Reviews*, vol. 12, no. 3, 1–19.

Kook A. I. 1951. *Shabbat HaAretz: Hilkhot Shevi'it*. Jerusalem.

Krauss Y. September 29, 2019. 'Call from Rabbis of the Religious Zionism Movement: Reduce the Use of Single Use Plastics', *Makor Rishon*. https://www.makorrishon.co.il/news/175025/, accessed August 1, 2021.

Maimonides M. 1958. *Mishneh Torah: Hu HaYad HaḤazaqah LeRabbeinu Moshe ben Maimon. Sefer HaMada.* Vol. 2., ed. M. D. Rabinovitz. Jerusalem.

Muzzarelli M. G. 2009. 'Reconciling the Privilege of a Few with the Common Good: Sumptuary Laws in Medieval and Early Modern Europe', *Journal of Medieval and Early Modern Studies* vol. 39, no. 3, 597–617.

Rolston H. 2006. 'Caring for Nature: What Science and Economics Can't Teach Us but Religion Can', *Environmental Values* vol. 15, no. 3, 307–13.

Rosen D. March 16, 2017. 'Is Any Meat Today Kosher?', *The Times of Israel*. https://blogs.timesofisrael.com/is-any-meat-today-kosher/, accessed July 29, 2021.

Roth C. 1928. 'Sumptuary Laws of the Community of Carpentras', *The Jewish Quarterly Review*, vol. 18, no. 4, 357–83.

Sefer HaḤinukh. 1952. Ed. H. D. Chavel. Jerusalem.

Shefer S. 2019. 'An Initiative in the Gur Court: Regulations to Limit Expenditures at Children's Weddings', *Kikar HaShabbat*. https://www.kikar.co.il/319392.html, accessed August 2, 2021.

The Shmita Project. 2021. https://shmitaproject.org/about-project/, accessed August 2, 2021.

Shmita Yisraelit. 2021. https://shmita-il.co.il/about/#hazon, accessed August 2, 2021.

Smith A. & S. Pulver. 2009. 'Ethics-Based Environmentalism in Practice: Religious-Environmental Organizations in the United States', *Worldviews: Global Religions, Culture, and Ecology* vol. 13, no. 2, 145–79.

Stein D. E. S. 2000. '*Halakhah*: The Law of Bal Tashchit (Do Not Destroy)', in *Torah of the Earth: Exploring 4,000 Years of Ecology in Jewish Thought. Vol. 1 Biblical Israel: One Land, One People. Rabbinic Judaism: One People, Many Lands*, ed. Arthur Waskow, 96–102. Woodstock, VT: Jewish Lights Publishing.

Tazmini G. 2018. "To Be or Not to Be' (Like the West): Modernisation in Russia and Iran', *Third World Quarterly,* vol. 39, no. 10, 1998–2015.

Tirosh-Samuelson H. 2017. 'Jewish Environmental Ethics', in *The Wiley Blackwell Companion to Religion and Ecology*, ed. John Hart, 179–94. Hoboken, NJ: Wiley & Sons.

Tsimpo C. & Q. Wodon. 2016. 'Faith Affiliation, Religiosity, and Attitudes Towards the Environment and Climate Change', *The Review of Faith and International Affairs*, vol. 14, no. 3, 51–64.

Wackernagel M. & W. E. Rees. 1996. *Our Ecological Footprint: Reducing Human Impact on the Earth*. Gabriola Island, B.C.: New Society Publishers.

Waskow A. October 12, 2018. 'Three Perspectives on Our Current Crisis', Keynote Panel at JOFEE Network Gathering.

Waskow A. 1992. 'What Is Eco Kosher?', *Jewish Quarterly*, vol. 39, no. 4, 5–10.

White L. 1967. 'The Historical Roots of Our Ecologic Crisis,' *Science*, vol. 155, no. 3767, 1203–7.

Yoreh T. 2010a. 'Environmental Embarrassment: Genesis 1:28 vs. Genesis 2:15', in *Vixens Disturbing Vineyards: Embarrassment and Embracement of Scriptures*, eds. Aubrey Glazer, Justin Lewis & Tzemah Yoreh, 558–91. Boston, MA: Academic Studies Press.

Yoreh T. 2010b. 'Ultra-Orthodox Recycling Narratives: Implications for Planning and Policy', *Journal of Enterprising Communities: People and Places in the Global Economy*, vol. 4, no. 4, 323–45.

Yoreh T. 2019a. 'Consumption, Wastefulness, and Simplicity in Ultra-Orthodox Communities', *Studies in Judaism, Humanities and the Social Sciences*, vol. 2, no. 2, 137–52.

Yoreh T. 2019b. *Waste Not: A Jewish Environmental Ethic*. Albany, NY: SUNY Press.

Zafrani H. & J. Vale. 1999. 'The Judaeo-Muslim Cultural World in Morocco: Written and Spoken', *Diogenes*, vol. 47, no. 187, 71–82.

Chapter 13

Confronting Environmental Crisis

What Do Orthodox Christian Traditions Teach about Using the World?

Elizabeth Theokritoff

Out of a growing literature on Orthodox Christian theology and practice in relation to environmental questions, we will focus here on an aspect of the tradition that is at once obvious, and often misunderstood: the ascetic tradition. This is an area where Orthodoxy has retained certain features that would have been common across the Christian world for most of Christian history:

1. Ascetic discipline, especially in the form of fasting, as a prominent part of everyday Christian life;
2. Close relations between Christians 'in the world' and monastic communities;
3. A sense of connection with saints, ancient and modern – many of them people who manifest the fruits of ascetic life and often leave their mark on places that have been transformed through their holiness.

In referring to monastic life, we should note that asceticism does not equate to monasticism: it is the common vocation of all Christians. But monks and nuns are certainly in the vanguard, the masters of the practice. And monastic communities provide examples of the sort of society that arises out of ascetic striving. Ascetic practice transforms relationships among people, but also between people and the natural world, because it transforms one's vision of the world. So it is no coincidence that in the Orthodox Church at least,

134   *Elizabeth Theokritoff*

monastic communities have also taken the lead in making environmental initiatives part of their everyday life.

First, there is an obvious but misleading connection between asceticism and our response to the environmental crisis. It was recognised early on that there is a remarkable coincidence between the ascetic practices of fasting and restraint of our appetites for material things, and the way of living habitually advocated by ecologists: 'Asceticism offers practical examples of conservation. By reducing our consumption – what in Orthodox theology we call *enkrateia* or self-control – we seek to ensure that resources are left to others in the world. . . . Asceticism provides an example whereby we may live simply' (Chryssavgis 2003: 219). Asceticism teaches us to 'walk lightly on the earth' and distinguish wants from needs, providing an antidote to a consumerist approach to the world (e.g., Metropolitan Kallistos, 1996).

It is of course quite true that some ascetic practices have direct, practical environmental benefits. Orthodox Christian fasting rules enjoin a vegan diet for approximately half the year: and if any such pattern, or simply the Orthodox practice of two fast days a week, were widely adopted in the developed world, it would significantly reduce our human ecological and carbon footprint. But the aim of fasting as an ascetic discipline is not to eat from lower on the food chain, but to cut off our self-will and conquer our self-love, our self-indulgence. Asceticism most certainly has practical implications – but less because of its techniques, more because it forms persons who are not hostage to their own desires. Metropolitan Kallistos (1996) sums this up by saying, 'Lent is a time when we learn to be free'. We become free to act out of self-giving love; but even beyond that, ceasing to look at our natural environment primarily through the lens of our own needs and wants transforms our *vision* of the world – a point to which we will return later.

The connection between asceticism and environmental crisis is based for Orthodox Christians on a deep-seated conviction that the ecological crisis is a symptom of a cosmic spiritual problem. That hostility on the part of our natural environment signals not a direct 'revenge of Gaia', but a rupture in our relationship with its, and our, Creator. We note for instance the use of Leviticus 26: 3–4 and 14–19 in the vespers service for protection of the environment (1 September): the land and the weather will cooperate with us and serve our needs if, and only if, we walk according to the commandments of the Lord. Hence the frequent calls to repentance, *metanoia*, in more homiletic Orthodox writings on the environment. This is not a denial of the immediate, physical causes of environmental damage; rather, it is a conviction that physical causality is but one part of a bigger picture of all things serving the Lord's purposes. In this picture, environmental degradation is a warning sign of sin. This does not correlate directly with the idea that environmental damage is *in itself* sin, which has been much used by Patriarch Bartholomew of Constantinople (Chryssavgis 2003) and enthusiastically adopted by Pope Francis (cf. the encyclical *Laudato Si,* § 8). But it does underline the idea of the natural world as integral to the relationship between God and humans, in both directions. God works through nature not only for our physical benefit but also for our guidance and chastisement; and we relate to Him through our attitude to material creation and our treatment of it.

This is reflected in the liturgical life of the Orthodox Church. Great Lent, the forty-day fast which is the most sustained ascetic effort for nonmonastic Christians, is immediately preceded by commemoration of the expulsion of Adam from Paradise. The fast is at once an expression of repentance and a return to the paradisal way of life: 'If we had fasted, we should never have been banished from Paradise', as St Basil says crisply (*On Fasting* Hom. 1.4, PG 31, 168B).

Church Fathers and modern writers alike have noticed that in Genesis, the difference between life in paradise and expulsion from paradise hinges on the way man uses the world as food. Is our eating, that most fundamental use of the world, a means of communion with God? Or will it be a way of asserting independence from God and opting for what seems to us 'good to eat'? Accordingly, fasting in Orthodox Christian practice is not an individual choice to 'give something up'. Fasting *and feasting* in the church mean that our most basic connection to the world on which we depend physically is not something private, but part of a relationship – with God, in the community of the church, through our attitude to and treatment of the rest of His creation.

The commands given to the first-created man about what to eat and not to eat are often interpreted by the church fathers in this sense: even our most fundamental relationship with the material world has to do above all with our relationship with the Creator. We find a useful summary of earlier patristic thought in St John of Damascus, who does not focus primarily on the prohibition of the one tree. Instead, he offers an eloquent interpretation of the positive command given to man, when God says, 'Let him eat of *every* tree': here, according to John, the Lord alludes to Himself who is *all* in *all*: 'Through all things [God is saying], ascend to me the Creator; from every tree harvest one fruit, namely me who am the life. Let all things bear the fruit of life for you: make participation in me the stuff of your own existence. Thus you will be immortal' (*On the Orthodox Faith* II.11 [25]).

John further identifies this 'eating of every tree' with the knowledge of God through his creatures which Paul talks about in the Epistle to the Romans; the way we perceive his 'eternal power and deity . . . in the things that have been made' (Rom 1.20). There is an echo here of St Gregory the Theologian, who describes the Lord creating Adam and placing him in paradise 'to till immortal plants, by which is perhaps meant the divine ideas' (Hom. 38, *On Theophany*, 12; Hom. 45, *On Easter*, 8). What Adam is to 'cultivate' is the ultimate meaning of things, the rationales according to which God has created them – what St Maximus the Confessor will later call their *logoi*. This does not exclude literally cultivating the land; but whatever man does with the world should at the same time teach him to perceive the Creator ever more clearly through it. This is the way of life which man was created to grow into. The fall, for Damascene, consists in a rejection of this contemplative dimension to our relationship with the physical world. The tree of knowledge thus represents physical, hedonistic eating, a surrender to the *natural* connection to things which man was intended to transcend. The fall thus solidifies man in his animal nature. He becomes merely a top predator, a 'consumer' of physical resources to satisfy his appetites.

Another patristic interpretation of 'tilling and keeping' makes explicit the connection with God's law and commandment – this was all that Adam in paradise needed to 'keep' (e.g., Ephrem the Syrian, *On Genesis* II.7; Brock 1990: 201–2). It is a short step from this to seeing the ascetic life as itself a tilling and keeping of the soil of the heart (an image that goes back to the fourth-century Macarian Homilies [Plested 2015: 172]) – only now in a world where that soil too is overgrown with thorns and thistles. 'Compunction is a "tilling" and a "keeping"', says the great Abba Poemen of the Egyptian desert (Poemen 39; Ward 1975: 145). It is in this sense that the ascetic is 'involved in a mighty battle against nature', meaning fallen human nature (Makarios 1992: 42). The passions that we struggle to transform include attachment to things, the sort of dysfunctional love that makes us hungry to possess and control. But there are also very important but less obvious ways in which ascetic discipline affects our response to environmental crises – the battle, for instance, against pride and self-will. We need to be on our guard not only against unnecessary consumption, but equally against any temptation to 'greener-than-thou' self-righteousness. Cutting off my own will may mean on occasion not insisting on *my* environmental agenda.

The traditional tool against self-will is obedience. And this may be the area where we can speak most accurately of an ecological asceticism, a way in which the present environmental crisis presents itself as an ascetic challenge. When it demands changes in aspects of life that we in the developed world have come to take for granted, these can become 'occasions for obedience in everyday life', in the words of Tito Colliander's wonderful handbook *The Way of the Ascetics* (Colliander 1983). We are increasingly aware (not before time) of the impact of our most mundane and seemingly trivial choices on distant parts of the earth and on future generations. Limitations imposed by limited natural resources, or land, or the environmental cost of energy generation are all things that can be used to discipline our wants, in obedience to the needs of those with whom we share the earth. To be sure, an ecological asceticism practised in this way brings new challenges. We hear of hermits avoiding the tyranny of worldly cares by buying the cheapest and most readily available items – but what to do if we know that those are precisely the most likely to be produced by exploited workers labouring amidst environmental and other hazards? In a globalised world, living simply can get quite complicated, and we shall doubtless make mistakes. But I would suggest that the core principle stands: even personal decisions about what we eat, what we buy, how and how much we travel, are not dependent simply on individual whim. They afford ways for nonmonastic Christians to learn what it means to live in community.

Asceticism, then, involves seeking obedience and service in our everyday choices. However dramatic its ultimate impact, it is not a matter of *setting out to* change the world or 'make a difference'. In the striking words of a contemporary monastic writer, 'My spiritual life begins when I realise that it is I, not another, who is the cause of the corruption in nature' (Makarios 1992: 43). It is thus a journey of self-knowledge. Dominion over the beasts starts with the 'wild beasts' within us; and it takes only a few mild skirmishes with these to recognise our limitations and our utter dependence on God's grace and mercy, like all other creatures. This is the beginning of the universal compassion and sense of the oneness of mankind that is so marked in the great ascetics (notable for instance in Fr Sophrony of Essex (1896–1993); see Sakharov 2002, esp. 99, 117–42). This sense of solidarity in creaturely frailty makes us aware, certainly, of our fellowship with those less fortunate, including those worst affected by environmental damage. But it makes us equally aware of our fellowship with all those others who also find it an uphill struggle to give up our comfortable way of life and the material security we have been led to expect. The first luxury we have to forgo, therefore, is that of seeing ourselves as the righteous and someone else as 'the problem' or 'the enemy' – climate change deniers, oil company executives, agri-businessmen, the older generation. . . .

Isaac the Syrian, one of the greatest of ascetic teachers, speaks of the blessing of knowing our own weakness (Homily 8; Holy Transfiguration Monastery tr. 1984). 'Asceticism, far from being a heroic or ecstatic journey, is for Isaac a profound learning of one's passibility, which makes of the solitary a creature capable of solidarity with the whole suffering creation' (Duca 2016: 438). It also allows him or her to recognise the strength of God's help. This is in sharp contrast with the prevailing environmental rhetoric, which may be outspoken about the damage done by human activities, but paradoxically then puts all its hope in what humans *can* achieve by their own efforts, if only they put their minds to it. The temptation is thus to measure what *my* efforts are able to achieve against the scale of the problems. It is perhaps not surprising that this leads to an epidemic of 'eco–anxiety', panic and despair. Christian ascetic endeavour removes the anguish about the obvious disparity. The paradoxical reassurance of knowing our limitations is nicely summed up

138   *Elizabeth Theokritoff*

in the titles of consecutive chapters in Colliander's *Way of the Ascetics:* 'On a resolute and sustained purpose' and 'On the insufficiency of human strength' (Colliander 1983).

Asceticism, to sum up, is a way of transforming *persons.* But it is precisely this inward labour that leads to such far-reaching practical effects. As no less a climate campaigner than Christiana Figueres acknowledges, 'Systemic change is a deeply personal endeavour. Our social and economic structures are a product of our way of thinking' (Figueres & Rivett-Carnac 2020: 50). But more fundamental than our way of *thinking* is our way of *seeing.* The ascetic way clarifies and thus radically changes our vision of creation, and it is this that transforms the way we relate to other creatures (our natural environment). Ascetic practice thus creates what the French theologian Olivier Clément calls a 'wondering and respectful distance' between us and the world (Clément 1993, 141). Some environmentalists would immediately pounce on any such idea of 'distance', associating it with a separation of man from other creatures, a sort of human exceptionalism that they see as the root cause of misuse of the natural environment. This is not the place to unpack that line of thinking, except to point out that it reveals a narrowly anthropocentric frame of reference. Orthodox thinking starts from the perspective that 'the earth is the Lord's and the fullness thereof', so that creatures all share the property of existing primarily in relation to God – relationships *among* creatures can be understood only on the basis of that primary relationship. Distance, in Clément's sense, is precisely what enables the perspective of each creature existing in itself and for its Creator, beyond and prior to any ecosystem services it might provide to us. It is not simply 'good to eat', in the language of Genesis, but a creature with its own integrity and dignity, existing for God's purposes and only secondarily for ours. Clément refers back to Christ fasting in the wilderness to teach that 'man does not live by bread alone, but by every word that proceeds from the mouth of God' (Mt 4:4), but then he adds the twist: 'and the world also is a word that comes from the mouth of God' (Clément 1993: 141).

This captures perfectly what we can call a contemplative vision of the world. Saying 'contemplative' does not imply that we simply look at the world and admire its beauty: in the vocabulary of the Greek Fathers, *theoria* (contemplation) refers also to a spiritual interpretation of Scripture. So a contemplative vision is one that gives an additional layer of meaning to everything that makes up our environment, and all the interactions with it on which our physical life depends. No longer is there any such thing as 'bread alone': nothing, natural or manufactured, exists only as resources for our consumption, however abstemiously and wisely.

Confronting Environmental Crisis

Clément's imagery here takes us directly to the understanding of creation elaborated most fully by one of the great ascetic writers, St Maximus the Confessor, which helps elucidate the connection between ascetic practice and a transformed vision of all creation. The world is 'a word that comes from the mouth of God' in that all things are created by the Word (Logos) of God. And this creation 'in word (*logos*) and wisdom' (Wisd 9:1–2) means that each thing is created according to its own 'word' (principle, rationale) of existence, its inmost reality. It is in these 'words' that the Creator Word is present in all things, even as he is infinitely beyond everything according to his own nature (Maximus, *Ambiguum* 22, PG 91: 1257A). Human beings are created to be able to 'tune in' to these words, to read the divine Word written in the letters of everything created through him. This is integral to what it means to say that man is 'rational', *logikos*; he participates in God's Word in a special way (creation 'according to the Image' of God is understood in this sense) (cf. Louth 2004: 189). Human 'logos' is seen as distinguishing us from other animals, even those capable of reasoning; but it equally enables us to perceive in them the echoes of the Word who is our own archetype. This capacity to discern the words, the inner meanings, of things is obscured in us as long as we are at the mercy of the disordered appetites and desires that cause us to 'see the world in relation to *our*selves and read into it *our* meaning' (Louth 1996: 37). This is why Maximus can say, strikingly, that 'virtues exist for the sake of the knowledge of created things' (*Centuries on Love* 3:45). Human nature as it is intended to be, including this 'knowledge of created things', is restored in Christ; and as Maximus says, the Word of God is constantly working to accomplish in each of us the mystery of His embodiment (*Ambiguum* 7, PG 91: 1084CD). Ascetic purification is the way we cooperate in this work, making room, as it were, for the Word of God to be embodied in us. In the words of one distinguished Maximus scholar, the spiritual life is 'a micro-drama of the larger macro-drama of salvation', whereby we participate in the transfiguration of the cosmos in Christ (Blowers & Wilken 2003:38).

'Transfiguration' is not something we do to the world: to participate in it means that we come to recognise it. To refer yet again to Maximus, it is those whose senses are purified that see and hear with the mind 'the ineffable and supernatural divine fire present in the essence of things as in a burning bush' (*Ambiguum* 10, PG 91: 1148CD). One of the great ascetic elders of our day, Aemilianos of Simonopetra, gives us a telling gloss on St Maximus's commentary on the transfiguration of Christ:

> According to St Maximus the Confessor, this vesture which is resplendent with 'a dazzling whiteness' (Luke 9:29) comprises the *logoi* of creation, that is, the ontological roots of created being, which have found their fulfilment, their *recapitulation,* in the divine–human person of the Word of God incarnate.

140 *Elizabeth Theokritoff*

> The elements of the natural world . . . become supple, luminous, bearers of the Spirit, and convey thus to humanity the radiance of God's glory. (Aemilianos 1996: 200)

When Elder Aemilianos speaks of the elements of the natural world conveying to humanity the radiance of God's glory, he is talking about – and from – the experience of *natural contemplation*. Referring to this 'essential category in Orthodox spiritual terminology for the relationship of man with the environment', another contemporary monk writes: 'Thus a person who has purified himself and been illumined with grace will have a unique perspective on how to live in the created world, one informed by his enlightened perception. . . . a unitary experience of the synergy of all created beings with the Creator, of which one is a part rather than a[n] . . . observer' (Jonah 2013: 46–47).

Often this synergy is expressed in liturgical terms. Many contemporary Orthodox have adopted with enthusiasm the idea of 'cosmic liturgy', an expression coined by Hans Urs von Balthasar to describe St Maximus's vision of the world (Balthasar 2003).

The full reality of all creation's relationship to its Creator, its offering of prayer and praise, is revealed only to some of the great ascetics and saints – like St Nectarios of Aegina (1846–1920), who was able to hear the grasses praising the Lord, and even through prayer to share the experience with his nuns (Clément 1967: 261). Such perception is far beyond the personal experience of most of us, but it should not be foreign to any Orthodox Christian – it is a reality embedded in Orthodox worship, not least through the Psalms. Just as there is a tradition down the centuries of holy people experiencing cosmic worship first hand, there is also a tradition that the Prophet David was among them. Commenting on the heavens 'telling the glory of God' (Ps. 18/19) and the praise offered by all creation in Psalm 148, Gregory of Nyssa gives the explanation: 'It was *because David had actually heard this hymnody* that he said in one of the Psalms that all the powers of heaven praise the Lord, as well as the light of the stars . . . and everything in creation' (*On the inscriptions to the Psalms* I.3).

The vision of a worshipping cosmos may be clearly represented in liturgical texts, once we know what to look for; but in the absence of contact with people who witness to it from their own experience, the liturgical testimony is easy to overlook or misinterpret. Such witness is not lacking. Long before human interactions with their natural environment were recognised as problematic, holy ascetics gave an example of a way of living that recognises other creatures not as resources, but as fellow servants of the same Lord (see further Theokritoff 2009: 117–53). The lives of the saints abound in stories of dangerous animals and even the elements cooperating with people of holiness, and it is important not to dismiss these as charming legends. In many

Confronting Environmental Crisis   141

contemporary examples, we see not only the same restoration of Adamic 'dominion' but also the attitude to all creation that underlies it. There is a saying from the Fathers of Mount Athos that anyone who loves God loves not only his fellow man but the entire creation as well: the trees, the grass, the flowers. *He loves everything with the same love* (Ioannikios 1997: 31).

We might recall the elder Porphyrios (1906–91) counselling his spiritual children to take delight in everything around them; all the plants and animals, and flowers and the elements are 'little loves through which we attain to the great Love that is Christ' (Chrysopigi 2005). To attain holiness is, after all, to grow into the likeness of the new Adam, so that the world round the holy person becomes a paradise, a place where the fruit of 'every tree' is a taste of relationship with God. And where, as Elder Paisios (1924–1994) once told some visitors, 'This grass is an icon; this stone is an icon; and I can kiss it, venerate it, because it is filled with God's grace' (Belopopsky & Oikonomou 1996: 55).

The principle of 'loving everything *with the same love*' is an important one today. For those who are concerned about environmental destruction, there is a real temptation to love 'nature' and see humans as 'the problem', even the real pollution. But we can see the contrast with a saint such as Seraphim of Sarov (1754–1833), who both enjoyed amicable relations with a bear that visited his hermitage and would greet each one of his stream of visitors as 'My joy!'.

The balanced relationship with all our fellow servants, human and otherwise, is something we see not only in individual holy lives but in the very structure of monastic communities, the way in which everyday life is ordered, the use of matter and space and landscape. Its object is not self-indulgence but, as Elder Aemilianos says, 'to render nature a participant in the glory of the children of God, that she may join in their song' (Aemilianos 1996: 205). It is hardly surprising, therefore, that once environmental conservation and sustainability became a focus of attention, several monasteries were pioneers in grafting new ecological practices and technologies into their traditional ways of living. Those under the guidance of Elder Aemilianos were prominent among them – Simonopetra on Mt Athos, Ormylia monastery in Greece, Solan monastery in France. There is a fascinating convergence between new approaches that emphasise a humble listening to nature, such as biomimicry and rewilding (Benyus 1997, Tree 2018), and the receptiveness of the ascetic who has learned to read in the natural environment the words of its Creator. A few monasteries have become involved with environmental projects or educational programmes (e.g., Chrysopigi in Crete – see Theosemni 2018). Many more teach principally by example, like the Monastery of St John the Baptist in central Greece (see http://www.saintjohns–monastery.gr/). Inspired, like Chrysopigi, by the advice of Elder Prophyrios, they have a particular interest

142   *Elizabeth Theokritoff*

in collecting and propagating heritage varieties of vegetable seeds; but the example of lived theology goes far beyond any particular project. The Sisters support themselves from their organic farm, producing dairy products, meat and herbs. Apple trees shelter nesting birds, feeding insects in the spring, and the nuns and their guests through the autumn and winter. Human artefacts also join in the hymn of praise. The wooden stalls in the church, like much of the monastery's furniture, were salvaged from the roadside in the local town; the Sisters worked for days stripping and restoring it. So instead of going to the landfill, the stalls serve in worship once again, glorifying the creator of wood beneath an iconostasis whose upper tier depicts the six days of creation.

BIBLIOGRAPHY

Aemilianos (Archimandrite). 1996. 'The Experience of the Transfiguration in the Life of the Athonite Monk', in *The Living Witness of the Holy Mountain,* ed. A. Golitzin. South Canaan PA: St. Tikhon's Seminary Press.

Balthasar H. U. von 2003. *Cosmic Liturgy: The Universe according to Maximus the Confessor.* San Francisco: Ignatius Press.

Belopopsky A. & D. Oikonomou. 1996. *Orthodoxy and Ecology Resource Book.* Bialystok, Poland: Syndesmos, The World Fellowship of Orthodox Youth.

Benyus J. 1997. *Biomimicry: Innovation Inspired by Nature.* New York: HarperCollins.

Blowers P. & R. Wilken. 2003. *On the Cosmic Mystery of Jesus Christ: Selected Writings from St Maximus the Confessor.* Crestwood, NY: St. Vladimir's Seminary Press.

Brock S. 1990. *St Ephrem the Syrian, Hymns on Paradise.* Crestwood, NY: St. Vladimir's Seminary Press.

Chrysopigi, Sisters of the Holy Convent of, ed. 2005. *Wounded by Love: The Life and Wisdom of Elder Porphyrios.* Limni, Evia: Denise Harvey.

Chryssavgis J. ed. 2003. *Cosmic Grace, Humble Prayer: The Ecological Vision of the Green Patriarch Bartholomew I.* Grand Rapids. MI: Eerdmans.

Clément O. 1967. 'Le sens de la terre (Notes de cosmologie orthodoxe)', *Contacts* 59–60 (1967/3–4): 252–323.

Clément O. 1993. *The Roots of Christian Mysticism.* London: New City.

Colliander T. 1983. *The Way of the Ascetics.* London & Oxford.

Duca V. 2016. 'Human Frailty and Vulnerability in Isaac the Syrian', in M. Vinzent & A. Brent eds. *Studia Patristica* LXXIV: 429–38.

Figueres C. & T. Rivett-Carnac. 2020. *The Future We Choose: Surviving the Climate Crisis.* London: Manila Press.

Holy Transfiguration Monastery, tr. 1984. *The Ascetical Homilies of St Isaac the Syrian.* Boston.

Ioannikios (Archimandrite). 1997. *An Athonite Gerontikon: Saying of the Holy Fathers of Mount Athos,* translated by M. Derpapa Mayson & Sister Theodora (Zion). Kouphalia-Thessaloniki, Greece: St. Gregory Palamas Monastery.

Jonah (Paffhausen). 2013. 'Natural Contemplation in St. Maximus the Confessor and St. Isaac the Syrian', in *Toward an Ecology of Transfiguration: Orthodox Christian Perspectives on Environment, Nature, and Creation*, ed. J. Chryssavgis & B. V. Foltz, 46–58. New York: Fordham University Press.

Kallistos (Metropolitan). 1996. 'Lent and the Consumer Society', in A. Walker & C. Carras, ed. *Living Orthodoxy in the Modern World*, 64–84. London: SPCK.

Louth A. 1996. *Maximus the Confessor.* London: Routledge.

Louth A. 2004. 'The Cosmic Vision of Saint Maximus the Confessor', in *In whom we live and move and have our being: Panentheistic Reflections on God's Presence in a Scientific World*, ed. P. Clayton & A. Peacocke, 184–96. Grand Rapids, MI: Eerdmans.

Makarios (Monk) 1992. 'The Monk and Nature in Orthodox Tradition', in *So That God's Creation Might Live*. 41–48. Constantinople: Ecumenical Patriarchate.

Plested M. 2015. 'The Ascetic Tradition', in *The Oxford Handbook of Maximus the Confessor*, ed. P. Allen & B. Neil, 164–76. Oxford: Oxford University Press.

Sakharov N. 2002. *I love therefore I am: The Theological Legacy of Archimandrite Sophrony.* Crestwood, NY: St. Vladimir's Seminary Press.

Theokritoff E. 2009. *Living in God's Creation: Orthodox Perspectives on Ecology.* Crestwood, NY: St. Vladimir's Seminary Press.

Theosemni, Sister. 'The Protection of the Environment as Applied to the Environmental Education Programme of the Holy Monastery of Chrysopigi, Crete': https://doi.org /10.1111/erev.12397 (Accessed 2 November 2021).

Tree I. 2018. *Wilding: The Return of Nature to a British Farm.* London: Pan Macmillan.

Ward Benedicta, tr. 1975. *The Sayings of the Desert Fathers: The Alphabetical Collection.* London: Mowbrays.

Chapter 14

The Challenge of COVID-19

Reflections of an Orthodox Congregational Rabbi

Michael J. Harris

Sitting in the British Library reading the *Times* one Wednesday lunchtime in December 2019, I noticed a brief article reporting the spread of a new virus in Wuhan, China. Years of reading about potential forthcoming crises of all kinds in the media which never materialised and were never mentioned again have engendered in me, as I suspect in many others, a kind of reflex psychic dismissal of such reports. But something about this particular article disturbed my customary sanguine response. The simple fact of our living nowadays in a global and closely interconnected village suggested that this danger was not one relevant only to a faraway place.

When the COVID-19 pandemic arrived on our shores a short few weeks later, it brought in its wake a host of unwelcome consequences for my congregation, as of course for so many other people around the world. Most serious, as the first wave struck in Spring 2020, was the loss to the disease of several members of our congregation, in each case individuals who had been much-loved by their families and community.

Like other synagogue congregations, we had to face an array of further challenges. Some of our older members were feeling isolated during lockdown and some were unable to shop even for necessities. The several-months-long total closure of our synagogue and adjoining Community Centre buildings, apart from rendering impossible our frequent in-person gatherings for worship as well as educational, social and cultural events, disrupted the natural rhythm of congregational life in which the weekly Shabbat services and social gathering are central. Once again it was more elderly members who

146 *Michael Harris*

were perhaps most affected since many of them derive great benefit from the human contact and community spirit engendered by a Shabbat morning at the synagogue among familiar and friendly faces.

An additional major difficulty, again faced by many others in both the Jewish and wider communities, was the enforced postponement of long-planned joyous occasions marking life-events – in the case of our congregation, weddings and Bar- and Bat-Mitzvahs. After nearly three decades in the communal rabbinate, I have become somewhat cynical about the widespread phenomenon of obsessive focus on every detail of the wedding day, as if it, rather than the marriage it ushers in, were the most important element. Yet I too did not find it difficult to empathise with the stress experienced by loving couples who had long set their sights on a particular wedding date and were now forced to alter their plans, assume further logistical and practical burdens and delay the long-awaited beginning of their married life. The postponement of Bar- and Bat-Mitzvahs was in some respects even more difficult, given that the celebrant is by definition either a thirteen-year-old boy or a twelve-year-old girl who has, moreover, been preparing for many months a section of the public Torah reading or a talk on a section of the Torah which are specific to the particular Shabbat on which they are marking the Bar- or Bat-Mitzvah. There is also the social element of such occasions, frequently spread over a whole weekend with family and friends travelling from afar to enhance the festivities, and most importantly for the young celebrant, being surrounded by his or her own friends. In one instance, a Bar Mitzvah due to take place at our synagogue on a particular Shabbat had to be cancelled when lockdown rules were tightened on the preceding Saturday night. To effectively have a very major birthday party, and one with deep religious significance to boot, indefinitely postponed at a week's notice is a cruel thing for a young person on the cusp of their teens to have to deal with. In the case of the postponed Bar Mitzvah, the ingenuity of the boy's parents in crafting a moving post-Shabbat ceremony on Zoom containing many of the classic elements of a synagogue Bar Mitzvah ceremony succeeded in marking the occasion in a substantive and meaningful way.

The pandemic threw up serious challenges to the traditional Orthodox Jewish practices surrounding death and bereavement. Due to the severe legal restrictions on the number of people permitted to attend funerals, bereaved families often had no alternative but to bury a close relative without the physical presence and support of many extended family members and friends who would have undoubtedly been alongside them under normal circumstances. Moreover, in Jewish tradition, the primary focus at the funeral service itself is the deceased person and paying due respect to that person, with the emphasis shifting to comforting the mourning family only when (though almost immediately after) the burial itself has taken place. Thus, in our congregation as in many others, fine people were laid to rest without being accorded the honour of the large gathering of admirers they deserved accompanying them on their final earthly journey. The traditional Hebrew term for a funeral, *levayah*, literally means just this, accompaniment, and the attenuation of this accompaniment was sad to witness and above all painful for families already suffering from their bereavement itself.

During the first wave of the pandemic in the Spring of 2020, a marker of how badly the London Jewish community was being affected in terms of COVID-19-related deaths was the permission given by some religious authorities for burials to take place, subject to certain restrictions, on the Second Day of Passover because of fear of a backlog of funerals building up – something especially undesirable in Orthodox tradition due to the religious obligation to bury the dead as promptly as possible. Although technically burials are permitted in Jewish Law on the Second Day of a Festival, such an event is an extremely rare occurrence nowadays, certainly in the major Orthodox Jewish cemeteries in London, since by Rabbinic Law the many restrictions attaching biblically to the First Day of a Festival apply, outside Israel, to the Second Day also. Thus many forms of work are prohibited, as well as standard modes of travel such as car or public transport. In practice, therefore, burials on the Second Day of a Festival are avoided as they throw up serious logistical and practical challenges preventing many of those who would wish to attend being able to do so. The conditional permission for Second Day burials at Passover 2020 was a sure sign of the gravity of the pandemic situation.

As soon as the funeral is complete, the focus of the Jewish laws of mourning shifts to the mourners and to comforting and supporting them. The distinctive and central Jewish practice in this connection is *shiva*, literally meaning 'seven', when the immediate relatives of the deceased person remain at home, usually all of them together in the home of the deceased or in one of their own homes. They are visited and comforted throughout the days of the *shiva* (seven by inclusive counting, usually including the day of the funeral and a very small segment of the seventh day), by family and friends. Family and friends traditionally provide meals and take care of the needs of the mourners so that they have the time and space to begin the grieving process and to be nurtured by the love and support of those close to them. For the mourning family (defined for the purposes of Jewish legal obligation as a parent, spouse, sibling or child of the deceased), the *shiva* constitutes the first and most intense stage of the mourning process, one during which many restrictions on the normal conduct of life apply. Throughout my many years as a communal rabbi, countless congregants have remarked on how therapeutic they found the experience of *shiva* to be.

The pandemic restrictions have usually made the traditional visits to mourners during the *shiva* impossible, other than in cases in which an appropriate outdoor space such as a private garden have been available. The physical embrace of the mourners by family and friends has in most instances had to be replaced with as much love and empathy as can be communicated in online gatherings or over the phone. The 'Zoom Shiva' has become a feature of Jewish communal life. But the full healing force of the powerful institution of *shiva* has in significant ways been blunted.

Nevertheless, in other respects the pandemic restrictions have sometimes seemed, paradoxically, to enhance the spiritual and religious calibre of Jewish mourning practices. I have long noticed, as I am sure have many other rabbis and indeed clergy of other faiths, that funeral gatherings in normal times, while almost always decorous and dignified, inevitably contain a social element. Family, friends and acquaintances, some of whom might not have seen each other for some time, are likely to be present, and a fair measure of *sotto voce* (and even insufficiently *sotto voce*) social 'catching up' takes place, particularly on the often five- or ten-minute walk from the cemetery prayer hall (where the funeral service commences) to the graveside and back. With an enforced smaller attendance at funerals, at times during the pandemic limited to the immediate family and the rabbi, I have noticed that family members were able to focus without distraction on the proceedings and on saying farewell to their loved one, something of which they were often conscious and appreciative. In a similar vein but in still sharper relief, congregational rabbis are keenly aware of how the inevitable social element of the *shiva* can frequently overwhelm the proceedings. A rabbinic friend and colleague, looking at night in an unfamiliar street for a *shiva* house at which he is due to lead the prayers, reports that he is often guided to the correct address by the loud noise of conversation, as if a party were being held. A far cry indeed from the religious requirement that a *shiva* visitor must not speak until the mourner has spoken first, and from the ancient practice of sitting on the floor alongside the mourning family. The 'Zoom shiva' service, while denying the mourners the huge benefit of the physical presence of loved ones, is inevitably far more focused, eliminates the 'social gathering' element and has sometimes seemed, again not infrequently to the mourners themselves, more meaningful than the in-person *shiva* prayer services of pre-pandemic times.

An additional, more obvious benefit of online *shiva* prayers or gatherings has been the simple fact that people who find it inconvenient or difficult to leave home have been able to participate and to communicate with the mourning family, as indeed have extended family members and friends from abroad.

A major impact on traditional Jewish mourning practices during the pandemic surrounds the recitation of the Kaddish prayer. Kaddish is recited by a member or members of the deceased's close family for a little under one year following death. It is then recited every year on what, in Ashkenazi Jewish tradition, is known as the *yahrzeit*, the anniversary of the death. Although some authoritative Jewish legal sources insist that the recitation of Kaddish is not the most important way of honouring the deceased, insisting that the most important means is by living an upright life (Ganzfried 1864: 26:22), Kaddish exercises an extremely powerful hold on the Jewish religious imagination. If the opportunity to recite Kaddish is denied, a relative will sometimes feel that they are not doing their duty to the deceased. In classical Jewish Law as followed in most contemporary Orthodox communities, however, Kaddish, as a prayer of special sanctity, may be recited only in the presence of a quorum, a *minyan*, defined as a minimum of ten Jewish males above the age of Bar Mitzvah. During periods of the pandemic in which government restrictions prohibited the gathering of such a number, the recitation of Kaddish became impossible for many Orthodox Jews who followed the consensus of rabbinic authorities that a quorum can be constituted only in person and not online. I, like many of my Orthodox rabbinic colleagues, encountered congregants who were deeply upset about this issue. One solution suggested was the recitation of a medieval version of Kaddish which does not require a quorum. A remedy that I personally preferred to offer to congregants was the traditional alternative to Kaddish of studying some short passages of rabbinic law in memory of the deceased. But it is certainly a relief to many that quorate synagogue services have, at the time of writing, resumed, albeit with social distancing and masks, so that Kaddish can be recited in the normal way as well as enjoying the other religious and communal advantages of near-normal regular prayer services.

Turning from rituals surrounding life-events to the routine life of the community, very many key regular activities had to be rethought and reframed. In common with many other congregations, ours took full advantage of Zoom and other online platforms to run adult education programmes and social and cultural events virtually when doing so in-person was impossible. Although, quite obviously, the warmth of real human contact is lacking in such settings, as well as, for a person taking a class or leading a discussion, the energy one draws from a live audience, there were compensations in terms of accessibility, especially for older and more frail synagogue members who even in normal times might be reluctant to physically attend an evening programme at the Synagogue. For very many such events, the attendance was significantly higher than at parallel pre-pandemic in-person events, in large measure due to the desire to connect with the community in difficult times but in part also for the more mundane reason of convenience – no travel time to and from the Synagogue, no deterrent of inclement weather, and everything available from the comfort of one's own home with a few clicks of the mouse. Textual discussion in online adult education sessions, initially difficult, worked increasingly well as people became used to the technology of shared screens, and a real sense developed of multiple pairs of eyes focusing on the same text, bringing their unique perspectives to bear upon it. We also ran an international day of Jewish learning online in partnership with JW3, the Jewish Community Centre in London, featuring lecturers from Israel, North America and the UK – something which would have been much more logistically complex and financially costly to achieve at an in-person event. I have noticed, as pandemic restrictions have lifted and at least some physical gatherings have become permissible, how congregants seem now to nevertheless often prefer educational events and classes online. Online educational programmes look like they are here to stay, and it seems clear that 'blended' educational and other communal events available both in-person and via video-conferencing will become increasingly popular.

During lockdown periods when our synagogue building was completely closed, the continuation of the weekly Shabbat service of worship, the centrepiece of congregational life in normal times, posed a particular problem because of the very wide consensus among Orthodox Jewish legal authorities that online activities may not take place on Shabbat. We were able to provide a kind of substitute for the traditional Friday evening service by holding a weekly Friday afternoon online gathering before the commencement of Shabbat featuring some of the Friday evening liturgy, but for the lengthier Shabbat morning service there was not much that could be done other than sending out detailed weekly guidance to the congregation on how to recite the Shabbat morning prayers at home without a *minyan* and offering some thoughts on the weekly Torah reading which sadly could not take place in the Synagogue using the Torah Scrolls.

I have already identified several 'silver linings' compensating in some measure for the many difficulties facing congregational life during the pandemic, but others are also worthy of mention. The pandemic enriched my own Jewish legal knowledge and our communal adult education classes by throwing up a range of fascinating issues that tend to be overlooked in normal times. Some examples: (1) In Orthodox congregations, the text of the Torah, that is, Genesis through to Deuteronomy inclusive, is divided into weekly portions which are read from the Torah scroll in the synagogue every Shabbat in such a way as to complete the reading of the whole Torah annually. If the synagogue is closed for several months and therefore the weekly public Torah readings cannot take place, should the missed readings be made up once services are able to resume? (2) Under normal circumstances, a number of people are individually honoured at the public Torah reading by being called to the Torah, standing next to the reader and reciting the traditional blessings. Can this be done when social distancing rules are in force and if not, is some valid alternative available in Jewish Law? (3) In normal circumstances, Orthodox

The Challenge of COVID-19 151

communal prayer requires a *minyan*, meaning, as mentioned earlier, a quorum of ten Jewish males aged thirteen or above. What are the spatial constraints on a quorum? If, for example, pandemic regulations permit only six people to gather together in an outside space, can two groups of six in adjoining front or back gardens or standing on adjacent balconies be considered as if they are in one synagogue or one room? (4) On the Festival of Purim, the Book of Esther is read publicly from a scroll in the synagogue or in other settings. The traditional requirement of Jewish Law is that one must hear the reading in person. What happens when synagogues are closed or gatherings of more than a handful of people are prohibited? Does listening to someone read from the scroll on Zoom count as hearing the reading? If so, must one hear the reading live or is a recording sufficient? (5) A broader, historical issue: how were the ramifications of epidemics, pandemics and plagues for traditional Jewish practice handled by Jewish legal authorities in previous generations? The famous scholar Rabbi Akiva Eiger (1761–1837), for example, rabbi of Posen during the second cholera pandemic that lasted from 1829 until 1837, wrote a number of important letters on this topic (Reichman 2020).

From a philosophical perspective, the pandemic brought the problem of evil to the forefront of many people's minds. Orthodox tradition has a wide array of responses to the problem, drawing from interpretations of the Book of Job, Talmudic and medieval discussions, and contemporary thinkers. The many approaches are not only different from each other but often mutually exclusive. The pandemic invited reflection in adult education classes on this rich and nuanced literature.

A further silver lining related to the cycle of the traditional Jewish festivals. While, on the negative side of the ledger, celebration in the synagogue was restricted and indeed entirely impossible when the synagogue was closed, and at home the welcoming of guests was prohibited or severely limited, there were some positive outcomes. At our Passover Seder at home, usually happily crowded with family and guests, having to confine ourselves to our household enabled my wife and I to focus more on interacting with our teen-age son. In a similar vein, whereas we usually hold an all-night Torah study session at the synagogue on the Festival of Shavuot in commemoration of the revelation at Sinai, my son and me were able to study on Shavuot night just with each other (though whether he enjoyed it as much as I did is open to question). On Chanukah, the Jewish legal requirement to light the nightly candles specifically in one's home has become somewhat overshadowed by the recent fashion of lighting the Chanukah *menorah* (candelabrum) in all kinds of venues, including even Trafalgar Square and Downing Street. Pandemic restrictions on Chanukah meant that the *menorah* lighting reverted to being, as tradition requires, a home-focused practice.

Paradoxically, too, there were even some in-person festival gatherings which would not have taken place in normal times. The central religious obligation of the New Year, Rosh Hashanah, is to hear the blowing of the *shofar*, the ram's horn. In previous years, we had always simply performed the blowing during the synagogue service and catered for those who wished to hear the blowing but were too unwell or frail to attend by visiting them at home. In a situation in which capacity in the synagogue was restricted on Rosh Hashanah because of social distancing requirements and in which many congregants felt unsafe attending an indoor venue in any case, we had to consider how to facilitate the hearing of the *shofar* for the majority of the congregation who would not hear it at the synagogue. We therefore arranged a *shofar* blowing on Rosh Hashanah afternoon in the outside forecourt of our local Jewish Community Centre. We also organised one for later in the afternoon outside my house, simply by advertising it on our street's Whatsapp group. To see neighbours and friends from our local area, as well as other people whom I had never met before, gathered (while socially distant) around our home to fulfil the key tradition of Rosh HaShanah in such unusual circumstances was one of the most moving things I have witnessed in my rabbinic career.

Yet another silver lining – one which was of course evident across large swathes of society – consisted in the many acts of extraordinary interpersonal kindness and generosity sparked by the adversity of COVID-19. Selfless volunteers in our congregation shopped, cooked and delivered food for synagogue members and others who needed assistance. The community gave generously to a special fund set up to help people through the crisis. Another set of volunteers worked the phones, reaching out to those who were isolated and often striking up new friendships. Paradoxically, the bonds of community in our congregation have been in many ways strengthened rather than weakened by the exigencies of the pandemic.

Two further beneficial outcomes of the reorienting of Jewish life enforced by the pandemic may have a long-term positive impact. First and quite simply, many have observed that some things that seemed necessary or important pre-pandemic have been shown not to be, and indeed Jewish communal life is better off without them. The enormous success of online fund-raising campaigns for a host of good causes showed that grand charity fund-raising dinners are not the only or even the best way of recruiting charitable support. In a broadly similar vein, while the proper celebration of a wedding or Bar/ Bat Mitzvah is totally appropriate and indeed encouraged from a religious perspective, overelaborate and ostentatious festivities are not, and the mandatory scaled-down nature of many such events during the pandemic served at some level as a salutary reminder that it is the life-event itself, rather than its excessive celebration, which is the proper focus. Secondly, as rabbis never tire of emphasizing, Judaism is primarily a religion of the home rather than the synagogue. It is the home which is the main focus of central religious practices and home which is the key factor in transmitting Jewish tradition intergenerationally. The retreat into the home when synagogues were closed was therefore in some ways a helpful indication of which institution ultimately matters more.

Finally, a personal reflection on how I have found the pandemic period impacting on my life as a congregational rabbi. Maintaining the necessary physical and mental stamina for a job in which free evenings or weekends are very rare is challenging at the best of times. In worse times it is more difficult still, especially when the opportunities for travel and a change of scene are very restricted. Like many other ministers of religion, I cancelled several planned breaks during the pandemic period due to unwillingness to be unavailable when I felt I was needed by my community. I have no regrets, but there is inevitably a price in terms of loss of perspective, narrowing of horizons and missing out on the richly re-energizing nature of time away, particularly when spent in a location with deep religious resonance, such as the Holy Land.

As I write these words in the Summer of 2021, with the United Kingdom about to jettison most legal restrictions surrounding COVID-19 but the path forward far from assured, one can only pray with the psalmist that God release us fully from narrow and confined spaces and bring us into the broad expanses of a brighter future.

BIBLIOGRAPHY

Ganzfried S. 1864. *Kitzur Shulhan Arukh.* Uzhhorod.
Reichman E. 2020. 'From Cholera to Coronavirus: Recurring Pandemics, Recurring Rabbinic Responses'. *Tradition*: https://traditiononline.org/from-cholera-to -coronavirus-recurring-pandemics-recurring-rabbinic-responses/

Chapter 15

The Challenge of COVID-19 to Rituals around Death in Orthodoxy

Ian Graham

In the last eighteen months or so the COVID-19 pandemic has forced many changes of social practice in many societies. 'Lockdown' and 'social distancing' have entered our vocabulary, and the realities to which those words point have inevitably had significant impact on the ways in which we live and express ourselves. Spiritual life and practice have not been exempt, coming under direct and explicit regulation from both our national government(s) and our religious authorities in ways that would formerly have been unthinkable in our liberal democracies. In all the time of the pandemic I have not had to confront the direct consequences of COVID-19 – I know of only one person under my pastoral responsibility who tested positive for the illness, and they suffered it only in a mild form – and so the thoughts I offer here relate more to the generalities than to the specifics. I have, however, consulted with a number of my colleagues, some of whom have had more direct experience than I. I hope, therefore, that what I write here will reflect a wider view than the perspective of one parish priest, although still parochial, as I can speak only of how things unfolded in the UK, and specifically in England.

As, through early March 2020, the UK government advanced towards the first lockdown the churches moved in step with it. Thus, for example, when the prime minister announced on March 16 that those with COVID symptoms should stay at home for fourteen days, and that those who were COVID free should avoid unnecessary travel and social contact, the Archdiocese of Thyateira and Great Britain, under the jurisdiction of the Ecumenical Patriarchate of Constantinople, issued guidance to its clergy that all activities other than religious services were suspended at all churches. On March 19, when the prime minister reiterated the advice to practise social distancing, and said that he thought 'the tide could be turned within the next twelve weeks', the archdiocese issued further advice that all services other than the Sunday Liturgy (which was to be served without a congregation) should be postponed. An exception was made in the case of funerals (and also some baptisms), but at these only the immediate family was permitted to be present. The archiepiscopal announcement closing the churches indefinitely was issued on March 24, the day after the prime minister had instituted the first national lockdown.

The most notable effect here was, of course, the restriction of those attending funerals to close family only. Although many funerals are, in practice, private affairs, the Orthodox principle is that no service of the Church is restricted, and many funerals are indeed (in 'normal' times) corporate celebrations. Both in its social, Mediterranean roots and in its theology Orthodoxy sees the Church as a society, a body, and as each organ rejoices with those who celebrate so each grieves with those who mourn. The lockdown regulations made such expressions of solidarity impossible, and this was so, be it noted, whatever the cause of death. To some extent this problem may have been partially resolved in the later stages of the response to the pandemic by the possibility of streaming services via Zoom or another platform (I celebrated a funeral in the Spring of 2021 which involved the participation of an Outside Broadcast team whose leader told me they had diversified from such events as the British Grand Prix at Silverstone). But in the early days many churches lacked the facilities and the skill for such broadcasting, and this has by no means ceased to be a problem.

Then there are the practical questions connected with the celebration of a funeral. One of the most notable features of a traditional Orthodox Christian funeral is the fact that the coffin is open throughout the service until at the end family, friends and faithful give the departed a final farewell kiss. Only then is the coffin closed and taken for burial. Even before the COVID crisis there were many funerals in which the open coffin did not feature. Sometimes this was because the undertakers refused to allow it on 'health and safety' grounds. But more commonly it was because the family, or some of its members, had absorbed the general British distaste for viewing corpses. This was often expressed as 'We don't want to upset the children', but it was often clear that the adults were even more upset than the hypothetical children at the prospect. Here the regulations surrounding COVID have perhaps confirmed and strengthened a trend that was already apparent. In my own experience undertakers have continued to vary in their approach to the question of an open coffin, although some are now citing the need to protect people from the threat of COVID as a reason for having a closed coffin. But many families have made the connection themselves, and expressed relief that the traditional path need not or cannot be followed. The same differences and tensions have been apparent in the question of the provision of an earth box at the graveside which is supposed to be used by the priest to sprinkle earth on the coffin in the grave, and is often (again in 'normal' times) then used by family and friends as another farewell gesture. Flower petals provided by the family have sometimes formed an acceptable alternative in the undertakers' eyes, but carry a different symbolic resonance.

The final kiss, whether delivered to the corpse or to the closed coffin has, of course, not been permitted during the lockdowns, and this, too, may have accelerated an already existing trend. In traditional Orthodox societies many things which are seen as conveying sanctity are kissed: icons, bibles, the priest's or bishop's hand, etc. But all of this is counter to British habit, and I have noticed that at funerals people seem increasingly to prefer to make their farewells from where they are standing or sitting without any overt gesture.

In some (especially Slavic) Orthodox traditions the funeral service is celebrated with richly harmonised choral singing (think of the funeral scenes in *Doctor Zhivago* or *The Deer Hunter*). The prohibition on choral singing has therefore led some people to question whether their loved one has been given a 'real' funeral or memorial service. This has been less of a problem in traditions such as those of the Greek or Arab Orthodox, where a single cantor is fairly common.

As there was never a prohibition on funerals during any of the lockdowns, and as the rites and ceremonies covered by the word 'funeral' were fairly clear in this area, it was simply a question of adapting practice to government and archdiocesan guidelines. But Orthodoxy, like many other religious groups, observes other rituals around death, and in these cases matters became slightly more complex.

The Orthodox tradition does not formally recognise 'Last Rites' for the dying, but there are a number of prayers provided in the service books for the sick and the dying. These include the sacraments of Unction and Holy Communion, and prayers to be said at the departure of the soul from the body. In older days these would probably be said at home at the family's request as they kept vigil over the dying family member, but now death is often a matter for hospitals and so these services frequently take place under hospital conditions. Popular piety stresses the importance of a final Communion, and many relatives who are not otherwise particularly practising Orthodox will call in the priest to try to ensure that the dying person is able to receive this benefit. Unfortunately they sometimes wait until the last minute from a misplaced sense of kindness or duty (I was once asked to step out of the room in which the sick person lay lest he should recover consciousness, see the priest and become afraid that he was dying).

158 *Ian Graham*

Since a person incapable of swallowing cannot easily be given the sacrament of Communion, the more common final rite is that of Unction, or Anointing. This sacrament is not specifically associated with dying – it is a sacrament 'for the healing of soul and body' – and can be received in any illness or difficulty where healing is sought, even as part of the resolution of a family quarrel, for example. It involves the priest blessing some oil and anointing the recipient on their sense organs (eyes, ears, nose, mouth, heart, hands and feet). As it requires no responsive participation, it can be received even when the patient is unconscious.

Both Unction and Communion, however, involve physical contact with the body and will require those things which have been in such contact to be dealt with. In the case of the chalice and spoon for Communion it would be usual in any case to rinse them with hot water, but the cotton swabs used for Unction need to be disposed of securely. For this the hospital may take charge of incineration, or the priest may burn them at home.

Hospitals take different views on what is permitted in ministering to the sick and dying. In some cases, even the request of relatives that the priest attend has been ignored, as only the sick person is recognised as being able to request pastoral care, and there is no way of recognising a proxy even in the case of delirium or unconsciousness. Fortunately, other hospitals operate a more reasonable policy, but clearly security has needed to be heightened in the face of the serious potential infection and transmission of the COVID virus. In some places, therefore, in the initial lockdown pastoral care of the sick and dying was reserved to those who were formal representatives of the hospital chaplaincy, which could mean that some Orthodox Christians were unable to receive the services of their church. With the easing of regulations, however, it became possible once more for priests to visit their parishioners in hospitals where this was ordinarily permitted, and although there were some restrictions (a requirement to wear PPE, for instance, especially in the context of the ICU), my own experience has been that hospitals have been happy to facilitate pastoral visitation of the dying as much as possible. Although usually one is not present for the precise moment of death, some of the prayers said at the departure of the soul from the body may be incorporated into the more general service for the visitation and Anointing of the sick.

After death the traditional role of washing, dressing and preparing the body is now usually reserved to the undertakers. A common custom, especially in Mediterranean countries, is that the funeral and burial will take place very soon after death, and so the prepared body is taken to the church and the community keep vigil over it until the funeral with a continuous reading of the Psalter in the case of a departed lay person, or the Gospels when the deceased is a clergyman. This again was not possible during the COVID lockdowns, but once more I would have to note that the inability to pray in this way confirmed or advanced an already existing trend. In normal circumstances there is a delay of about a week between death and funeral in England, and so for most of this time the deceased will be kept at the undertaker's, perhaps at most being brought to the church for a vigil the night before the funeral.

In the Orthodox tradition memorial services, known as *Mnimosyna* in Greek and *Pannykhida* in Russian, are served on significant days. The full schedule is: on the day of death, on the third, ninth and fortieth days following a death (counting inclusively), on the third, sixth, ninth and twelfth month anniversaries of the death and thereafter annually on the anniversary.

At these services it is a common practice to offer *kollyva*, which will be made by the relatives and shared with all who attend the memorial. *Kollyva* is a dish based on boiled wheat or a similar grain. To this base are added (usually – the exact recipe varies from household to household) anise seeds, flaked nuts, raisins, pomegranate seeds and sugar. Although it certainly goes back to pre-Christian Greek traditions of honouring the dead, it is now understood to have a Christian significance. The wheat symbolises the death and resurrection of the body, recalling the words of Christ in St John's Gospel 12:24: 'Very truly, I tell you, unless a grain of wheat falls into the earth and dies, it remains just a single grain; but if it dies, it bears much fruit'. The anise is said to symbolise the bitterness of death, the sugar the sweetness of the life to come.

This tradition of memorial services created complications. Initially, of course, there was no practical problem. With churches closed to worshippers between March 23 and June 15 there was no possibility of holding these memorials, and between June 15 and July 4, when churches were open only for private prayer, the situation was unchanged. But from July 4 things became more complicated. The government regulations, perhaps understandably, tried to cover as many eventualities as possible for all religious groups, subsuming many activities, therefore, under sweeping headings. The memorials would normally take place on the nearest Sunday to the anniversary of death, at the end of the Liturgy, and with many family members in attendance. They could thus, perhaps, be covered by the permission given for 'communal worship, including led prayers, devotions or meditations by a Minister of Religion', although the number attending would be restricted according to the social distancing capabilities of the venue (in Oxford our church was restricted to a maximum of twenty attending any one service), and this might mean that if the memorial was attached to the Liturgy it might be impossible for the full complement of family members wishing to attend to do so. This last point could be resolved by holding the service as a separate event, though this immediately removed the communal dimension and turned the memorial into a *de facto* private service. The question, however, would then become whether the memorial counted as among the 'life cycle events', defined as: 'Religious ceremonies to mark rites of passage, which are separate, self-contained ceremonies as opposed to marking a life cycle event or rite in the course of routine communal worship' – which were permitted with a capped attendance of thirty. As far as I am aware, most churches made the decision that these services were permitted under one rubric or the other.

The blessing and distribution of *kollyva* also needed consideration. The guidelines for July 4 onwards from the UK government discussed, again in blunt instrument terms, the use of 'food and drink' ('consumables') in acts of worship. 'Where . . . consumables are essential to the act of worship, they can be used, however the sharing of food should be avoided.' The necessary loophole appeared in a later clause allowing 'mitigations . . . for example, foodstuffs should be prewrapped." Even before the first lockdown the Archdiocese of Thyateira had instructed its priests in the letter of March 19 that the *antidoron* should no longer be distributed by the priest, but should be left at the back of the church for the faithful to help themselves. The *antidoron* is bread taken from the loaf used for the Communion after the section to be consecrated has been removed. It is therefore considered blessed but not consecrated, and is distributed by the priest at the end of the Liturgy. In some churches all who wish are invited to partake; in others only those who are Orthodox, or only those Orthodox who have not received Communion (*antidoron* means 'instead of the Gift') are offered it. In many churches the practice of bagging the portions separately was added to this precaution. *Kollyva* thus continued to be offered, but if it was to be distributed wider than the family bubble, it was offered already portioned out.

This summary covers the main areas in my experience where COVID-19 and the associated regulations affected Orthodox rites and practices around death. What I have not been able to touch on at all is the impact on folk traditions which, for many first-generation immigrants, form part of the essential ritual surrounding death. This is because, although these rituals are of such significance to those who observe them, they are often impenetrable to 'outsiders' (like me), and also because they lack consistency, linked as they are to the life of the particular village or region from which those observing them originate. They are, in short, too many and too varied.

I would be remiss if I did not also note that Orthodoxy was not immune to a suspicious approach to the COVID question. Some Orthodox Christians joined others of like mind in deciding that the virus had been unleashed on the world by a vast international conspiracy, and that the safety regulations that we were being asked to observe were intended to deliver us into the power of the conspirators. Although they formed only a minority, they included some clergy and prominent laity. Others, overlapping with these, saw COVID as ultimately demonic in origin, and designed to attack Orthodox Christianity. For them it was a matter of faith not to comply with the safety regulations, and those who did were publicly called out as cowards and even heretics. This, of course, goes far beyond the question of the impact of COVID-19 on rituals around death, but it has affected the way that some approach the matter, and it will, perhaps, continue to impact the life of the Orthodox church for some time to come.

Chapter 16

Euthanasia and Assisted Dying
What Jewish Texts Can Teach Us

Sylvia Rothschild

Judaism is a religion that is supremely focussed on life. From the moment God forms a human being from the earth and breathes a living soul into it (Gen 2:7), creating humanity in the image of God (Gen 1:27) the bible gives human life a particular sanctity unlike any other.

The salutation when drinking wine '*L'chaim*' – to life – is documented as far back as Rabbi Akiva, the first-century sage (Babylonian Talmud, *Shabbat* 67b)*,* and the almost ubiquitous prayer of gratitude thanking God for keeping us alive to reach this moment – the *shehecheyanu* prayer – also dates back till at least the first century CE. It is recorded in a number of places in the Talmud (Babylonian Talmud, *Pesachim* 7b, *Sukkah* 46a, *Berachot* 37b, 44a, 59a, etc.), along with the prescribed blessing for evil times or news of a death, *Baruch Dayan Ha'Emet* ('Blessed is the True Judge'). We wish mourners *chaim aruchim* ('a long life'), and express the hope that they will live '*ad meah v'esrim*' ('till one hundred and twenty').

The bible sees God as uniquely being the source of life, and while animals might be killed under particular circumstances, human life is different. Early in the book of Genesis we read 'But for your own life-blood I will require a reckoning: I will require it of every beast; of humans too, will I require a reckoning for human life, of every person for that of their fellow! Whoever sheds the blood of a person, by a human being shall their blood be shed; For in God's image did God make humankind' (Gen 9:5–6).

That 'but' is critical. As explained by twelfth-century French tosafist Yosef Bekhor Shor:

164 *Sylvia Rothschild*

> Because it permitted to spill the blood of beasts, it forbade the spilling of human blood, even one's own blood. [This is] so that they will not say, 'Is it not that [since] the blood of a beast is permitted for us to spill because they live through us, [so] too a person who lives through himself should be permitted to kill himself? Hence it is stated, 'but of your lives I will require a reckoning.' (Yosef Bekhor Shor on Gen 9:5)

We are commanded at Sinai not to murder. In Moses' final exhortation to the people of Israel, he has God say 'See, then, that I, I am God. There is no god beside Me. I deal death and give life; I have wounded and I will heal: None can deliver from My hand' (Deut 32:39).

The covenant between God and the Jewish people, as repeatedly asserted in the Hebrew bible, is about life, and specifically life in this world. We are promised the reward of a long and prosperous earthly life, should we keep its conditions. So, for example, the preface to what becomes a central tenet and prayer in Judaism (the *Shema*) tells us:

> Now these are the commandments, the statutes, and the judgments, which the Eternal your God commanded to teach you, that you might do them in the land where you are going to possess it: That you might fear the Eternal your God, to keep all God's statutes and commandments which I am commanding you, you and your children, and your children's children, all the days of your life; so that your days may be prolonged. Listen therefore, O Israel, and observe to do it; that it may be well with you, and that you may increase mightily, as the Eternal God of your ancestors has promised you, in the land that flows with milk and honey. (Deut 6:1–3)

The biblical narrative repeatedly stresses the values by which we should live, exhorting us to behave according to God's will so that we will live good long and comfortable lives.

Rabbinic Judaism, while it shifted somewhat towards the concept of an afterlife, never lost focus on the importance of living one's best life in this world. So we have, for example, the statement, 'This world is like a vestibule before the world to come; prepare yourself in the vestibule, so that you may enter the banqueting-hall' (Mishnah, *Avot* 4:16). It continues 'more precious is one hour in repentance and good deeds in this world than all the life of the world to come' (Mishnah, *Avot* 4:17).

For the rabbis of Mishnah there is a real sense of existence after death, but we cannot know anything about this world to come. What matters is the world we live in now, and our actions in it. We should not yearn to reach the world to come, but instead try to live as long as possible in this world. Time spent here will allow us to perform more good deeds and so earn a greater reward in the afterlife. Once there, good deeds and repentance will not be available

Euthanasia and Assisted Dying 165

to us – and so the message is driven home: we should live our best lives, use our time on earth wisely and well because our actions have consequences beyond our limited lifespan.

The specialness of human life asserted in the bible is underlined throughout the rabbinic literature. So, for example, the life of one individual human being is equated with that of all of humanity – life is of infinite worth. The Talmud records, 'Anyone who destroys a human life is considered as if he had destroyed an entire world, and anyone who preserves a human life is considered to have preserved an entire world' (Mishnah, *Sanhedrin* 4:5). The saving of life, *pikuach nefesh*, takes precedence over every Torah prohibition (and every rabbinic prohibition) save for three. One must not choose martyrdom except where one would otherwise desecrate God's name by transgressing the commandments against sexual offences, idolatry and murder (Babylonian Talmud, *Sanhedrin* 74a–b). This is based on the verse in Leviticus 18:5 that the commandments are given to us to live by – understood by the Talmud as also meaning 'not die because of them'.

The preservation of life takes precedence over every other ethical and moral consideration, and indeed the obligation to save one's own life applies to everyone – a sick person is obliged to seek medical care in order to find a cure (Feinstein 1996: 76), and a doctor is obligated to respond to the sick person or would be considered a shedder of blood (Solomon ben Adret (Rashba), *Sefer Issur v'Heter* 60:8–9).

Time and again rabbinic texts support the sustaining of life in complex situations. So for example we have the Talmudic discourse about feeding a seriously ill patient on Yom Kippur – thus breaking an important commandment to fast (Babylonian Talmud, *Yoma* 83a). If the patient feels the need to eat, even though the doctor does not think it necessary, the patient's will prevails and they eat. But if a doctor thinks it necessary that they eat and the patient does not, then the doctor's will prevails; the presumption is that the patient has become confused and is unable to judge their critical need for food. In each case, the argument is focussed towards sustaining strength and life rather than listening to either the expert or to the individual.

This value of sustaining life right up to the point of death can be most clearly seen in the laws of the *goses* – one who is expected to die imminently. The Talmud tells us:

> A dying person (*goses*) is regarded as a living entity in respect of all matters in the world . . . , as it is stated, 'Before the silver cord is snapped asunder and the golden bowl is shattered, and the pitcher is broken at the fountain, And the dust returns to the ground as it was, And the life-breath returns to God Who bestowed it' (Eccl 12:6–7). We may not move him, or place him on sand or salt until he dies. We may not close the eyes of a dying man. Whoever touches and moves

166   *Sylvia Rothschild*

him is a murderer. For R. Meir used to say: He can be compared to a lamp which is dripping; should a man touch it he extinguishes it. Similarly whoever closes the eyes of a dying man is considered as if he had taken his life.' (Babylonian Talmud, *Semachot* 1–4)

All of the actions mentioned here were understood to hasten death.

The principle of doing nothing that may hasten death stands in the rabbinic literature, but Rabbi Judah heHasid extended it by ruling that one could – and even should – remove obstacles that are preventing death. This view was codified by Moses Isserles who in his commentary to the Shulchan Aruch wrote, 'If there is anything which causes a hindrance to the departure of the soul . . . it is permissible to remove [it] from there because there is no act involved, only the removal of the impediment' (on Shulchan Aruch *Yoreh Deah* 339:1).

The idea that death should not be actively hastened, but that impediments to the process of dying can be removed in order not to prolong the experience is critical in many subsequent responsa on euthanasia, allowing for passive euthanasia if not for actively hastening death. The texts on which Rabbi Judah – and others – base this view can be found in the very different deaths of Rabbi Judah haNasi and of Rabbi Hanina ben Teradyon.

The story of the martyrdom of Rabbi Hanina ben Teradyon by the Romans is explicit and painful:

They brought him to be sentenced, and wrapped him in the Torah scroll, and encircled him with bundles of branches, and they set fire to it. And they brought tufts of wool and soaked them in water, and placed them on his heart, so that his soul should not leave his body quickly, but he would die slowly and painfully. His daughter said to him: Father, must I see you like this? . . . His students said to him: Our teacher, what do you see? Rabbi Hanina ben Teradyon said to them: I see the parchment burning, but its letters are flying to the heavens. They said to him: You too should open your mouth and the fire will enter you, and you will die quickly. Rabbi Hanina ben Teradyon said to them: It is preferable that God who gave me my soul should take it away, and a person should not harm themself in order to speed their death. The executioner said to him: My teacher, if I increase the flame and take off the tufts of wool from your heart, so that you will die sooner and suffer less, will you bring me to the life of the World-to-Come? Rabbi Hanina ben Teradyon said to the executioner: Yes. The executioner said: Take an oath for me, that what you say is true. Rabbi Hanina ben Teradyon took the oath for him, and the executioner immediately increased the flame and took off the tufts of wool from his heart, causing his soul to leave his body quickly. The executioner too leaped and fell into the fire and died. (Babylonian Talmud, *Avodah Zara* 18a)

Rabbi Hanina ben Teradyon himself follows the dictum that one should not hasten one's own death, yet goes on to agree to the removal of the soaked

Euthanasia and Assisted Dying 167

wool which is delaying his death. His daughter's agony and his students' suggestions that he himself speed his martyrdom are rejected, yet in his agreement with the executioner shortly afterwards, he assents to what may be understood as passive euthanasia or even – at a stretch – assisted dying. Does the reality of the increasing pain motivate Hanina to change his mind? And are the actions of the executioner – who is immediately granted eternal life for his act of compassion towards Hanina – make him someone to be praised? The text can be read in multiple ways.

The story of the death of Rabbi Judah haNasi is also one of removing obstacles to dying. In this case the prayers of his students are preventing his soul from leaving his body. But it takes us further into the compassionate hearts of the rabbis who understand the desire to pray for the death of a beloved person who is suffering deeply.

> On the day that Rabbi Yehuda HaNasi died, the Sages decreed a fast, and begged for divine mercy so that he would not die. . . . The maidservant of Rabbi Yehuda HaNasi ascended to the roof and said: The upper realms are requesting the presence of Rabbi Yehuda HaNasi, and the lower realms are requesting the presence of Rabbi Yehuda HaNasi. May it be the will of God that the lower worlds should impose their will upon the upper worlds. However, when she saw how many times he would enter the bathroom and remove his phylacteries, and then exit and put them back on, and how he was suffering with his intestinal disease, she said: May it be the will of God that the upper worlds should impose their will upon the lower worlds. And the Sages, meanwhile, would not be silent, they would not refrain from begging for mercy so that Rabbi Yehuda HaNasi would not die. So she took a jug and threw it from the roof to the ground. Due to the sudden noise, the Sages were momentarily silent and refrained from begging for mercy, and Rabbi Yehuda HaNasi died. (Babylonian Talmud, *Ketubot* 104a)

The appropriateness of praying for someone to die in order for their suffering to be ended threads through rabbinic texts. So, for example, Rabbi's maidservant is praised. We find too stories of the students of Rabbi Akiva who did not visit a sick colleague and are criticised by their teacher who tells them: 'Why didn't you visit your sick colleague? You could have helped him or prayed for his recovery. If you were convinced that there was no hope of a recovery, you could at least have prayed for him to die quickly. Even that little help you withheld from him!' (Nissim of Gerona on *Nedarim* 40a).

Suffering is not seen as bringing any spiritual benefit. We find in the Talmud, responding to a debate as to whether suffering will bring rewards, a clear rebuttal of the idea. In a series of stories about rabbis who are visited on their sickbeds (Babylonian Talmud, *Berachot* 5b), the question is repeatedly asked, 'Is your suffering dear to you?' – and the answer repeatedly given, 'Neither the suffering nor its reward'.

168   *Sylvia Rothschild*

Judaism concerns itself with both physical and emotional suffering. So even in the case of a person condemned to death by a court, there is concern for their feelings – before their execution the Talmud tells us they should be given wine containing some frankincense in order to intoxicate them and reduce their anxiety (Rashi on *Sanhedrin* 34a). Loneliness and existential angst are recognised too – the story is told of the Talmudic Sage Honi HaMa'agel who woke after a sleep of seventy years to find that no one recognised nor believed him when he told them who he was, and everyone whom he had known was long gone. In great distress he prayed for mercy and he died. 'Rava said: This explains the folk saying that people say: Either friendship or death, as one who has no friends is better off dead' (Babylonian Talmud, *Ta'anit* 23a). The Talmud also tells of the people in the city of Luz, where the Angel of Death was forbidden to go. 'Rather, its Elders, when they have decided that they have reached the end of life, go outside the city wall and die' (Babylonian Talmud, *Sotah* 246b).

Jewish texts protest against suffering: it has no moral or character-enhancing effects. We should do what we can to alleviate it in every circumstance and there is consensus in every rabbinic response on terminal care that analgesics and narcotics are given to relieve pain and suffering, even if they have the effect of depressing respiration in the patient and potentially hastening death – known as the 'double effect' (Auerbach 1995: 2(2–3) 86).

Suicide – by one's own agency or with assistance – and active euthanasia are forbidden in Jewish law, yet one can see great compassion for the distress of the suicide: in stories such as the death of Saul or of Samson (Jud 16:30) there is a recognition of the mental anguish which led to their choice. The Talmud also, while upholding the prohibition, finds ways to exempt many from being judged to have transgressed the prohibition; mental distress, temporary lack of competence, a feeling of compulsion, lack of witnesses – even poverty are all used as reasons to not call such a death a suicide.

Any review of the sweep of Jewish texts leaves no doubt that the focus is on preserving and sustaining life at almost any cost. The quantity and quality of that life is irrelevant – one can break the laws of Shabbat, for example, in order to try to preserve the life of a clearly dying person. Yet at the same time there is an awareness – possibly most succinctly put in Ecclesiastes – that there is a time to die (Eccl 3:2). Life is finite, we are all at some point 'gathered to our ancestors' and the generations move on. We find in the Midrash the explanation of the emphatic in the verse 'and behold it was very good' (Gen 1:31) as signalling that God saw an extra goodness when surveying the almost completed creation – God saw the goodness of death. Spending one's last days and hours in suffering is to be avoided – the medieval text *Sefer Hasidim* rules that 'when a person is moribund and his soul is departing, we do not pray that his soul return to him because he would in any event be able to live only a few more days, and those days would be in pain' (*Sefer Hasidim* 234).

Rabbinic texts hold fast to the sanctity and integrity of life – one life is not worth more than another, no one's blood is redder than anyone else's, and our bodies and souls belong to God who created us. But at the same time they demonstrate a great generosity of spirit, and compassion for those who are suffering from physical, emotional or spiritual distress; and empathy too for those who have to witness that suffering. Our tradition offers a variety of texts and lenses through which end-of-life decisions can be made and how once made they may be judged.

We have the principle of *shev, v'al ta'aseh* – sit and do nothing heroic to preserve a life which will have little quality and much suffering. At the same time we can remove impediments to the process of dying, including, amongst other impediments, any feeding that is more medical than social, or artificial breathing for an unconscious patient.

We have the principle also of the *mitah yafah* – a phrase which maps exactly onto the more common word 'euthanasia', in its radical meaning of 'a good death' rather than its common idiom of helping someone into death.

The phrase *mitah yafah* is used originally in the Talmud in the context of alleviating the anxiety of a person condemned to death, or of not also humiliating them in the execution process, or of not unnecessarily prolonging the execution and therefore the pain of dying (Babylonian Talmud, *Sanhedrin* 45a, 52a, etc.). It is not used to describe facilitating the process of dying of a person who may be suffering or fearful and who has had enough of life; however, it remains an intriguing phrase for more modern commentators to utilise. The Talmud derives the principle from the verse known as the golden rule – 'Rav Nachman says that Rabba bar Avuha said: The verse states "And you shall love your neighbour as yourself," which teaches that even with regard to a condemned prisoner one should select a good, compassionate death for him' (Babylonian Talmud, *Sanhedrin* 52a). If one should choose a good death even for a condemned prisoner, how much more so for an ordinary individual?

The question facing the Jewish world, as it faces other religious worlds, is how to facilitate a *mitah yafah*, when we must weigh it against the principle of the inalienable importance of the value of life.

Rabbinic Judaism frames its thought within the legal structures of halachic responsa. But a good death cannot simply be framed according to legal argument, nor – as is clear from the texts – is the expertise of the doctor alone sufficient to facilitate it. There are spiritual dimensions at work here, and of course there is also the individual and their own experience in life, their own perceptions and increasingly their own autonomy. The tension between the absolute value of life per se and the complexities and nuances of how life is experienced by a dying person means that a purely medico-legal approach to a good death can never be sufficient.

Jewish tradition is heterogeneous and multivocal. Halachah is a dynamic process that evolves and adapts, basing itself on earlier texts but arrogating to itself the right to interpret and extend from those roots. As rabbinic understanding grows, so often rabbinic opinions moderate and mitigate what has gone before.

Our lives are finite, and we all hope for a good death. But Jewishly what does that mean? We have many stories in our texts about the deaths of our ancestors, and can bring forth diverse readings from them to help us understand what a good death might look like. Abraham put his affairs in order, leaving his estate to Isaac but giving legacies to his other children in his lifetime, and died an old and contented man (Gen 25:5–11). Isaac too breathed his last as an old man, and like his father was buried in the family sepulchre by his sons who came together to fulfil this last honouring act (Gen 35:28–29). Surrounded by his family having given deathbed instructions that he too would be buried in Machpelah, Jacob breathed his last (Gen 49:29–33). These were completed lives and peaceful – good – deaths.

Moses climbed a mountain, was shown all the land that had been promised in the patriarchal covenant, but was told he would not enter it. He died 'at the mouth of God' – which midrash interprets as dying by a divine kiss – and was buried by God in a hidden grave and mourned deeply by the people (Deut 34:6). Moses' death took place on the cusp of a new time – he could see it but not go into it – and there is a whiff of a suggestion that Moses felt cheated of the completion of his life's work, but that emotion is mitigated by his extraordinary relationship with God.

Later in the bible the death stories are somewhat darker. King Saul's death is told twice – once where he kills himself to avoid humiliation, and once where he tries to do so but fails, and has to be helped to finish the job. King David in his old age became weak and vulnerable and could not stop the political intrigues of his sons as they fought each other for power. His last days were filled with attempting to maintain his legacy and establishing his succession against a backdrop of conspiracies and attempted coups (I Kgs 1–2). Solomon died peacefully but after his death the kingdom was divided – his son Rehoboam had no statecraft and quickly caused a rebellion (I Kgs 11:43ff., II Chr 10:1–4).

A good death seems in the bible to be connected to having made good decisions in life, finding ways to resolve family tensions and pass on the values and traditions that have meaning to the dying person, to the safekeeping of the next generation. One might say that this is not much different today.

Euthanasia and Assisted Dying   171

The process of dying – the desire for a good way to die – is something that exercises us greatly in modernity, as medicine gives us options and dilemmas that were unknown in earlier times. The struggle that is engaged between authority and expertise and the autonomy of the individual is real. Who ultimately can dictate the course of the life of an individual if not the individual themselves? But the tension between individual autonomy and what we might call the common good is also real – how does the decision making of one individual or group impact on the behaviour and self-understanding of the rest of the community? And where does the boundary lie between acts of personal autonomy and the medicalising of accelerated dying?

Legislation that allows assisting people to die has enormous impact on society and how it views life's value. We know that suicidal behaviour is contagious: exposure to it in one's family or peer group can greatly increase the risk of others following suit. Disability advocacy groups are fearful that once the principle to protect every life is breached, there will be pressure to assess the quality of lives, and that the distinction between disability and terminal illness is not so clear-cut as to protect them (Campbell 2019). Disabled activists have warned that the latest bid to persuade parliament to legalise assisted suicide is a threat to their 'lives, independence and peace of mind' (Pring 2021). In the current pandemic, disabled people have been disproportionately affected because of discrimination in the healthcare system: they are 60% more likely to die of COVID than their able-bodied counterparts. Hundreds of 'do not resuscitate' notices were applied to disabled patients, without discussion or consent. Once assisted dying becomes a legitimate option for competent terminally ill patients, a door opens that may facilitate the earlier deaths of others in society – those without competence, or whose quality of life is seen as less than ideal.

Should assisted dying become just another option when life becomes too heavy a burden? Is it a legitimate response to existential distress or will it normalise suicide rather than address the causes of that distress? Have we lost the balance between seeing life as infinitely precious while working to minimize the areas of suffering: physical, emotional, psychological and spiritual? Will removing the burden of life for a few mean that many more will continue to live without the investment needed for sufficient social and emotional support and palliative care?

Dame Cicely Saunders, the founder of the modern hospice movement, famously said 'How people die remains in the memory of those who live on.' It is intolerable for anyone to watch a beloved person living with pain and fear, with humiliation and lost dignity, without agency and dragging through days which hold little meaning or hope or joy. The rabbinic texts understand this, they offer compassion and empathy, and oblige us to treat the terminally ill with full respect for their worth and humanity. The dignity and agency of the dying person is mandated, it is recognised that 'the heart knows its own bitterness' (Prov 14:10) and so the individual experience is validated and upheld. There are texts that oblige us to visit and comfort the dying person; the Talmud teaches that 'one who visits the sick takes away one sixtieth of their pain' (Babylonian Talmud, *Nedarim* 39b). The rabbinic tradition is well aware of both physical and spiritual distress, and commands us to mitigate both as strenuously as we can.

Judaism has a tradition rich with texts that support a process of dying well, as well as of living well. In its strong aversion to active euthanasia or to suicide it holds to a principle expressed most eloquently in the book of Job – God gives and God takes away (Job 1:21) – yet it offers pragmatic and considerate responses to the suffering of the seriously ill and of those who care for them. It offers texts which may help us as we struggle with the multiplicity of options facing a terminally ill person, and with the legal framework of *lechatchilah* (the better way initially) and *bediavad* (practices that are acceptable after the fact) it holds what might be mutually opposed positions of the absolute value of life and the desire for someone to live as long as possible, and the need to mitigate suffering and remove any impediment to death in order to do so, in a carefully calibrated balance.

Can we continue to maintain such a balance as individual autonomy weighs into the arguments along with many variations of the common good? Time will tell. Judaism adapts and evolves to current realities and the dynamic nature of halachah and responsa allow for a fluid future iteration. Judaism is a religion of life, and life is the arena in which we exist and from which we bring forth meaning, and we are covenanted to find the ways to live until we die.

BIBLIOGRAPHY

Auerbach S. Z. 1995. *Minchat Shlomo.* Jerusalem.
Campbell J. 2019. 'Disabled people like me fear legal assisted suicide: it suggests that some lives are less worth living', in *The BMJ Opinion.* https://blogs.bmj.com/bmj /2019/02/06/disabled-people-like-me-fear-legal-assisted-suicide-it-suggests-that -some-lives-are-less-worth-living/ (accessed 21.10.21).
Feinstein M. 1996. 'Responsa: Care of the Critically Ill', in *Quality and Sanctity of Life, a Torah View* tr. Moshe David Tendler, vol. 1. New York.
Pring J. 2021. 'New bid to legalise assisted suicide "threatens disabled people's lives and independence"' in *The Disability News Service.* https://www .disabilitynewsservice.com/new-bid-to-legalise-assisted-suicide-threatens-disabled -peoples-lives-and-independence/ (accessed 21.10.21).

Chapter 17

Do We Have the Right to End Our Own Life?

Orthodox Christian Responses to the Debate on Euthanasia and Assisted Dying

Joanna Burton

The debate about euthanasia and whether individuals should have the legal right to choose to deliberately end their own life is very much current in Western societies. The arguments both for and against are often pleaded with passion. The pro-euthanasia lobby cite examples of unendurable pain, and the indignity, wretchedness and injustice of having to travel abroad as a very ill person to fulfil one's wish where euthanasia is illegal in one's home country, a journey needing to be made while a person is still physically able to make it and so arguably sometimes before the person is really 'ready to die', which further augments the injustice of the situation. A central argument of the pro-euthanasia lobby is that an individual has the right to make a decision about his/herself by reason of an inalienable autonomy we each have in regard to our own person. The anti-euthanasia lobby emphasize the dangers if the protection of life and the prohibition of deliberately choosing to end one's life is weakened or taken away, including negative effects on the character of a society where the deliberate ending of lives is current.

This chapter will focus on Orthodox Christian responses to central themes in the contemporary euthanasia debate. The ethical question of the personal individual right to choose whether to continue to live or die is central to much of the present debate. It is one with the strong and often overriding emphasis placed on the autonomy of the individual as a value and as a right in Western

174 *Joanna Burton*

societies. Some would claim that it is simply a particular cultural overemphasis that has intruded into the euthanasia debate (e.g., Pitcher 2010, 25–32).

The great value we place on autonomy also conditions our view of what it means to be a dignified human being, commonly seen as one who is autonomous and nondependent on others, and results in major arguments for the choice of euthanasia for those who are thought to have lost their dignity as dependent on the help of others for their basic bodily needs or psychologically damaged or dependent beyond acceptable limits. The emphasis placed on rationality as the defining and distinguishing characteristic of human beings encourages this view.

Greek and Roman societies practised infanticide, suicide and euthanasia but Judeo-Christian societies have traditionally believed that human life is sacred and different in kind, not just in degree, to that of other creatures, and that to take it is to usurp a right that is God's alone. An emphasis on the superiority of rationality has led to a similar distinction in the philosophical tradition, while at least part of the philosophical tradition in the West has seen taking life as a violation of natural law which resolutely promotes life (Kuhse 2009, 294).

It might be said that the question of deciding to end another's life, not simply one's own, needs to be considered within the debate. This simply because where a person lacks capacity, the ethics of best benefits applies (Mental Capacity Act 2005). This, it might be argued, greatly widens the debate and introduces other ethical questions and conundrums (Pitcher 2010).

A central feature of the pro-euthanasia argument is an emphasis on autonomy and freedom of personal choice. It is also fundamental to the palliative care healthcare approach: the wishes of the dying person are to be central in holistic end-of-life care provision. Those involved in caring for a dying person must seek to find out and respond to what the person desires and needs on a physical, psychological, spiritual and social level (Saunders et al. 1981). Popular debates tend to place autonomy above all else, coming close to Nozick's extreme Libertarian and classic Self-Ownership thesis: I belong to myself alone; no one has any claim on me, unless I choose to share what is mine alone (Nozick 1974, 160–74).

Secular debaters (e.g., Nedelsky 1989) point out the inadequacy of the liberal view of autonomy, which takes the individual as the basic unit in legal and political theory, ignoring the fact that human beings are also social beings. A new vision of autonomy is sought, that adequately expresses both the individual and the social nature of human beings. In a more middle-of-the-road healthcare approach, as in Beauchamp and Childress's influential Four Principles approach (Beauchamp & Childress 2009), autonomy is just one of four central principles to consider when making end-of-life care decisions. Euthanasia is usually defined in a healthcare context as ending someone's life because this is thought to be in their best interests. It carries the idea of doing good to and not doing/causing harm. The Four Principles question the priority of autonomy and further discuss good and harm in the particular situation. In the end-of-life care context, they are used to determine what is good for the dying person, yet the palliative care movement has always spoken of ministering to the needs of loved ones as well as to those of the dying person. The Principles make us understand that individual autonomy has to be seen within the context of a number of autonomies, needs and interests. They implicitly recognize that others have rights and that the dying person may well have relational duties and responsibilities, as well as rights, usually emphasized in the euthanasia debate.

Jennifer Nedelsky argues that we do not usually make serious choices in isolation, but in the context of our families, loved ones and friendships. Autonomy has this relational dimension and normally is exercised in and through relationships. So too with decisions about whether to end our life or not. Autonomy is more complex than isolation and non-interference. Nothing substitutes for the unique particularity of a context and its unique relationships.

Orthodox Christianity also places great emphasis on the importance of the choices we each make, both for our present life and for eternal life. The Orthodox spiritual-ascetic tradition calls us to make choices pleasing to God and congruent with our human vocation, a vocation that calls us to continual growth. The recognition that there are tendencies within us and without that pull us away from good choice allows us to see our state and condition as being one of constant choice (Breck 1998, 29). Orthodox Christians often use the biblical term repentance (*metanoia*) to speak of this continual choice of turning from evil to good (Zizioulas 2006, 3–4).

Yet there are choices that are not ours to make as created beings, given life by God (Gen 1.26–27). Here we enter the realm of faith conviction. As Christians, we receive our lives as given; we also receive them as a gift. The consequences of seeing life as God's gift rather than as a possession are great. If something is our possession, we can legitimately do as we wish with it, discarding it if we wish. If something is given to us as a gift, we often need to follow the giver's desires and intent in giving the gift, in our use of their gift. There is also the need to trust that the gift is good, even in difficult circumstances (Breck 1998, 213–20). Some Christians today do see assisted suicide as the working out of Jesus' command to love the neighbour. Others think that the right to decide when to die is included in God's gift of choice and free will to human beings. For these Christians it is acceptable to kill oneself, deliberately handing oneself back to God if life becomes too much to bear. Orthodox Christians do not usually hold such convictions.

Orthodox theology does not support the vision of isolated autonomous choice, especially with the end of life choices. Dying human beings do not suddenly lose their responsibilities to and for others; they may not be able to carry them out practically, but these remain. Orthodoxy wishes to emphasize the continuity of the person in life and in dying: we do not suddenly become other in illness and in our dying. In the particular cases where illness includes dementia or other mental incapacity, it is for the community to keep alive the reality of the person and to make decisions according to the person's best interests.

Orthodoxy bases its vision and understanding of human beings on the biblical witness of God creating human beings in His own image. There have been various reflections within the Orthodox tradition as to what makes the image of God in humankind, none definitive and exclusive (Ware 2005, 11). However, Orthodox are convinced of the sacredness of every human life, in any condition. This view makes it difficult to put an end to a life in which God is mysteriously but really present and imaged. It situates the image beyond the conceptual rational and intellectual capacities of a person (Palmer et al. 1979, 362), so that people with severe mental or psychological incapacities still bear God's image within them and may not be killed or thought of as less precious than other human beings.

Orthodox reflection has made a distinction between image and likeness (Ware 2005, 18–22) as a way of describing the long journey of growth which is human life. All human beings bear God's image, by reason of the fact that God created human beings in His image, an image that can be sullied but never lost. We each bear the likeness of God to the extent that we have actually become like Him in our attitudes, values and actions. Such a vision is essentially dynamic and ongoing: we may hope that if we do our part, God's likeness will grow ever greater in us. Orthodox see becoming like God (*theosis*, deification, transformation) as the purpose of life: everything experienced may be a vehicle for this transformation of a person into a loving, compassionate and Godlike human being.

Yet we also know from experience that we do not always make use of our life experience to become loving human beings in God's image: human experience is of both capacity to choose the good and of incapacity (Zizioulas 2006, 206–49). If the Orthodox funeral service sings, in Ps. 118, of the one who delights in God's law and God's values, it also laments the sinfulness in human life and brings it to God for forgiveness and healing (Hapgood 1996, 368–93). A vivid contrast is made between the glory of being created in the image of God and the pitifulness of the present image of the deceased lying before us, made after our own image, calling us, the mourners, to learn from the contrast and choose aright in our own lives (Hapgood 1996, 390). This valuing of what we might call good and bad experience is another element present in the Orthodox view on life and death decisions. There are experiences that can crush and harm a person, but also all experience can be a vehicle for existential learning, and salutary, if sometimes very difficult. As human beings, we cannot always discern which is which, and prefer to entrust that decision to God and God's love, doing all we can to help and accompany the person, rather than simply cutting off experience by ending someone's life. This too is the difficult path of trust in God in circumstances we do not always understand.

The human vocation does not cease as death draws near. Dying and death itself is recognised as an important and significant event, the completion of a life. It is not simply a fading away and diminishment of the person, but the entrusting of oneself to God's love, practised throughout the many events of our life, yet never so radically as in the helplessness of death. Surprisingly to some contemporary ideas of a good death ('in my sleep'), Orthodox pray to be spared a sudden death and privilege a fully conscious one in which the person is able to consciously entrust her/himself to God (Breck 1998, 224). Death is seen thus in both a negative and positive light: negative, because it is the consequence of human sin. God never intended us to die, but human wrong choice led to the reality of death as experienced. Death is also the potentially terrifying place of judgment when the quality of our life and its choices will be clearly revealed. Yet it is also the place of the opportunity for radical trust in God in our helplessness and inability to do anything to save ourselves. It is the final act of our *ascesis*; it thus becomes a passage, and not the end of everything. At Easter we cry out in the liturgical services, 'Christ is risen from the dead, trampling down death by [His] death, and to those in the tomb he has given Life'. Such a testimony changes our experiences of death and dying.

The biblical narrative also points us to an adequate understanding of the relation between the individual and the social, founding that understanding in God's own being. There is the mysterious suggestion of plurality in one God, 'Let us make humankind in our image', which since the second century has been read by Christian authors and readers as a reference to the Holy Trinity (Ware 2005, 48). God is not solitary, but a community of Persons and Relations. It is in this total *exstasis*, this being for the other, that they are/ eternally become Themselves. Human language stutters but tries to show that 'the being of God is a relational being' (Zizioulas 1985, 17; 2006, 167–69).

If human beings are created in God's image, they are persons in relation, beings who become themselves by being for the other/s, unique persons, individuals, but also bound together in relationships of love and care. Man and woman together are created in God's image, two, not one, the primordial community, from whose shared love a third is born (Ware 2005, 48). Descartes showed the logical truth of 'I think, therefore I am', but there is a deeper, existential truth, 'I love, therefore I am': love and loving create the reality of our being as persons. I am loved, therefore I am (Ware 2005, 15). We also need the love of others to become the unique persons we are called to be. In such a vision others most certainly and deeply play a part in the creation of our particular personal being. Nozick's view that I alone create my being and therefore I alone own myself, unless I choose to share it with others, is inadequate from the Orthodox vision of people as interdependent persons. This interdependence expresses itself in a call for loving and caring for each other and everything (Ware 2005, 50). It also signifies the process of each unique and particular person being created through such loving inter-action and interdependence. This inevitably builds the essence of Christian life in the Church around continual repentance (Zizioulas 2006, 4), continual change from evil to good, continual building of the image and likeness of God in ourselves.

A central issue in the pro-euthanasia argument is of course the presence of severe and dreadful pain. These are difficult and very distressing situations for everyone who experiences and reflects about the euthanasia debate. There should be no question of allowing people to suffer when it is possible to con-trol their pain, as it often is today. There are Orthodox who have argued that patients should not be given palliative relief because their suffering is 'a share in the sufferings of Christ' (Breck 1998, 216–17). Breck calls these extreme arguments and pleads for the avoidance of glib pronouncements about the value of suffering, 'not to deny that value but to set it in its proper perspec-tive and acknowledge its proper limits' (2005, 221). Orthodoxy does indeed see that suffering and distress of any kind, including and perhaps especially that at the end of life, can be joined to Christ's own sufferings and death and become mysteriously fruitful for the Church and the world. How we react to it can also be part of that purifying growth of becoming a truly loving person in God's own image, which is the whole journey of life. But surely our duty is to help those in pain to the best of our ability. Good pain control is a first requirement of palliative care. Only when we do that can we consider how to view and tackle pain that is intractable.

The doctrine of double effect is generally accepted and accepted in law: healthcare providers may give a suffering person doses of morphine or other pain killer, even if it will or may hasten death, as long as there is no intention to deliberately bring about death. To allow this doctrine to work as it should, we must create a trustful attitude towards the actions of physicians and their intent to do good to their patients, else the fear of prosecution will stop them from providing relief in a way that is morally and practically helpful to those who suffer: this is not always evident today.

Orthodox may too, in principle, accept the doctrine of double effect and generally do so as the intention is to alleviate and/or make tolerable a dying

Do We Have the Right to End Our Own Life?

person's pain, not to deliberately end their life, as in active euthanasia, or to deliberately hasten their death. Garrard and Wilkinson (2005, 64–68) argue that for passive euthanasia to occur there must be the intention to hasten death, while the World Health Organisation's definition of palliative care (2004) says that it intends neither to hasten death, nor to prolong dying. However, others, both in the secular debate (e.g., Manninen 2006, 647) and in an Orthodox context (Breck 1998, 205; 2005, 220–30), have asked whether intention can so easily be discerned and whether the practice of double effect is sometimes a hidden form of passive euthanasia.

Both Breck and secular reflection lay out similar conditions to guard against hidden euthanasia, while others propose an important distinction between intending and foreseeing. A doctor may foresee that a painkiller may hasten death, but he or she does not intend it. Gillon argues the differences between intending and foreseeing on logical, experiential, conceptual, legal and moral levels: 'If you intend to do something, you necessarily aim to make it happen, but that is not necessarily true if you merely foresee it happening' (Gillon 1999). Breck states that it is unrealistic in certain hard cases to expect a doctor not to hope that his greatly suffering terminal patient will die more quickly because he has administered an augmented dose of painkiller (Breck 2005, 226). Yet from a faith standpoint, hoping and foreseeing allow a space for God's will to manifest itself, for God to act.

The same question about passive euthanasia may be asked for selective nontreatment, withholding or withdrawing treatment. Our very technological capacities have created problems at the end of life: the capacities that keep people alive longer may also prolong their dying. Orthodoxy does not work with a Vitalist approach. While all must be done for a person if there is a realistic possibility of cure or effective palliation, there is a time to die: when someone is in a terminal condition, where vital functions are breaking down, treatment may be withheld or withdrawn and the person allowed to die. The spectre of keeping the physical body and organs working while the person is no longer present is one which we have all become aware in publicized cases. Human beings are created in God's image: when the person is no longer present, they are dead (Breck 2005, 231–38).

Palliative or termination sedation is another arsenal in extreme pain control. Terminal sedation is when, in the last days or hours of a person's life, they are given sedative drugs, so that they become either semi or fully unconscious; this is usually maintained until death occurs. Once a person is unconscious, nutrition and hydration are usually withdrawn. The decision to make a person unconscious and the withdrawal of nutrition and hydration make it controversial. Breck argues that it is acceptable if appropriately used: as a last result when other forms of both physical and psychological pain relief have clearly failed, and proportionally, only to the degree necessary to control pain (Breck 2005, 226–27). He also notes that withdrawing nutrition does not mean that a person will die of starvation or thirst (Breck 2005, 228) and that continuing nutrition and hydration at this point in the dying process can cause more pain and distress to the person, whose vital functions are shutting down (Breck 1998, 234–38). The withdrawal of nutrition and hydration is, however, often very difficult for the dying person's family to understand and accept. In some cases this may perhaps be a situation where the needs, rights and interests of family members are part of the considerations in decisions regarding best benefits. Breck situates his remarks in the context in which intolerable physical or psychological pain incites people to call for euthanasia; palliative sedation, when used appropriately, offers a more acceptable way of dealing with such pain.

Pain is not only physical but existential and emotional. In so far as this pain is treatable by drugs and therapies, it must be. Treatable depression should not lead to euthanasia. Yet some would plead that severe untreatable existential pain is a sufficient reason for allowing euthanasia. Some countries have recently legislated in this direction. While palliative sedation may have its part to play in case specific situations, the need to deal with pain spiritually and humanly is vital from an Orthodox standpoint. We need to mention the importance of human and spiritual accompaniment of the dying within parishes and communities, if there is to be a viable alternative to euthanasia. Becoming familiar with the major themes of the liturgical services, Holy Unction, the Parting of the Soul from the Body, the Order(s) of Burial and the Requiem Office of the Dead can give us a heightened awareness and sensitivity to what is really happening when one of our community or any human being is dying. It is an understanding which we need if we are to effectively accompany the dying through this final stage of earthly life, comfort ourselves, and not fall by default into purely secular attitudes to the phenomena of the dying process. As human beings and fellow members of the faith community, we are all involved by our concern, compassion and prayer.

Breck suggests that effective accompaniment of the dying is a neglected area and that we need to do it better (Breck 2005, 229–30) and suggests that a new form of Christian ministry might be developed, in which specially trained laypersons or medical professionals might provide such 'aid-in-dying'. A female diaconate might fruitfully be developed or rediscovered, focused on offering a recognized ministry to the dying and their loved ones. Parishes might sponsor suitable individuals to be trained in end-of-life care would carry out their *diakonia* in the name of the whole community (Breck 1998, 239–40). Such initiatives would make concrete our responsibilities for each other along the journey of growth to 'a place of brightness, verdure, repose, whence all sickness, sorrow and sighing have fled away' (Hapgood 1996,

369). They would also show and illustrate that there are feasible and positive alternatives (Breck 1998, 241) to the practice of euthanasia.

The right to choose euthanasia is often linked with the right to a dignified death. Here fears come together, the fear of pain, the fear of uncertainty, and most of all, the fear of a lack of control. For our society a dignified death is a controlled/controllable death (www.dignityindying.org.uk). Yet death is the place of no control, of helplessness, where we can do nothing for ourselves except – and it is an almighty BUT – accept such helplessness ('Father, into Your hands I commend my spirit'; 'It is done' – each life done, complete, as Jesus' was). We practise this final acceptance of a lack of control in the events of life which afford us little or no control, if we choose to accept helplessness and not being in control. Old age, physical incapacity, serious and debilitating illness, or simply big disappointments when our plans and desires do not come to the fruition for which we hoped. Every life has these and they are difficult to bear. Taking initiative, acting are good, but accepting and adapting ourselves to what is are at least as important. I found there was a courage and real dignity listening to an elderly person of 90, speaking of the difficulty of accepting an increasing physical and mental incapacity. Among the TED talks, there is one in which Lucy Kalanithi (2017) talks of living with her young husband's cancer and death: 'It's painful, messy stuff and pretending it isn't doesn't help. Death is part of life and engaging in the full range of human experience doesn't happen despite suffering, it happens in it, helping each other through'. Again the theme of not cutting off experience when it becomes very difficult, but learning and growing through it. She also says, 'You don't go back to the place you were before, you grow'. This acceptance of life as it comes and growing through such experiences and the acceptance it requires, seems to me to be a better and fuller definition of dignity than one centred only on individual control. We all surely understand the desire to cut off and avoid what is painful, messy and frightening in our lives, but perhaps we might also cut off an opportunity for growth. Orthodoxy does not encourage the seeking of suffering, yet if it appears in an unresolvable way in a life, we trust that it holds its own blessings and growth for us and those we love.

Lucy also says, 'You help each other through'. Today people fear dependence on others – this too is part of the rhetoric of being autonomous, independent, self-owning persons who interact with each other from separate individual self-contained centres. Neediness makes us vulnerable. Do we fear dependence because we are not sure that our loved ones and others truly love us and will be willing to care for us in our neediness and vulnerability? Physical disintegration, paralyzed limbs, leaking bodies, dementia and other mental illnesses, personality changes, vegetative states, unconsciousness . . . the list is not easy reading, nor easy to experience, either for the dying person or for their loved ones and those around them. Some of the literature in the euthanasia debate centres on the burden a dying person can be for others and at least one study has argued that those with relational duties to others might have a duty to kill themselves so as not to burden either their loved ones or the State!

Such an attitude is totally foreign to many people and to Orthodox Christians. In its own idiom, the Orthodox funeral service acknowledges the bitterness that can accompany the experience of dying for both the dying person and for their loved ones and the wider community: 'The spirit has vanished from its tabernacle; its clay grows black. The vessel is shattered, voiceless, bereft of feeling, motionless, dead . . . all comeliness stripped off, dissolved in the grave by decay. . . . As we gaze on the one lying before us, let us all accept this example of our last hour' (Hapgood 1996, 390). Again, the call to learn and grow through difficult experiences.

It is true that caring for a dying relative, especially for a long period, can be draining, exhausting and sometimes financially devastating. Yet it can also be a precious, even transformative experience. Difficult love does happen. Lucy says, 'You see each other through'. Relationships grow and develop and learning happens to all those involved. It is not simply one sided caring and giving; the dying of a person gives gifts to all those who are present. Death is to be lived within loving community and the dependence it often entails lived in love and compassion, which can make it less terrible. For Orthodox Christians there is a terrible aspect to death: it is the tearing apart of a person in their full bodily and spirit reality; this was never meant to be in God's original plan. Yet that reality, through God's merciful action in Christ is now a passage to Life, to 'a place of brightness, verdure, repose, where all sickness, sorrow and sighing have fled away'.

> 'Christ is Risen from the dead, Trampling down death by death,
> And to those in the tomb He has given Life.'

BIBLIOGRAPHY

Beauchamp T. L. & J. F. Childress. 2009. *Principles of Biomedical Ethics*. Oxford: Oxford University Press.

Breck J. 1998. *The Sacred Gift of Life: Orthodox Christianity and Bioethics*. Crestwood, NY: St. Vladimir's Seminary Press.

Breck J. & L. 2005. *Stages on Life's Way: Orthodox Thinking on Bioethics*. Crestwood, NY: St. Vladimir's Seminary Press.

Garrard E. & S. Wilkinson. 2005. 'Passive euthanasia', *Journal of Medical Ethics*, 31, 64–68.

Gillon R. 1999. 'Foreseeing is not necessarily the same as intending', *British Medical Journal*, 318, 1431–32.

Hapgood I. F. 1996. *Service Book.* Englewood, NJ: Antiochian Orthodox Christian Archdiocese.

Kalanithi L. 2017. 'What makes life worth living in the face of death?' TED, May 2017.

Kuhse H. 2009. 'Euthanasia' in P. Singer ed., *A Companion to Ethics*, 294–303. Oxford: Blackwell.

Mahmood S. 2012. *The Politics of Piety: The Islamic Revival and the Feminist Subject.* Princeton, NJ: Princeton University Press.

Manninen B. 2006. 'A case for justified non-voluntary euthanasia', *Journal of Medical Ethics*, 32, 645–51.

Nedelsky J. 1989. 'Redefining autonomy', *Yale Journal of Law and Feminism*, vol. 1, no. 7, 255–95.

Nozick R. 1974. *Anarchy, State and Utopia.* Oxford: Blackwell.

Palmer G., P. Sherrard & K. Ware. 1979. *The Philokalia*, vol. 1. London: Faber and Faber.

Pitcher G. 2010. *A Time to Live: The Case against Euthanasia and Assisted Suicide.* Oxford: Monarch Books.

Saunders C. et al. 1981. *Hospice: The Living Idea.* London: Edward Arnold.

Ware K. 2005. *L'île au-delà du monde.* Paris: Cerf.

Zizioulas J. D. 1985. *Being as Communion.* Crestwood, NY: St. Vladimir's Seminary Press.

Zizioulas J. D. 2006. *Communion and Otherness.* London/New York: T & T Clark/ Continuum.

Index

Abraham, Archbishop, 26
agunot, 54
Anthony of Sourozh,
    Metropolitan, 69–70
Apostolic Constitutions, 84–85
Arida, Patriarch Anthony Peter, 29
Armenian Orthodox Church, 26
asceticism, 123, 127, 133–38
Axia, 72
Axios, 113

bal tashhit, 122–24
Bartholomew I of Constantinople,
    Patriarch, 37, 134
Behr-Sigel, Elisabeth, 69
Benjamin of Tudela, 18
Bethlehem, 27, 46
Bouteneff, Patricia Fan, 71–72

cheirotonia, 70
churching, 72–73
circumcision, 82, 90, 94–96, 112
Clément, Olivier, 138–39
conspiracy theories, 160–61
Constantinople (as New
    Jerusalem), 6–10
Coptic Orthodox Church, 26
Crusades, 4, 6, 8, 10, 18
Ćulibrk, Bishop Jovan, 30

Daniel, Abbot, 8
Daniel al-Kumisi, 16
deaconesses, 67, 70–71
dhimma, 25–28
Didascalia, 83–84
Diodoros of Jerusalem, Patriarch, 46
Dionysius of Alexandria, 77–78, 83

Ecumenical Patriarchate, 36, 116
Eirenaios of Jerusalem, Patriarch, 45

Georgia, 6–10
Golitzin, Archbishop Alexander, 31
Greenberg, Blu, 57
Greenberg, Rabbi Steven, 100–101, 105
Gregory of Nyssa, 9

Hananel ben Hushiel (Rabbeinu
    Hananel), 100
Hartman, Tova, 57
Heschel, Abraham Joshua, 124–25, 128
hierotopy, 2
Hirsch, Samson Raphael, 91

Ibn Ezra, Abraham, 100
Irshai, Ronit, 56–58, 61

Johanan ben Zakkai, 15
John of Damascus, 135–36

185

186   *Index*

Judah Halevi, 17

Kaddish, 148–49
Kallistos of Diokleia, Metropolitan,
    69–70, 134
kashrut, 89–91, 127
Kizenko, Nadieszda, 72
kollyva, 159, 160

levayah, 147

Maimonides, Moses, 17, 123, 127
Maronite Church, 28–29
Maximus the Confessor, 139–40
Melito of Sardes, 4
menstruation, 73, 77–86, 91–94
mikvah, 96
milah, 94
Mirvis, Chief Rabbi Ephraim,
    53, 54, 58–60
mitah yafah, 169
Moscow, 8–9
Moscow Patriarchate, 8, 109
Mtskheta, 6–7
Mubarak, Archbishop Ignace, 28–29

nazirite vow, 127
Nikon of Moscow, Patriarch, 8–9

Old Believers, 9–10

Partnership Minyanim, 58–60
pikuach nefesh, 165

pilgrimage, 6, 9–10, 17, 26, 46–47
purity laws, 72–73, 77–86, 92–94

rape, 96, 100, 101, 103
Rapoport, Rabbi Chaim, 105
Rashi, 90, 103
relics, 6–7, 9
Romanian Orthodox Church, 30
Ross, Tamar, 56–57, 60–61

Sabbatai Zevi, 18–19
Schachter, Rabbi Hershel, 54
semikhah, 55
Serbian Orthodox Church, 30
shemittah, 124–25
Shira Hadasha, 57
shiva, 147–48
sodomy, 101–2, 107, 109
sumptuary laws, 125–26

Tawadros II, Pope, 26
Taylor-Guthartz, Rabba Lindsey,
    53–55, 57, 58
Theophilos III of Jerusalem,
    Patriarch, 1, 44

Weiss, Rabbi Avi, 55–56
women, ordination of: in Orthodox
    Judaism, 53, 55, 57–58; in Orthodox
    Christianity, 68–71

yahrzeit, 149
Yeshivat Maharat, 53, 55, 57, 59

About the Editors and Contributors

Nicholas de Lange is professor emeritus of Hebrew and Jewish studies in the University of Cambridge. A rabbinic graduate of Leo Baeck College, he currently serves as Visiting Rabbi to Etz Hayyim Synagogue, Haniá, Crete.

Elena Narinskaya is an academic researcher in Abrahamic religions and a founding director of Women's Ministries Initiative, an Orthodox Christian educational initiative open to everyone.

Sybil Sheridan is a freelance rabbi currently working with Newcastle Reform Synagogue. She has written and edited books largely in the area of women's studies and interfaith dialogue.

Michael G. Azar is associate professor of theology/religious studies at the University of Scranton in Pennsylvania.

Nikita (Krastu) Banev has published on Christian asceticism, Byzantine hymnography and later Orthodox spirituality. He is currently an associate professor of Byzantine and Orthodox theology at Durham University (UK). He also serves as deacon, ordained with the name Nikita, in the Archdiocese of Thyateira and Great Britain (Ecumenical Patriarchate).

Joanna Burton is a nun and past part-time teacher in the ecumenical Cambridge Theological Federation and initial director of studies and director of pastoral studies at the Institute for Orthodox Christian Studies; (retired) associate lecturer, The Open University (Healthcare-Death and Dying). Her specialisms are Christian Spirituality, Liturgy, Carmelite Studies, Death and Dying.

188 *About the Editors and Contributors*

Mary B. Cunningham is honorary associate professor of Historical Theology at the University of Nottingham. She has published books and articles in the fields of Orthodox Christian theology and Byzantine Studies.

Misza Czerniak is an Orthodox human rights activist and theologian, born in Moscow and living in Warsaw. A translator and musician by training, he has been actively involved in advocacy, capacity-building and research work at the intersection of human rights and faith/religion.

Miri Freud-Kandel is fellow and lecturer in modern Judaism in the Faculty of Theology and Religion at the University of Oxford and co-convenor of the Oxford Summer Institute on modern and contemporary Judaism. Her research focuses on the development of Orthodox Jewish theologies, the distinctive features of Judaism in Britain, and gender issues in modern Judaism.

Ian Graham was ordained as a priest to assist Bishop Kallistos of Diokleia in the Greek Orthodox Community of the Holy Trinity, Oxford, in 1986. Since 2001 he has been the priest-in-charge there.

Michael J. Harris is Senior Rabbi of The Hampstead Synagogue, London, and Senior Research Fellow at the London School of Jewish Studies.

Petra Heldt is professor for the history of the Church in the Middle East at the Jerusalem University College in Israel and the director of the Ecumenical Theological Research Fraternity in Israel.

René Pfertzel is currently serving as rabbi of Kingston Liberal Synagogue in Surrey, UK. He also teaches Bible at the Ecole Rabbinique de Paris.

David Rosen is the international director of interreligious affairs of the American Jewish Committee. He is a president of the world interfaith body Religions for Peace, and is a past chair of the International Jewish Committee for Interreligious Consultations (IJCIC), that represents world Jewry to other world Faiths.

Sylvia Rothschild has worked since her rabbinic ordination in 1987 in communities in South London. She is now the spiritual care lead at Heart of Kent Hospice and rabbi of Lev Chadash, Milan.

Marc Saperstein is a Reform Rabbi. A former principal of Leo Baeck College, he continues research and publication on Jewish history and homiletics and has published books on Jewish preaching from the twelfth century to the present.

Elizabeth Theokritoff is an associate lecturer at the Institute for Orthodox Christian Studies, Cambridge.

Tanhum Yoreh is an assistant professor at the University of Toronto's School of the Environment.

Milton Keynes UK
Ingram Content Group UK Ltd.
UKHW011315240823
427424UK00006B/58